Light Your Torches
and Pull Up Your Tights

Light Your Torches

and

Pull Up Your Tights

by

TAY GARNETT
with Fredda Dudley Balling

ARLINGTON HOUSE   *New Rochelle, N. Y.*

Library of Congress Catalog Card Number 72-91639
ISBN 0-87000-204-x

MANUFACTURED IN THE UNITED STATES OF AMERICA

To Tiela

Introduction

By Frank Capra

THERE IS A SPOT OF LAND ON THIS PLANET—NO BIGGER THAN THE STATE OF Georgia—which spawns a special people. A people poor in wealth but wealthy in spirit, very wealthy. A people who, with their wit and poetry, their blarney and laughter, enrich the lives of *all* humanity and lighten the load of man's pilgrimage on earth.

They call themselves the Sons of Erin. We call them Irishmen.

It has been said—and if not, it's time somebody said it—that among the leprechauns and the pixies there is a puckish rumor making the rounds of the Fairy Rings that God loves the Irish. Yes. And that He talks to them in their dreams. Yes. And that it was Queen Mab herself—she has special powers about such things, you know—who reported that one fine Saint Patrick's Eve, she actually heard the Ineffable Voice command their Irish friends as follows:

"Hark ye, men of Erin!" said the Lord. "My peoples on earth are weary and full of woe. Life is a drag to the Gentiles, and a schlock to the Jews and the Arabs. And this is my command to ye Irish of Erin: Go forth and quicken their hearts with my joy, and with my song arouse their spirits and bring a greening to the lands of my peoples.

"And this shall be a sign that ye will fulfill my command: Ye shall kiss the stone on Blarney's wall, ye shall wear the green on Saint Pat's day, and lo! the whole world will do likewise. Quail not, ye lads and lasses of Erin, for I will gird your loins with courage and loose your tongues with honeyed words; and for your hunger will I send manna shaped like unto potatos. Selah!"

And so, the lads and lasses of Erin heeded the Lord and set forth for other lands as evangelists of Spring. Warriors, politicians, artists —champions they became, even in pulpits and theaters. On Manhattan's Broadway, George M. Cohan and Eugene O'Neill added luster to the Golden Age of the American stage.

And then—it happened. In a sleepy outskirt of the sleepy petticoat town of Los Angeles, a new and strange show biz giant was taking its first Brobdingnagian steps on legs awkward and unsure. Detractors called the new phenomenon the "cheap and tawdry fillum business."

But the theatrically-minded Irish, intuitive about such things, surmised correctly that film would be a new and powerful communications medium. Wearing the green, they rushed West to embellish the imagery and polish the manners of the raw, crude, phenomenon—and, of course, to dig for its gold.

Entrepreneurs came: Mack Sennett, Winfield Sheehan, Joseph P. Kennedy.

Thespians came: Spencer Tracy, James Cagney, Walter Huston, Pat O'Brien, Frank McHugh, Victor McLaglen, Frank Morgan, Lloyd Nolan, Ronald Reagan. And Barbara Stanwyck, Maureen O'Sullivan, Maureen O'Hara, Loretta Young.

Irish writers and playwrights came. And film directors too: John Ford, William Wellman, Marshall Neilan, John Farrow, John Huston. Two of our top Irish directors didn't have to come far to reach Hollywood: Leo McCarey and Tay Garnett were both born in Los Angeles. And one of them, Tay Garnett, has given us an extraordinary book about an extraordinary man—himself; a book that bubbles with witty, earthy anecdotes about the witty, earthy guys and dolls of Hollywood whom Tay worked with and loved—particularly the dolls.

He tells us outlandish tales about such off-beat but little-known characters as "Beanie" Walker, Wilson Mizner, Akim Tamiroff, Gregory Ratoff; scores of delightful never-told yarns about Clark Gable, Spencer Tracy, Greer Garson, Loretta Young, Joan Blondell, Lana Turner, Alan Ladd, Robert Mitchum, Robert Walker, Robert Taylor, John Barrymore, John Garfield, John Wayne, and Marlene Dietrich; and a few satirical jabs at Mack Sennett, Harry Cohn, Darryl Zanuck, and Irving Thalberg.

But it is the fun-loving, lovable Irishman himself that emerges as the star of Tay's high adventures. He relates how he grew up in Los Angeles without aims or goals—unless the seeking of laughs and excitement can be called goals.

[8]

But badly-timed laughs are seldom very funny, as Tay learned when, as a boy acrobat, he joined a group of professional tumblers and made his theatrical debut in one, and *only* one, disastrous performance. He debuted and retired from vaudeville in less than five minutes. A record.

In another badly-timed laugh, Tay accidentally "souffléed" the school principal with thrown eggs that were meant for his pals. For that laugh he was expelled from the Los Angeles Polytechnic High School as a juvenile delinquent.

World War One was going strong. Tay joined the Navy for laughs, and was assigned to naval aviation. He loved to fly; became an instructor. On checking out a student's solo flight, on an old N-9 pontoon plane, the student put the "tub" into a full-power tailspin, and spun it into the drink. Tay came up laughing—but with a smashed right leg that gave him a life-long limp.

Came the Armistice—and boredom caused morale at the naval air base to "crash-dive lower than an abalone's anus."

"Ensign Garnett," the skipper commanded, "you're Irish and you're gabby, and you're now my morale officer. Put on some shows."

The show bug bit hard. When discharged, Tay made eatin' money as a film extra. Discovering studios paid more for an extra who would take "falls," Tay became a stunt man—and girls discovered him. Being Irish and handsome, and boyish and lovable, mothers and daughters alike found him irresistible. "Love was everywhere," writes Tay, "but an honest dollar was hard to find."

But Tay blarneyed himself into a few dollars, honest or not, with a job writing titles for silent slapstick comedies at the Hal Roach Studio. His titles got so many laughs he graduated into a Mack Sennett gagman. And that's where Tay and I met as "prisoners of Edendale" condemned to solitary confinement in the top cell of Sennett's Tower.

There are many ways two people can size each other up: ride out an artillery barrage together in a fox hole, play two rounds of golf, or team up as gagmen at Mack Sennett's. Tay was not only witty, he was also a most likable companion—the kind that wears well. All men will know what I mean.

But for Tay gags and scripts were still for laughs—something to occupy his time between amours. It wasn't until he directed his first film, *Celebrity,* starring Robert Armstrong and Lena Basquette, that

[9]

meaning and purpose infiltrated into Laughing Boy's life. Directing films is what he had been looking for, what he was born for. He became known as a surefire "doer." Did a studio or an independent producer want a film shot in Tibet, in Baffin Land, the Sahara, or the Holy Land? Get Tay Garnett. Did a producer with "the shorts" want a picture shot under schedule and under budget? Get Tay Garnett. Was it a comedy, a drama, or a melodrama? Get Tay Garnett.

For over fifty feature films, they got Tay Garnett. And from that output came such powerhouses as *One Way Passage, China Seas, Slave Ship, Trade Winds, 7 Sinners, Mrs. Parkington, The Postman Always Rings Twice, A Connecticut Yankee in King Arthur's Court, Wild Harvest,* and many others.

And when Television panicked Hollywood, and things got so tough for filmmakers that John Barrymore quipped: "If you run, they bite you in the ass . . . if you stand still, they hose you," Tay neither ran nor stood. His mission was to enliven the day for humanity, whether they were audiences in movie houses or TV viewers in living rooms.

The cry, "Get Tay Garnett!" was repeated again and again by such top TV shows as *Wagon Train, The Untouchables, Naked City, The Virginian, Rawhide, Gunsmoke, Bonanza,* and a dozen other programs.

And Laughing Boy knew he had found himself in his own talents; knew that there is no greater satisfaction in life than knowing who you are, and what place you occupy in time and place and magnitude and achievement.

There is much, much more to the universe than electrons and gravity. Science can only observe and measure the tip of the iceberg. Hidden from us is how life, mind, and matter, and time, imagination, and energy fit together. Poets glimpse flashes of the unknown through knotholes in their imagery. Saints see fleeting visions through a glass darkly. The Irish, being part poet, part mystic, often *feel* more than meets the eye or beats the ear. Perhaps the elves and pixies have something. Perhaps the Irish, and those like them, *have* a vocation to brighten the drab and leaven the dull.

If so, Tay Garnett's book is "exhibit A" in defense of clowns who go to jail for laughing at troubles.

Foreword

I STOOD SHIVERING ON THE CHILLY NIGHT-SET FOR *The Hunchback of Notre Dame.* As the only high school correspondent for a magazine entitled *Photoplayer's Weekly,* I was earning summer money by reporting what REALLY went on in Hollywood's studios.

Lon Chaney was playing the hunchback in makeup so grotesque that even the jaded extras avoided looking at him. I remember that, among other blemishes, his right eye had been masked out and a glittering artificial eye hung on his cheekbone.

The girl beloved by the monster was a newcomer named Patsy Ruth Miller. Her great brown eyes and her long reddish-brown hair were superior to anything I had ever seen at Los Angeles High School. I ogled her. She smiled a routine smile; I was wrapped up and ready for mailing.

If some seer had told me that Miss Miller would be my first wife, I would have dropped dead and saved several people, including Miss Miller, a lot of trouble. On the other hand, all of us would have missed a lotta laughs.

When I could pry my gaze off the star, I was fascinated by the vast mob scene in front of the facsimile Cathedral of Notre Dame. The scene being shot with great difficulty was that in which Quasimodo races from crenelation to crenelation, pouring boiling oil on his tormentors far below. First one thing went wrong, then another. After each flub, the forest of extras would douse their torches, slump onto the floor, and grumble about the passing of the hours.

The hang-up would be adjusted, then the assistant director would shout, "Light your torches, and pull up your tights."

The exhausted extras, still earning their $1.50 per day—far into the night—would struggle to their feet and have another go at it.

"Light your torches, and pull up your tights."

Gradually it has come to mean more to me than a remembered moment on a set long, long ago. No matter how many times my torch has been extinguished, no matter how hard I've been hammered to the floor, tights gone slack, the invocation of those words has brought me up fighting.

Men live by words. For me those words are, "Light your torches, and pull up your tights."

Light Your Torches
and Pull Up Your Tights

1

A FEW YEARS AGO THE WORRIED HOLLYWOOD CHAMBER OF COMMERCE looked up and down Hollywood Boulevard at the honky-tonk conglomeration of bars, souvenir and junk shops, surplus outlets, blatant banners announcing clearance sales, and decided they must do something to Bring Glamour Back to the Boulevard.

The problem having been descried, heavy thinking was directed toward a solution.

The genius who came up with the answer is rumored to have been a paving contractor. Promptly bulldozers fouled up traffic, airhammers tortured eardrums, and upended sidewalks looked like a Disneyland for mountain goats.

It was a big undertaking, but it paid off.

On Hollywood Boulevard from Argyle Avenue to La Brea, and on Vine Street from Yucca to Sunset, the Hollywood sidewalks were inlaid with star-shaped bronze plaques, each bearing the name of a theatrical "great," including actors, directors, writers, producers, musicians, art directors, and cinematographers. At that point they ran out of sidewalk.

Of course, the Boulevard was still a honky-tonk conglomeration of bars, souvenir and junk shops, surplus outlets, blatant banners announcing clearance sales, but the happy assumption of the Chamber of Commerce was that tourists, plodding along with their eyes firmly fixed on the stars underfoot, would be unaware of the landscape above their knees.

For hours I personally have stood on Hollywood Boulevard at the foot of Whitley Avenue, casually leaning near the entrance to a chili parlor which fronts upon my star. I have watched an endless procession of hippies, dopies, prosties, newsies, and boozies traipse across my name; all hope of having someone ask me for an autograph was abandoned the day I noted two dogs squatting in business conference directly over my star.

Much caustic criticism has come my way through forty years in Hollywood during which I've written and/or directed and/or produced nearly one hundred feature films, and more than that number of television segments. But I still maintain that those dogs were hypercritical.

There is, I believe, no single formula for getting one's name well-trodden and extensively desecrated on Hollywood Boulevard. Of course, a proper esthetic background is essential, although the means of achieving such a background are, you might say, varied.

One of our finest directors was originally a butcher. Another was an acrobat, another a plumber, and still another a highly-paid gigolo. Then there was a bartender, a barber, a chorus boy, a boxer, a bookkeeper, and a bookmaker.

It is my great good fortune to be asked occasionally, "But what does a director DO? Actors act, cameramen operate cameras, and sound technicians handle the mikes, but a *director* . . . ?"

The writer/producer Nunnally Johnson, upon being asked that question, quipped, "Oh, a director's the guy who tells the actors when to go home." Thereafter Mr. Johnson made the mistake of becoming a director, it says here, but no one was kind enough to tell *him* when to go home.

Dan Dailey, while under contract to 20th-Century Fox, was once handed a script in which appeared the sweeping line, "At this point, Dan Dailey goes into a dance that would stop any Broadway show."

Dan, shaking the script in the director's face, demanded, "What are YOU going to do about this?"

"We'll look at some old Fred Astaire movies," replied the director innocently.

Which explains why, now and then, a director appears in public wearing a black eye patch, *without* having a military command in Israel.

My own trauma was inflicted by a script that finally suffered the hero to be gagged, bound, nailed in a packing crate, and dropped into the East River. This situation, calculated to starch every hair of the composite audience head, was dismissed with a scriptwriter's airy solution: "By a clever device, he escapes."

So that's what a director does: if he can come up with a clever device, *he* escapes.

Yet I couldn't have escaped Hollywood. There came a series of moments in my early life when I knew beyond the slightest doubt that I was fated for the hippodrome.

When I entered Los Angeles Polytechnic High School, I had no talent for baseball and insufficient beef for football, so I spent much of my spare time working out in the gym, hoping to entice a muscle here and there.

Coincidentally, a professional acrobatic team became stranded in Los Angeles. While awaiting some word from their agent, they, too, worked out daily in our school gym. This is as good a time as any to report the late Fred Allen's crack about agents (to which I don't subscribe, of course): "All the sincerity in Hollywood could be hidden in a gnat's navel and there'd still be room for four caraway seeds and an agent's heart."

And so, back to the gym. Every afternoon, in open-mouthed admiration, I watched the acrobats. They had lost their "top-mounter" and were looking for a likely successor. Noting my size and enthusiasm, both compatible with their needs, the acrobats asked if I'd like to work out with them.

The big German "understander," who was also the act's manager, explained that they had been booked into a Long Beach auditorium for one performance; from that start, they hoped to tour California. Their booking jibed loosely with the end of the school term—give or take a couple of weeks—so I agreed to join the act. I spared my parents any knowledge of my professional vaudeville debut.

Not until opening night was I supplied with my costume. It consisted of a skin-tight, torso-encasing leopardskin upheld by one frail shoulder strap. I looked like a spotted sausage bursting its cage. One glance into a mirror gave me a full set of opening night jitters, including hiccoughs.

I had heard somewhere that chewing gum relieved tension. I tried it with a stick of peppermint; turned out to be a very dry flavor, so I added another type to lay the dust, then a third and a fourth. By

[17]

the time the orchestra started gallop music, signaling curtain rise for our act, I was working on a two-pack cud.

At the rise we were to be discovered in a three-man high formation: Upright on our understander's shoulders was the middle man, and erect on the middle man's shoulders was the top mounter (me). The two remaining members of the troupe were cantilevered by the understander, one on either side, each supported by a handhold and foot pressure against the understander's thighs.

It was intended to be a sock opening.

Unfortunately we had been unable to rehearse in the auditorium before the show, so we had overlooked an element vital to the success of this pyramid: the height of the proscenium arch.

As I was boosted upward and the curtain opened, I found that I had to bend my knees and crane my neck to avoid being pushed through the plaster mask of tragedy. Terror seized me: Intent on keeping my balance, I began to chomp my gum in time with the rapid fire music.

The audience murmured, then giggled, then howled.

The louder they howled, the more desperately I chomped and shook. I shook our formation to pieces.

The curtain was closed as we spilled all over the understander. This momentary pileup gave me about three lengths lead on the maddest acrobat I've ever seen.

Grabbing my shirt, trousers, and shoes as I passed the chairs that were our designated dressing room, I scorched down the alley with the giant thundering after me. Youth and weight began to tell as I put distance between us, finally plunging into the concealing shrubbery of a public park.

I was still wondering where I'd dropped my heart when a sweet voice with laughing overtones asked, "Are you all right?"

"Is he gone? The guy that was chasing me?" I whispered through the leaves.

"I don't see anyone. Are you a purse snatcher—or maybe a burglar?" the voice wanted to know.

I pulled on my clothes and shoes, then crawled out to meet one of the prettiest girls I'd ever seen. I confessed my only crime: stage fright.

The girl suggested that I walk home with her for a cold Coke, an

[18]

invitation that I accepted with a grateful croak. One of the graces of my life has been that whenever I've been in serious trouble, I've been rescued by a girl. In this case, my champion turned out to be the daughter of the mayor.

I joined his honor, his wife, and his daughter in a sandwich and an iced tea, then the mayor walked me to the streetcar line. "Got any money?" he asked as we waited for the big red Pacific Electric Car of that era.

Money? I'd forgotten it existed—another of my weaknesses. I went through my pockets. Someone else must have thought of the same thing. I was broke.

The mayor gave me fare to Los Angeles. "And stay out of show business," he advised, patting my shoulder.

"I intend to, sir," I answered fervently.

My subsequent activities remind me of the time Peter Lorre asked Humphrey Bogart if he had ever given up the grape and gone on the wagon. Moving a frosted glass from his lips, Bogey said, "Once. It was the most miserable afternoon of my life."

My own abstention (from drama) lasted until I was about seventeen. Word went around Poly High that President Theodore Roosevelt was coming to California. Rumor added that the presidential parade would proceed along Washington Boulevard, past our school. We were to be freed from classes for an hour of cheering.

Although I was normally apathetic toward politics, I found this news inspiring. I conferred with a buddy who had access to his family's Stoddard-Dayton touring car. If you've never heard of a Stoddard-Dayton, forget it. Your own grandchildren will never believe the Edsel.

After making a deal for transportation, I bought a pair of steel-rimmed spectacles at the dime store and manufactured a supply of charcoal from cork.

Just before noon on the day Roosevelt was due, several of us cut classes. We assembled at the Stoddard-Dayton where I donned spectacles, combed my hair at random, and covered my upper lip with an exuberant charcoal mustache.

Sitting on the top of the back seat, bowing and flashing a dazzling dental display, I was chauffeured grandly past the assembled student body. Here and there a derisive student, whose parents had undoubtedly voted Democratic, extracted a tomato or a hard-boiled egg from his lunch pail and hurled it at me.

The critical aim was poor and I was an expert dodger, but the incident gave us a further idea. We chugged to the nearest grocery and bought a crate of eggs. Unboiled.

Once again I presided, bowing toothily as our ersatz parade moved along Washington Boulevard. Once again we were hailed with boos and catcalls, plus a well-hurled banana. That was our cue. We souffled the entire student body.

Unfortunately, the principal—assuming from the uproar that the authentic President had arrived—hastily took his place in the midst of a particularly attractive target area. By the time I recognized him, it was too late; he looked like an omelet on its way to the stove.

So I transferred to Los Angeles High.

I left Poly with such speed that I was unable to check my performance against that of President Roosevelt, but I was assured by my partisans that the Roosevelt parade was anticlimactic.

Speaking of junior goof-offs, the phrase "juvenile delinquent" had not been coined when I was one. I was just a dopey, fresh kid; if my immature, insecure, awkward, rebellious condition had been labeled, it would have scared me half to death. Yet, once I had grown accustomed to the term, I would have done my best to live up to it, which brings up the old debate as to whether art follows life, or life follows art.

In any case, I grew up amid a generation that was taught that the ability of a man to play a fine game of pool indicated a misspent youth. During my L.A. High days, I began to insure my future by frequenting a smoky basement room that appeared to have been sown, wall to wall, in green baize.

The sign above the door read, "Sneed's Pool Room," and I'm sure my conventional mother would have been scandalized if she had known exactly where I spent my spare time. As kids have done since time began, I answered vaguely when questioned about where I had been, where I was going, and why.

I never learned to play billiards or pool even passably, but I made some fascinating friends at Sneed's, not one of whom became a number behind bars: Nacio Herb Brown became a composer; Leo

McCarey was one of the ablest directors ever to call out, "Roll 'em" —cameras, not dice; his brother, Ray, was very nearly Leo's equal; Dudley Logan formed his own advertising agency and was an ornament to his profession; David Butler was one of the top silent picture directors, and when films began to speak, David made talking pictures that also moved. I believe he was one of the first to mount a microphone on a fishing pole and delegate a sound man, off-camera, to follow the principals around, recording speech while the camera recorded action.

A final member of this group was my beloved friend, Frank Borzage, who won two Academy Awards and who directed such sensitive motion pictures as the original version of *A Farewell to Arms,* starring Gary Cooper and Helen Hayes, plus the never-to-be-forgotten first version of *Seventh Heaven,* starring Janet Gaynor and Charles Farrell, and the eloquent *I've Always Loved You* with lovely Catherine McLeod.

All those men were alumni of Sneed's.

The moral is: If you wish for artistic excellence, wealth, and fame —to the poolroom, men.

The tragic realization that I was never destined to unseat Willie Hoppe was somewhat softened by concern with larger matters. In a burst of patriotism, a group of us joined the Navy in the midst of World War I. When discussing this bold move, we had anticipated salt-sea training, and had talked laconically of blowing the enemy out of the water, and sailing our gunboat right up the Rhine River to Berlin, a triumph of sheer guts over geography.

We wound up in an airless warehouse, designated as "barracks," in San Pedro, fighting rats for the right to sleep on our cots at night. During our working day—roughly sixteen hours—we loaded and unloaded cargo in heat that would have prostrated a camel.

A few years ago I made a sentimental journey to the area and noted that the warehouse had been converted into a submarine base, in which capacity it was still standing inspection, although lurching slightly to starboard. That is the Navy Way: to revere the past until it has disappeared into the alimentary canal of a termite.

We were issued uniforms, typhoid shots, and inferiority complexes by chief petty officers whose job, then as now, was to convert a crop of lead-footed landlubbers into able seamen in the shortest possible time.

At the end of a six-week training period, we were navigating our warehouse with consummate ease. We were pronounced seamen first class, and rewarded with weekend "shore" leave.

The uncle of Bob Stephens, one of my shipmates, owned a cabin cruiser, the *Silverado,* tied up at San Pedro. My parents were staying at their summer home in Manhattan Beach. These two facts encouraged a bunch of us to navigate from San Pedro, around Point Fermin, to Manhattan Beach. I notified my family to prepare a gala homecoming dinner featuring fried chicken and chocolate cake.

Resplendent in our spanking new uniforms, we embarked on the voyage without knowing how to read a chart or sound a foghorn. Luckily the weather was clear, so our navigation problem consisted merely of seeing and being seen.

Arriving at Manhattan, we dropped our mudhook well offshore, lowered our skiff and started for the beach. We were a taut company, shipshape, very spit and polish, and *VERY* navy.

As our landing party neared shore, we noted that word of the gallant heroes' homecoming had gotten around. Most of the population of Manhattan Beach had gathered on the sand to welcome us.

There was no band, yet there was that silent fanfare on the air trumpeting the pride of the Navy on review.

In all academic training there are omissions. Our boot camp indoctrination had included nothing at all about the art of maneuvering a small boat through breakers.

The first comber lifted our skiff and sent it end over end toward the high-water mark, sprinkling the tide with assorted Navy personnel, white hats, oars, and personal belongings.

Several of us, dodging debris, started to swim.

Training definitely pays off. If you've had it. Before abandoning our position, we called the roll and discovered that some of our crew didn't know how to swim. They clung pitifully to our turtled boat, which tried to buck them off with every wave.

It was an uneven match. By the time we had organized an adequate lifeguard system, the boat was out in front by several lengths; when we reached shore, drenched, scraped, waterlogged, and sanded from head to heel, the boat was on the beach, waiting for us. It wasn't even breathing hard.

The expressions on the faces of the welcoming committee were studies in self-control and/or incredulity. There was not so much as a snicker on the summer air.

As we sloshed toward our house, my father gingerly rested a hand on my shoulder. He spoke thoughtfully, "Let's see. You've had six week's Naval instruction?"

"Yes, sir. Why?"

"Mmmmm—I was just wondering whose Navy your instructors are working for: ours or the Kaiser's."

Thereafter we maintained a taut ship, eating and fraternizing with indigenous personnel until the last minute. Then, with the help of the local lifeguard, we managed to return to the *Silverado*, and hoist the skiff on board.

We reported to the warehouse several hours AWOL, looking like the remnants of the *Titanic's* crew.

We drew the spud detail until further notice.

Disgusted, we employed the traditional military protest against the status quo; fourteen of us put in for transfer, applying for pilot officer training in the newly inaugurated Naval Air Service.

To our amazement, all fourteen passed the rigorous tests and were accepted.

When the rumor went around (with a certain amount of help from us) that we were being sent to Massachusetts Institute of Technology in Boston for training—college types, yet—we sank to the social status of a civet cat. Our CPO posted us for daily latrine duty from that moment until we should depart for the east. The result was that fourteen of us superior recruits were chambermaiding for five thousand careless men. We were outraged. We held bitter conferences about eliminating the human race and vice versa.

(Excuse me, dear Navy, for using the word "latrine." I mean "head," of course, but no branch of the military service has ever employed a worse misnomer.)

Not being totally without defensive resources, the fourteen of us devoted hours of brainstorming to find a way to beat the rap. I am still proud to announce—even in memory of later misery—that it was I who came up with a Navy-proof solution.

I knew a two-striper, a medic named Dr. Cohn, who had been an urologist in San Francisco before joining the Navy. I outlined our predicament to Lt. Cohn, and asked how long a man should remain in sick bay after undergoing circumcision.

"At least two weeks," said the sympathetic doctor.

"Sold," I said.

All fourteen of us signed up for surgery, and all were treated the same morning.

In sick bay that night I had a horrible dream. I imagined that I had been chosen to race the blazing Olympic torch from Athens to Johannesburg. Somewhere along the line I had fumbled the torch and it had set fire to my clothing.

I awakened with a clear knowledge of the flame's location.

It is altogether absurd, considering the acreage involved, that so many stitches should be required to conclude the type of alteration our group had undergone.

On that bygone night in sick bay, I remembered that I was sleeping on a mattress supported by a white enameled iron bedstead. I staggered to the foot of my bed and applied the chill metal to the conflagration.

Nearby I heard a groan of relief duplicating the involuntary moan I had just uttered. Another groan joined the refrain, then another.

Opening my eyes, I squinted into the gloom. Gradually it dawned on me that I was anchor man in what had to be the world's most grotesque chorus line. There we were, all fourteen of us, lined up in identical pose, each at the foot of his icy iron bed. A frieze of outstandingly male Rockettes.

For me it was the moment of truth.

I had been the author of this tableau, the very epitome of show business; my intent, like that of the theatre since time began, had been to provide an escape from boredom and drudgery, and to give the Good Guys a victory over the Bad Guys.

What I had overlooked, in my youth and inexperience, was that art is born in agony, and there is no easy way to doublecross a CPO.

And so, on to Boston.

2

In the spring of 1967 I received a letter from my lovely second ex-wife, now living in London. She has published many successful novels and has sold the motion picture rights to most of them. She asked me to come to England to help set up production for filming a novel of which she is particularly proud. Justifiably.

My lovely third ex-wife felt that the trip was unnecessary. At the time we were still married.

I relayed this ruling to my second ex-wife, who responded with an irresistible argument: She sent me a first class airline ticket—round trip. It was that round trip that sprang me.

As I jetted along, crossing the continent in five hours, I remembered an earlier transcontinental trip.

It was preceded by my having completed preflight training at MIT in the early days of WW I, and having been transferred to San Diego for primary training in the Curtis N–9, a Navy rebuttal to the Army's Curtis JN–4, the famed Jenny.

I managed to stay alive in San Diego, so I was committed to Pensacola and the proposition that some force, other than reverse gravity, would keep that era's pusher prop planes in the air.

I recall that our trip from San Diego to Florida took six days: five on the Southern Pacific to New Orleans, and one on the L & N to Pensacola. We wool-uniformed flight students suffocated. One guy asked tentatively, "Think we're about right for carving?"

In the middle of Texas one blistering afternoon, the train stopped for water. A furtive character sidled up to me and asked out of the corner of his mouth, "Like to buy some—ah—TEA?" In those Prohibition days, that meant ambrosia.

"How much?" I asked. A mere formality, and the bootlegger knew it.

"Ten bucks a fifth," he whispered.

The engineer whistled, the wheels lurched forward; I handed over the ten and boarded, hotfooting it to the men's room followed by a trail of thirsty pilots. Licking our dry lips, we uncorked the handsomely labeled bottle. As host and accredited wine-taster, I took the first swig—and nearly strangled.

In subsequent analytical session, we were forced to concede that the man HAD asked if we wanted to buy tea.

Still parched, we reached Pensacola only to experience further surprises. We were transported from railhead to base via narrow gauge railway, under attack by mosquitoes in squadron formation, the biggest, meanest, ugliest mosquitoes I've ever seen. Along the way we were treated to visual indoctrination against crash-landing in a swamp: bank to bank alligators.

Upon arriving at the station, a friend and I approached an isolated telephone booth to call our families (collect), and discovered that—as usual in military installations—there was a communications snafu. The booth was occupied by an aggressive water moccasin.

My accompanying buddy studied the serpent at a safe distance and mumbled, "I still can't figure out how the Seminoles get those goddam things on their feet."

The horrors of the local fauna were trivial when compared to the dedicated hostility of the H-boat, a lumbering seaplane powered by the massive Liberty engine. This H-boat was a three-seater with a snout to drive a pelican mad with envy. Our bombardier sat in this forward cockpit in a circular machine-gun scarfmount that swiveled 360 degrees, and could be lowered or raised as necessary in combat.

Heavier than a goose gorged on buckshot, the H-boat was sluggish on takeoff, capricious in the air, and landed like a battlewagon's mudhook. Rumor had it that Baron von Richtofen personally had prepared the blueprints for this aeronautical monstrosity and slipped them to an American spy.

In our outfit there was a twenty-year-old lad (we'll call him

Beauregard) from a small Southern town. He picked up the fundamentals of flying with such speed that he was the first in our class to be condemned to H-boat training.

Like many a youngster, Beauregard dissipated his apprehension by denying it in a letter to his parents. He wrote, in part, "Tomorrow I start H-boat training. These boats are called Flying Coffins, but I have no fear."

Looking back on it, I find that bold statement infinitely pathetic. Like most of us, he was scared spitless, but even with a dry mouth he was trying to whistle.

Parents will be parents. Beauregard's turned his letter over to the hometown newspaper, which published it under the portrait of a Confederate flag snapping in the breeze. A clipping of the published letter found its way to our base and was duly posted on the bulletin board outside the mess hall.

That night two of us spotted Beauregard making for one of our H-boats without goggles, helmet, or one hour's solo experience in our aerial exterminator.

We overpowered him and took him back to our barracks where we removed his side arms and hid his razor and belt. We completed his cure with man's ultimate solace: a fifth of 100-proof.

Eventually Beauregard's stomach settled and his sense of humor revived. However, his subsequent lessons in self-control, administered by our squadron, were as character-building as his flight instruction. His letter had given us a slogan: "I have no fear."

It was used to express confidence in the madly implausible, to wit:

"My dough will last until payday, I have no fear."

"I've got it made with the admiral's daughter, I have no fear."

And, of course, "When I get to France, I'm going to blast Richtofen out of the sky, I have no fear."

I thought at the time that our slogan would make a good title for a service comedy starring Harold Lloyd. Or, nowadays, Dick Van Dyke.

In any case, Beauregard and I completed all required training in one piece, along with most of our classmates and were commissioned Ensigns in the Naval Air Corps. We couldn't leave well enough alone; in the course of our celebration we had to get mixed up with a flight of parachutists from our nearby dirigible section.

Since man took to the air, the heavier-than-air guys have been scornful of the lighter-than-air guys. We called them feather-pushers and kiwis, kiwis being the birds who "flew desks" in military offices.

Anybody with any sense never challenges a jump champ, but we were drinking bootleg bourbon, a beverage low in sense calories. I recall observing, "So what's a parachute jump? You step out of your blimp, your umbrella opens automatically, and you knit all the way down."

A two-striper who had been drinking Coke, asked mildly, "Like to try it?"

"Why not?" demanded Beauregard, full of flit. "*We* don't want to miss any of the recreational opportunities on this base, because *we're* going to be in France a long time."

I hate a guy who volunteers twice—once for himself, and once for me.

On the way to the blimp, we were encouraged by our hosts. "Don't worry about your chute. If it doesn't open, they give you a new one," they explained.

Also, "If you land just right, you don't break both ankles. If you're blown off course and land in the swamp, don't panic. Lots of guys have made it out with only a bite or two."

The jumping arrangements were more primitive then than now, but not much. The parachutes were hung in a cone on a lifeline OUTSIDE the gondola. A parachutist snapped himself to the cone, leapt out of the hovering blimp, and the cone automatically released a parachute—it was devoutly to be hoped.

"You go first," yelled Beauregard, ever the gentleman.

I looked at the grinning officers in the gondola; I looked at the jeering dirigible complement far, far below. I had a choice: jump, or have a yellow stripe a foot wide painted down the middle of my back. Thus are heroes made; I didn't have the courage required to admit I was chicken straight through to the bone. I jumped.

I've never had enough nerve to ride a ferris wheel since. As for Beauregard, he used a ladder to descend from his upper bunk until some clown stole it two or three weeks later.

I was awaiting shipping orders when I had coffee one morning with a morose guy named Deek Matthews (let's say), who had completed all the minimum requirements in all squadrons, but still lacked ONE hour's solo flight time for graduation. He was bitter about the likelihood of missing his commission through no fault of his own, but only because of a shortage of aircraft with which to log that last hour.

I comforted Matthews by saying I'd see what *I* could do. Everybody knows how easy it is for an Ensign to pull rank in behalf of friends.

Anyhow, I went over to Santa Rosa Island where the gunnery and acrobatic squadrons were stationed. I happened to know the skipper, so I put it up to him.

He chewed his lower lip, then said, "Yeah, I've got a spare crate here. It vibrates a little and most of the guys won't fly it, but it's held together so far. It may last out the war. You're welcome to it."

I looked it over. It was our old enemy, the N-9 pontoon plane. It had only one set of controls because it was rigged for gunnery practice. That made it legitimate craft for solo credit, even though I'd have to ride with Matthews since the plane would be checked out to me.

Sending for the jubilant Matthews, I took over the rear cockpit which was equipped with a machine-gun scarfmount; that is, a circular aluminum track, about the diameter of a hula hoop, was affixed to the top of the cockpit so that a skinny gunner could stand within its circle. The machine gun was fastened to a traveler that would raise, lower, or rotate the weapon on the track of the scarf circle.

We attained an altitude of about a thousand feet, then made a routine turn over the gunnery targets in the bay below—and continued to turn and turn and turn in a tight, full-power tailspin.

I couldn't reach Matthews or the controls. I couldn't yell instructions loud enough to be heard above the screaming engine. I could only hang on and watch Matthews make every wrong move in the book. We were going into the drink; I knew it, but there wasn't a thing I could do about it except swing the machine gun behind me and lock it into place so I could brace my hands and knees against the scarfmount.

The next thing I knew I was under water with a pile of assorted obsolete seaplane parts on top of me. I fought to the surface, mad as the devil. From the amount of blood on my hands, I was convinced that I'd lost both thumbs.

I looked around for Matthews. Apparently undamaged, he was sitting under a nearby palm tree, cussing his bad luck, the N–9, and the entire Navy. He had been catapulted through the upper wing of the plane and had landed in the arms of a palm that parted gently and lowered him onto the sand.

Our trip downstairs had been observed. As I started to swim, a fast sea-sled, manned by a pair of hospital orderlies, took me aboard. I still remember the blanched faces of the boys who lifted me over the side. They were stunned because I was alive, and because they didn't expect that state to continue.

"Lie down, sir," one of them said.

"I'm all right, sailor," I announced in the best tradition of the hardy young Naval officer.

When the sea-sled drew alongside the quay in the hospital wet basin, I stepped on the thwart, intending to hop lightly ashore. I was in a hurry to get my thumbs repaired before gangrene set in. Scorning the aid offered by the hospital men, I went SPLASH! into the bay. I had to be fished out with a boat hook. Even then it didn't occur to me to worry about my knee.

Nowadays, I have a half-moon scar on each thumb, but my hands function perfectly. I can't say as much for my right leg. Horseback riding, golf, and handball are sports of the past for me, and I can walk only short distances without discomfort. I bump along on one rim, piously genuflecting with every step.

Yet, as far as the Navy is concerned, Operation Garnett N–9 never took place. Along in the Fifties, I not only ran out of money; I lost my Irish luck. I was so hoodooed that I couldn't have gotten action in a three-dollar cat house if I'd had Errol Flynn's looks and Howard Hughes' money.

A friend of mine, a doctor who had treated my Navy knee, and who understood my fierce pride, came to my rescue in the only way he felt would be acceptable to me. "How about your service-connected disability?" he asked. "I've heard of guys who had hysterics during World War II; as a consequence they've been drawing monthly disability payments ever since. I'll bet you've never even applied."

I hadn't. I altered that situation at once. For a week I filled out forms in quadruplicate. For another week I submitted to laboratory tests. I spent so much time in a white jacket that pretty nurses began to call me "Orderly" and tell me their troubles. It was a switch; for years pretty girls had been calling me disorderly.

Time passed. After due consideration of my request for pension, the Veterans' Administration replied as follows: PENSION DENIED. EYES PRONOUNCED OKAY.

In spite of my 20/20 vision, I was still unable to pay the grocery bill by being a ski bum, a circus aerialist, *or* a Navy dependent.

Flashback to World War I: I've often wondered what became of Matthews after he left Pensacola, sans his commission. Sky-diver, probably. Or tree surgeon.

After my own discharge from the hospital, I was ordered to the San Diego Air Station to serve as an instructor. Teaching students how to get the ship off the water, keep it trimmed, and return it to the bay without submerging permanently was Sweat Medal duty with poison oak clusters.

I've watched a mother bird kick a fledging out of the nest in full view of the family cat, then fly away nervelessly. However, I might as well admit it: I haven't the guts of a bird.

On a first solo flight, as millions of civilians know, a flier is expected only to get up, circle once, and get down without disintegrating.

When I turned my first student loose to solo, I kept telling myself that he was a steady lad, that he had completed the required hours of takeoff and landing training satisfactorily, and that he had shown the essential savvy in all categories. So much for rationalization.

My boy took off with all the grace of a pair of red flannel longjohns being blown off a clothesline. I promptly lost my breakfast.

He described a wobbly smoke-ring in the sky, then fluttered back to the water. He landed and bounced, landed and bounced, landed and bounced.

He must have porpoised a dozen times before an idea occurred to him. Taking off, he circled a second time and made a zigzag approach to the bay. He landed, and landed, and landed.

After five touchdowns, each one higher and harder, he once more sought the safety of the wild blue yonder.

Our squadron leader was Josh Billings, Lt. (J.G.) who stood loyally

[31]

beside me, sharing my incredulous horror at this lampoon of the Brothers Wright.

At length he said expressionlessly, "Get a shotgun and shoot that s.o.b. down before he starves to death."

That proved to be unnecessary, because my penguin made a flawless landing on the next try.

Josh, who became a far-famed professional baseball player in later years, was a man of many facets. Deeply religious (an asset in the profession of training student flyers), he practiced his Catholicism devoutly.

One afternoon I stood rooted to the tarmac and watched Josh, in an H-boat, ride out a spin initiated by a student pilot. Josh pulled the plane out of it and landed in shock.

As we headed for coffee as fast as soft legs would take us, I blew out my breath and told Josh, "I thought for a couple of minutes we were going to have to send for the meatwagon."

Josh nodded vigorously. "We ought to have a fishcart on standby, too. I might crack up on a Friday."

Our youth and our highly hazardous profession inspired frequent and vivid social functions. As one long-ago October ended, our BOQ planned a Hallowe'en party; we rented a now-defunct night club on Point Loma, and invited the officers of the destroyer fleet to be our guests, promising witching music and appropriate spirits. We avoided mentioning that those spirits had been appropriated from the destroyer fleet's own private stock of torpedo juice.

At about 5 P.M. on October 31st, I had a call from the band; they were stalled in Los Angeles, having missed their train.

I told the manager to take a taxi to San Pedro. In that era of scant traffic and miles of open road, I thought a pair of cabs could transport our music to Paydro in time to catch the service mail plane bound for San Diego.

No luck. The manager telephoned at six to say they had missed connections by five minutes.

Both our captain and our exec were absent, so—as adjutant—the command decision was mine. After careful analysis, I ruled against giving up a good party, a mistake I have been making consistently right up to the present.

Turning the station over to the O. D., I had my ship fueled for the flight to Paydro. My transportation at the time was an F5L, a heavy twin-engined Liberty flying boat with all the aeronautical verve of a cow on water skis.

I couldn't locate my regular crew, so I collected some miscellaneous ratings who represented themselves as radio operators, navigators, engineers, and mechanics, and took off.

I studied the northern sky with disapproval. It was as bruised as the face of a sailor who has slid half a mile down skid row on his nose; even so, the flight was "uneventful," i.e., we made it.

By the time we had taken on seven musicians and their instruments, half a gale was blowing. The sea inside the breakwater was beginning to heave and churn, and visibility beyond Point Fermin was zero-zero.

In spite of our overload, we managed to take off and head south. We had been kiting around for maybe half an hour when, without preliminary gurgle, both engines conked out.

I had a problem. It was so dark I didn't know whether we were over liquid or solid. I hoped there was sea beneath, because I had no wheels, an embarrassment in case of a dry landing.

I flattened my glide and lost altitude in a series of steps, straining my eyes in search of a soft spot. The altimeter wasn't much help; it showed 300 feet when we hit. We bounced high enough to have spiraled down; without that refinement, we returned to the sea with enough emphasis to loosen the molars of every man aboard and snap two of the bass fiddle strings.

We were on water all right; it began to pour into the cabin.

I barked to a machinist's mate, third, barely visible beneath the drum, "Get onto these engines."

He rubbed colorless lips with his sleeve and blurted, "Sir, I'm an engineer, okay, but I don't know nuthin' about airplane motors. I'm a steam engine specialist."

We plunged and wallowed, shipping water with every wave. I tried everything I could think of to get the mills going, while my terrified passengers and crew (1) blubbered and cursed, or (2) were seasick.

While fiddling with an assortment of butterfly valves and petcocks, I must have done something right, because one motor came alive, sputtering resentfully and was shortly joined by the other in a sour symphony of internal combustion. It occurred to me that, before attempting takeoff, I should check the wings.

The upper and lower wings of those old biplanes were held *apart* by upright wooden struts, and held *together* by two sets of diagonal wires strung in each bay between struts; one set, the load wires, took the stress when the plane was in flight; the other set, the landing wires, took the stress of the impact as the boat touched down.

My wing check disclosed the interesting fact that most of the landing wires and fittings had been pulled out by the roots.

Half-frozen from my inspection tour, I crawled back into the cabin, which was knee-deep in water. Glancing around, I had the distinct impression that I was the only s.o.b. (soul on board) with any confidence in our future.

We had a two-man pump aboard, so I "volunteered" two of my crew for the job while I rummaged in the forward holds for something to glue on the wings.

Operating that pump provided all the simple pleasures of practicing dentistry on a shark, but we had to pump to keep afloat. The pumpers worked in fifteen-minute shifts, and as blisters formed, backs strained, and stomachs turned inside out, one of the pumping musicians snarled, "You got us into this; you get us out. If you want this goddam pump operated, you do it yourself."

I was faced by an orchestra in rebellion; mutiny on the high Cs.

I must have been a terrifying sight. My uniform was drenched and torn. I had bumped my forehead during one of the landings, and a trickle of blood continued to slide down my face and onto my collar. I couldn't man the pump alone, and I had other things to do in hope of keeping us afloat. The time had come for a command decision.

Reaching into the emergency rack, I brought out a Very pistol. Those old Verys looked as deadly as a sawed-off baby cannon, but their sole purpose was to fire a signal light.

Pointing my Very at my two ablest passengers, a saxophone player and a yeoman third, I yelled, "GET ON THAT PUMP."

They got. Their fury gave them strength. When the first pair was forced to rest, the second team was equally outraged and equally effective, and so on through the complement. Of such emergencies are naval heroes made. Often dead, of course.

[34]

Dawn came on, the seas subsided and the wind died. We were still afloat.

During the dark hours I had decided that as soon as I could see what I was doing, I'd try to start the engines and taxi in the general direction of San Diego. The light in the east provided a bearing, and —confounding all logic—the power responded.

At that heartening moment, a small cheer arose from my passengers.

Fame is brief.

Ten seconds later a massive fog bank rolled in, shrouding us in a blanket of goose down. I couldn't even see the wingtips. Luckily, I still had my Very pistol at the ready, or I would have been set adrift in the bass fiddle—the one with the two broken strings.

Around four that afternoon someone megaphoned through the fog, "Ahoy, there! Are you an F5L from San Diego?"

Never before in my highly ardent experience had I considered a sub-chaser an object to arouse permanent passion. Now, I yearned to rest my head on its rusted bosom.

Anyhow, the sub-chaser, sitting high in the water above the surface fog, threw us a line and towed us to home base.

I've never really cared a lot for seven-piece jazz combos since. I can see how a guy could learn to hate music. All of which may explain why, during my years in Hollywood, I confined my directing of musical pictures to two, only.

As Jimmie McHugh, the late celebrated composer and lyricist, once observed, "It's easier to deal romantically with something you know NOTHING about. All the really great Southern songs were written by Jewish boys from the Bronx who had never been south of the Jersey line."

3

ONE OF MY REASONS FOR BATTLING TO GET BACK TO THAT HALLOWE'EN party had been a green-eyed girl with curly russet hair and a flawless complexion. Add a figure that didn't slow down for curves, and you've got the picture.

Her name was Joan Marshfield. It occurred to me, many years later, that the feminine name I used most frequently in my scripts was "Joan," so obviously her influence persisted far beyond the days when her voice on the telephone turned me into a Creeple-Peeple.

Much of the time in those days, I was a little numb, which was probably Nature's way of fending off a Section Eight. I was flying eggcrates whose four fuselage longerons were made of strips of hickory less than two inches thick, then cocooned by treated silk into a fragile package. Christmas goodies are more securely wrapped these days.

Since the hazards of my profession weren't enough, I had to try something more lethal. I fell in love with Joan, who happened to be the wife of a four-striper, the skipper of a battlewagon. And I—a crummy ensign!

I met Joan half a dozen times before I really met her, as any ensign or shavetail will understand. She and the captain would appear with the other brass on gala occasions, and as she passed I sort of leaned toward her as if slanted by a strong wind. What made it worse was that all my fellow inmates of BOQ were affected the same way; from a distance we must have looked like a stripling forest of blue spruce, blown out of plumb.

We realized, of course, that Joan was ten or twelve years our senior, but the captain was ten or fifteen years older than Joan, so we felt that some sort of compensatory equation was working in our behalf.

One summer afternoon I went to our favorite local drugstore to pick up a cargo of Tincture of Orange Peel, a perfectly legal concoction—in spite of Prohibition—which was rumored to have some mystical medical purpose. It assayed at about 180 proof; a taste of it, uncut by ginger ale, produced Instant Laryngitis, and a second taste made it Permanent.

As I hugged my purchase, a retired admiral—living on Coronado —strode in. At nearly eighty he was still handsome; his bearing was military perfection, shoulders well back and spine as stiff as a marlin spike, and his thick crest of hair shone white in the bright drugstore lights.

Automatically shifting my package so that I could salute him, even though he was wearing civies, I was perplexed by the blankness of his gaze as he approached.

I've always been thankful for that salute, because a second later the admiral fell dead.

A civilian doctor materialized from somewhere but shook his head after a cursory examination. The body was covered by a large canvas, borrowed from painters who had been working on the building's exterior. In silent melancholy, we bystanders waited for military authorities to arrive.

It was a helluva moment for Joan Marshfield to stumble into my life. In a hurried attempt to step over what appeared to her to be a pile of painters' dropcloths, near-sighted Mrs. Marshfield tripped over the admiral's body and literally fell into my arms.

"Thank you, Ensign," she said formally as she started to withdraw from my support.

At that point a two-stripe medic hurried in and pulled the tarp away from the admiral's face.

Mrs. Marshfield glanced down; recognizing the admiral, she drew a long, agonized breath, and began to tremble violently. Spontaneously seeking comfort, she returned to my arms, pressing her face against my chest.

God bless that medic.

I took Mrs. Marshfield home and poured her a stiff drink from her husband's supply. (The captain's cellar was awash with grog, thanks to fleet maneuvers in Bacardi waters.)

We talked quietly for over an hour. I said the usual things aimed at condolence, mentioning the admiral's brilliant career, plus the gallantry of his signing out fast and efficiently without a prolonged, painful illness, etc.

Her ragged breathing eased and she was able to answer in a normal tone when the telephone rang. After a moment's conversation she turned to me saying, "I was planning to have dinner at the Coronado Hotel with Captain and Mrs. Harrison this evening. Could you join us? Captain Marshfield is at sea, you know."

And so it started.

I hit it off with Captain Harrison at once, and his wife, Orissa, was a member of an old line Navy family, so she knew all the right answers. While Harrison and I were outside, having a smoke, he confided that he had plenty of seniority on Marshfield, having been in grade much longer, and he added that he detested Joan's husband, always had, always would. That was The Word.

Thereafter we were a congenial *four*some, which precluded as much gossip as could be precluded on a Naval base.

Fleet maneuvers kept Captain Marshfield away for many months at a time, and intimate personal matters—more Navy gossip— seemed to take him ashore in San Francisco and Bremerton more often than in San Diego.

It was during a prolonged fleet absence that I awakened, slightly befuddled, one morning and deduced from the lacy canopy above the bed that I was NOT in my room at Bachelor Officers' Quarters.

By the time I had located my head and figured out how to turn it, I saw something else patently not government issue.

"Good morning," laughed Joan.

It turned out that—in the final moments of the night before—I had become the second body over which Joan had tripped.

Time—weeks and months—passed in comfortable comradeship; ultimately we drifted into talk of marriage. Of course there were problems.

In those quaint days a divorce might well scuttle the career of a Naval officer. I regarded my presence in the military as temporary, but Marshfield was bucking for admiral. Joan, although totally indifferent to her husband emotionally, was Navy enough to be unwilling to jeopardize Marshfield's advancement.

I had my own qualms. Joan came from a family of great wealth; when I thought of my ensign's pay stacked up against her monthly shoe bill, I vibrated like an N-9.

Meanwhile, it is possible that being in love with Joan kept me alive; it is impressive to note how cautious a man can be in the air when he has a helluva good reason for landing intact—and early.

An ensign is seldom clairvoyant, a fact that may explain my total lack of inkling that Joan Marshfield would reappear from time to time in my life, always when I most needed her. Until the very last.

4

ON THE MORNING OF NOVEMBER 12, 1918, THE BELLS CEASED THEIR clangor, the whistles fell silent, the instant romances dwindled to promises to write, and every duffle bag in San Diego was packed. The war was over. Put the fatted calf in the oven, Mom, we're coming home.

The Navy had a different idea. It was not to be hurried; discharges would be processed with all due delay.

Morale on our base crash-dived lower than an abalone's anus.

The skipper called me in and said in a tone that defied correction, "I understand you're a writer?"

By that time I had sold a few stories to the adventure magazines of the day, and had been inflated enough to show the checks to some of my big-mouthed fellow officers.

"Sir, I'm afraid . . ." I started to say.

"Good," said the skipper. "I must reestablish *esprit de corps*. Need an officer to bolster morale, stimulate interest in activities on base —shows, entertainment, and so on. Thank you, Ensign."

I returned his salute, swung smartly and left the office, wondering how—since I never volunteered for anything—I always drew the offal jobs.

Actually the skipper, bald, beet-faced and paunchy, was Fate's handmaiden. He was simply advancing me along my destined way.

From the age of ten, I had spent my spare time and money on vaudeville tickets. I had heard every variation of every joke used by the baggy pants comics of the day. However, to bring my education up to date, I advanced upon Los Angeles to see what was current on the Keith-Orpheum, Pantages, and Sullivan-Considine circuits.

I was thorough, which is standard procedure when one is operating on government cash. Also, I managed to spend quite a bit of time with Mother and Dad, somewhat to my astonishment, because I never suffered from lack of a lass. I've been forever thankful for those days with, particularly, my dad.

William Muldrough Garnett was born in Glasgow, Kentucky; at sixteen he signed on before the mast and came around the Horn to California on a sailing ship. His parents, older brother, and two sisters did it the easy way—by crossing the continent in a covered wagon.

The family met in San Francisco; my grandfather bought a ranch conveniently located near the general store and post office in Calistoga.

At eighteen, Dad enrolled at the University of California, Berkeley, intending to become a doctor. Somehow he managed to finance his education by saddle-breaking horses without becoming his own best patient.

Halfway through medical school Dad discovered that he lacked the emotional detachment that a doctor, to survive physically and mentally, must have. He switched to dentistry on the theory that what goes wrong in the mouth may be painful but is seldom fatal. He was further comforted by the concept of the tooth as curable; when incurable, removable; when removed, replaceable.

After getting his degree, he set up practice in Wellington, Kansas. (Why Kansas is not clear, except that he met my mother, Rachel Taylor, there.)

Dad was never strictly a molar man. His ingenuity ranged far beyond dentistry. He may not have been the inventor of rubber heels, but he was undoubtedly the first to manufacture his own—from castoff buggy tires.

He dreamed up what had to be one of the first fireless cookers. On Sunday, Mother would prepare a stew in a huge cast iron kettle with a close-fitting top. Once the stew had come to a boil, the kettle was lowered into a huge double-walled wooden crate. Dad used hundreds of newspapers to create an interior heat shield. The crate was closed with a lid insulated in the same way.

The Garnetts would gad about, visiting friends and generally en-

[41]

joying themselves for four or five hours, then come home to a hot Dutch-oven dinner. It is one of my fond childhood memories.

Long before I was born, this imaginative Dr. Garnett stared out over the golden stalks of Kansas and conceived the idea of confining western beef, range cattle, in pens and fattening them on corn. (Today, this is a standard practice called "beef finishing.")

Dad and a partner borrowed $100,000 from a Kansas bank, and fattened their first stock. They sold their prime steers for $150,000.

Dad was as jubilant as a man can get when flat on his back in bed with pneumonia. His sympathetic partner set out with the check to pay off the bank loan and bring back Dad's share of the $50,000 profit.

The partner went into a saloon, probably to gloat a little, sat in on a poker game, lost every cent, and shot himself.

As soon as Dad was able to get out of bed, he went to the banker and said, "I give you my word: every penny will be repaid."

The sympathetic banker suggested that Dad go through bankruptcy, but Dad said, "Not only will I repay the total loan, but interest at five percent per annum."

Then he went to call on Miss Rachel Taylor.

She announced that she still wanted to marry him, no matter how poor they would always be. Dad borrowed money for a marriage license and the minister's fee. He also borrowed the price of a team of high-steppers and a buggy in which to take a wedding trip.

They had scarcely pulled away from the minister's house before Dad, exuberant, clucked the team into overdrive. As he swerved around an approaching rig, he miscalculated and caught the back wheel of the other carriage behind his own rear wheel.

A huge man leapt from the other vehicle and strode belligerently toward the newlyweds. Dad, glaring at Mother and grabbing the lines as if she had been driving, bellowed, "Give me those reins. From now on I'LL do the driving."

The other man, sputtering, satisfied good manners by lifting his hat to Mother. Then he helped Dad extricate his buggy, as one fellow sufferer aiding another. That done, he again bowed to Mother stiffly and stalked away, his expression reading "Women Drivers!"

Dad never recommended this stunt as the ideal way to start a honeymoon.

Although Dad had a growing practice in Wellington, the city spooked him; ghosts were everywhere—dead dreams, a monstrous debt, and the life of a friend pitiably wasted.

When a college pal turned up one day with a rave review of opportunities in Southern California, Dad was a responsive audience.

Assuring the bank that distance would not lessen his sense of obligation, Dad borrowed train fare for two, and my parents moved to Santa Ana. The stork, with me aboard, let down among the orange groves nine months later. Dad, in his innocence, regarded my arrival as a good omen.

During my childhood and early youth I was never told of my father's dedication to paying the bank every borrowed penny. I often wondered why, since Dad was perpetually tired, he couldn't take a little time off. When I said as much to Mother, she answered with a sigh and a soft smile, "Your father must do what he thinks is right." Her smile brightened as she added, "I don't believe he has ever lost a friend. He always does the right thing."

That only increased my bewilderment.

At the time when I was briefly at home, during my investigation of the vaudeville circuits, I noticed that Dad was suffering slightly from the Dentists' Occupational Disease—aching feet.

I told him, "Why don't you build yourself some arch supports?— You've always been an inventor at heart."

Shrugging slightly he said, "These feet have done for me what had to be done. I think they'll last as long as I'll need them."

I was too young to examine that statement for more than surface meaning, but when Dad took me to the depot that foggy February morning, he seemed suddenly bent and tired. I stood on the rear platform and waved with a growing sense of melancholy as he gradually disappeared in the mist.

That was my last sight of him.

Time passed; eventually Mother told me the extent of my father's integrity. Then it was too late for me to put my arm around his shoulders in recognition of his sacrifice, his courage, and his high honor; too late for me to tell him that he was a great guy and deeply loved by his son.

5

BACK ON BASE, I SET ABOUT FASHIONING "BLACKOUTS" FROM THE BEST OF my purloined comedy material.

My top actor was a machinist first named Gompert, who—many years later—became a detective in the L.A. county Sheriff's office. I have often regretted the scarcity of cameras on base. Pictures of Gompert in some of his costumes for his starring roles would have been memorable art for the bulletin board in the Sheriff's office.

Gompert was broad and heavy, with the hairiest legs I've ever seen outside a zoo. He often played the leading lady in ballerina skirts and a decolletage that revealed his bushy chest and weight-lifter's arms. His blonde, curly wig, floppy white hat, and twirly flowered parasol set sex back two generations.

I made a study of our officers and—in exaggerated form—exploited their idiosyncracies. (An exercise in observing generic man in uniform that has stood me in good stead ever since.) I even used distortions of the guys' names in skits that ranged from the malign to the murderous. The enlisted personnel howled at our corniest contrivances, and morale—loosely speaking—was restored.

Our efforts were encouraged by the interest taken in our base by Hollywood. It was natural, once the war was over, for film producers to look longingly at San Diego and its flying complement.

Alan Holubar, an independent producer-director, was one of the first to request Navy flight cooperation for a film entitled *Hell Morgan's Gal,* starring his wife, Dorothy Phillips. I was assigned to put my F5L through a series of lumbering maneuvers that delighted the ground crew who had two pools going: one that paid off if I made it, and the other vice versa. I realized that there was disappointment among a majority of the grease monkeys when the Made It pool paid off, but I'm convinced there's a limit to what a morale officer is obliged to do.

I personally picked up a bonus. In the process of making the picture, Holubar and I became friends. It's true that the average film friendship terminates when the picture is finished, but Holubar made several subsequent trips to San Diego to see the service shows I was "writing" and directing. He laughed along with the military audience, which was perceptive of a civilian. One evening he asked if I would get in touch with him once I was out of uniform.

That "get in touch" pitch is the oldest con on earth, but I was young and naive. With my honorable discharge papers in one hand, I knocked on Holubar's door with the other.

He was actually *glad* to see me. I'm sure that was a historic First, and I shouldn't be surprised if it were a historic Last. Normally the returned fighter of wars at home or abroad is a drug on the Hollywood market.

"Gotta place to live?" Holubar asked. "No? Well, find a place to park your typewriter, then come back—tomorrow morning, maybe? I've got a job for you, doctoring a script."

"Yes, SIR," I said. I was not only a writer, I was a sort of super writer—a script doctor. On my first day in Hollywood, too.

I set out to find a room.

Housing, throughout the world, has always been a clue to status.

In that particular era, *the* place for inconsequential motion picture employees to live was within an area bounded on the east by Western Avenue, and on the west by Highland Avenue; on the north by Franklin Avenue, and on the south by Melrose Avenue.

Pickfair was perched on a hill in a remote section called Beverly Hills, as distant as a castle on the Rhine; Rudolph Valentino had a house called Falcon's Lair, teetering on a pinnacle above Hollywood, and Antonio Moreno occupied an aerie overlooking most of Southern California. But those people had it made.

Unmarried stars, getting their first big break, lived at the Hollywood Hotel (then situated at the northwest corner of Hollywood and Highland where the Federal Savings & Loan Association of Hollywood is now located), or in one of the elegant hostelries such as the

Garden of Allah on Sunset Boulevard, or the Garden Court Apartments still standing at the west end of Hollywood Boulevard (now debauched by a red sign advertising rooms at $7 per night.)

Featured players lived in bungalow courts. Extras and free-lance writers like me, even if one were a *script doctor,* lived in "guest houses."

The standard guest house was a rambling redwood-sided two-story building that had once been occupied by a large family, now moved—in their affluence—to an ambitious subdivision called Brentwood.

The guest house was usually fronted by a wide veranda; access was through a plate glass door set in a three-inch oak frame; this opened into a central hallway from which a stairway ascended to the upper floor.

Ordinarily the living room, distinguished by a fireplace with a massive cracked marble mantel, opened to the left of the entry, and a dining room with a built-in buffet boasting stained glass doors, opened to the right. Behind these major rooms there were, on one side of the house, a butler's pantry, kitchen and screened service porch, and a family bedroom and bath on the other. The number of bedrooms upstairs depended upon the opulence or fertility of the original owner, but there was never more than one bathroom to a floor. There must have been several hundred thousand of these edifices built in Los Angeles after the turn of the century, and many of them are still standing.

After close study of the fine print in the newspaper, I picked out a likely spot in a desirable location, and pressed the doorbell.

It was answered by a woman with orange hair and a body like a brace of basketballs under a flowered tablecloth.

She asked my profession; when I said, with all the nerve in the world, that I was a motion picture writer, she announced that she, too, had been in show biz all her life. "Vaudeville headliner," she said over her shoulder as she undulated up the stairs toward the advertised room. "I'm a singer." She uttered a few notes. The roses on the wallpaper turned brown.

"Here it is: a nice, big room, just ten steps from the convenience. You'll have to share the room with another young man in pictures, but it's a good deal when you're between jobs. Writing's a chancy business; usually I like to rent to more substantial types. No fly-by-nights for me."

There were two beds, two dressers, two straight-backed chairs, and a three-legged wicker fern stand, fernless, in the room.

My prospective landlady explained that local telephone calls and kitchen privileges were included in the rent, adding that my roommate usually fixed his dinner between six-thirty and seven. She preferred "to dine" at eight.

I nodded appreciation of this advantage while hoping, privately, to be financially able to take most of my meals at Musso-Frank's on Hollywood Boulevard. Incidentally, you can still get the world's finest flannel cakes at Musso-Frank's which hasn't changed locations in all these years.

The place seemed to be clean and the price was slightly less than I had expected to pay, so I handed over a week's rent in advance and unpacked my suitcase, a four-minute chore. My civilian wardrobe was Spartan and my most cherished possession was my Navy .45 automatic pistol, into the butt of which I had filed a notch every time I scored with a dame during my brass-button days.

I had just returned from the shower when my roommate came home. He was a wiry little guy with a touseled head of dark brown hair, lots of shoulder width, and a dazzling grin. "I'm Dick Grace," he said.

The name rang a bell. "Naval Air?"

"Sure as hell."

"Pensacola?"

"Dam' right."

We both began to talk at once.

This Dick Grace had been among the very early fliers to graduate from Pensy; he and two other pilots had been assigned to a seaplane base in Italy in the midst of World War I, and all three had become legendary heroes among Naval Air personnel.

Their story ran something like this: On the night of their arrival at the Italian seaplane base, Dick and his brother officers were honored at a dinner party given by their new Italian squadron leader and his men. Dick's reputation as a stunt flyer had preceded him, so his new comrades-in-arms began to boast of *their* prowess.

Few Americans have a reputation for silent modesty, so—after their share of vino—Dick and his buddies told some flight yarns that would have impelled an honest angel to turn in his wings.

Abruptly the Italian squadron leader arose and challenged Dick to a few chukkers of Follow The Leader.

On the field Dick discovered that the Italian Air Force was flying land planes, not the seaplanes in which Dick had been trained; however, on the wings of alcohol, that seemed a minor detail.

Dick and the squadron leader matched for first shot, and the Eye-tie won. Into the summer's twilight they flew, doing Immelmans, barrel rolls, spins, and a few contortions that had no formal names. The squadron leader was unable to shake Dick.

Landing at last, the Italian officer said, "You are good, Ensign. I now follow you—unless you care to postpone until another time."

"What I have in mind won't take long," Dick said. He had liked the surging power of the Italian plane; he studied the brief landing strip with careful calculation.

Starting at the extreme end of the runway, he gave the plane full throttle and held her nose down until he was getting every knot she had in her, then he pulled her up in a screaming loop and landed back on the runway.

The squadron leader copied the stunt perfectly, except for the landing. He splattered a nice plane all over the landscape but luckily was thrown clear into bushes and mud, both comparatively soft. After a few days in the hospital he was back on base, bugging Dick to explain the technique of the backward somersault.

"First of all," Dick said solemnly, "you can't have anything to do with a dame for a month beforehand—can't risk fouling up the inner ear."

The squadron leader studied Dick's guileless pan for signs of fraud. Finding none, the Italian shrugged and walked away, saying over his shoulder, "Is not *that* beautiful, that stunt."

When the war ended, Dick returned to the U. S., was mustered out, and promptly discovered that a pilot who wanted to stay in the air had his choice between barnstorming and stunting.

Dick liked California, and movies wanted more than the early flight services were willing to give, so Dick went into business for himself. He was the first pilot to put a plane into a tailspin and crash it, actually crash it, before a hand-cranked camera. As a sideline, he liked to bet anyone foolhardy enough to try to take his money that he could cream a plane inside a forty-foot circle; that, of course, specified the point of impact and had no reference to the area over which debris was scattered.

So that was my new roommate, Dick Grace.

I looked him over and summoned up an idea. "Why not give up this locoed bird profession? How about selling real estate? You've got the sex appeal for it."

He just grinned and I realized that I was set up for a chronic case of the heebie-jeebies. For a long time I was to grit my teeth and cross my fingers every time I heard a plane screaming across the sky.

Meanwhile, I reported to Holubar who handed me a script entitled *By Hate Possessed,* written for silent production. (Sound was still several years in the future.)

Holubar explained, "We paid thirty-five grand for this property; look it over and see if you can get a shooting script out of it. The big job is to reduce everything to action; rely as little as possible on titles. Look at some Lubitsch footage. He's the best in the business."

I studied several Lubitsch productions. I was fascinated; he could run ten or fifteen minutes without using a single subtitle; although the action took place at different times and in different locales, plot twist and plot advancement were clear.

I returned dubiously to the problems presented by Holubar's script which had little in common with the passions of Vienna and the sexcapades of royalty.

Our yarn dealt with an architect, a lean, idealistic man given to contemplating city streets that, he felt, had been deformed by ugly buildings. His dream was to build The City Beautiful, the gleaming metropolis serving the aspirations of mankind. He was hopelessly in love with a debutante, a "flapper" who was, according to the dialect of yesteryear, "wild." (Just crank this formula story forward a few years and you come awfully close to *The Fountainhead* by Ayn Rand, starring Gary Cooper and Patricia Neal.)

I told Holubar that I was worried about the silent action potential of the script, even if it *had* cost $35,000—long green in those days.

My initiation in How to Make a Sow's Ear out of a Silk Purse was instant and complete. "You're right," growled Holubar. "We've got to have a leading man with balls; none of this moody-doody business. Make him a tug boat operator. He has this stinking old barge, see, but he has a vision: some day he's going to own the goddamdest barge on earth. Show him boarding the *Leviathan* or something, as master. Now, about this babe. Forget the debutante business; our heroine is a working girl. On the waterfront. Atmosphere: she works in a fish cannery."

I ventured, "In the original script, the girl has an illegitimate baby."

"Are you kiddin'?" roared Holubar. "We gotta think about censorship. She picks up this kid from a box floating in the harbor. Now, about that marquee title. We gotta change that. *By Hate Possessed* —naw, it doesn't grab ya. Let's name it *The Adored Alice.* Give it kind of a *Seventh Heaven* flavor. Ya got it? A cannery kid, a tugboat captain, and a bastard. By Jesus, we gotta picture."

Holubar's next commitment was to be shot in Canada's Northwest Territories. He wanted to take me along so we could work on another gut-buster. I was ready. I had the plot for *The Adored Aurora Bory-Alice* nicely worked out: This French trapper meets this Eskimo broad, see? She's working in a mukluk factory and she finds this orphan in a snow bank.

Unfortunately for posterity, the budget wouldn't stretch to permit a script rewrite, so Holubar went off to Canada to shoot his frozen turkey without me.

I was left in a condition that *Variety* euphemistically describes as "at liberty."

I dug into the trunk for a couple of minor masterpieces and a major opus that an agent named Adeline Alvord had read, liked, and tried to sell without success. With these under my arm, I set out to canvass the studios.

I started on Gower Street, working what were then called "Poverty Row" operators. (It was probably at this period Gower Street picked up its generic tag, Gower Gulch, because of the number of quickie Westerns foaled there.)

Nobody has seen more secretaries guarding closed doors than I did, with the possible exception of a *Daily Worker* advertising salesman calling on Mr. Paul Getty.

Finally I ran into a samaritan named Ralph Ceder, a two-reel comedy writer–director for Monte Banks Productions. Monte Banks, incidentally, was fated to marry Gracie Fields and to live out his life luxuriating on the Mediterranean.

Ceder said, "Look, kid, your stuff is funny enough, but you're going at this in the wrong way. Carrying around an armload of scripts marks you as an amateur. Get yourself an idea: one GOOD comedy situation. Pick out a comic, and make an appointment with his director. Outline the suggestion verbally. Those guys are flashes at fleshing out an idea. Next, don't try to sell only the idea; sell yourself. That way, you've got a job when you put over an idea."

It was sound advice. Right today, the only way to sell a story for television is to make an appointment with a TV producer or story editor, tell him a yarn appropriate for his series, and hope he says, "Write it."

If he does, that's a commitment.

Then, as now, the amateur had little chance. To get a job, a writer must have been published, or he must have a sponsor. Ceder served in the latter capacity for me. He introduced me—via telephone—to the head title writer at the Hal Roach Studio, a helluva guy named Beanie Walker. He had been the dean of Los Angeles sportswriters during his years with the Hearst newspapers.

"Come into my office for ONE day," Walker suggested, "to get the feel of our operation. No pay, you understand. This is strictly a sightseeing excursion. But, maybe . . ."

It was that "maybe" that did it. After a day's indoctrination, I sat in, with Beanie, on the screening of an unfinished picture. Returning to the office, I whipped out some gag titles for the flick and submitted the finished job to Walker.

He looked them over and grunted, "Yeah." I was to learn later that his "yeah" was a round of applause.

He added, "Come back tomorrow—on salary."

Dress extras today get more for eight hours' work than I collected for a week of twelve-hour days. Nevertheless, I had a job.

I hurried home with the news to find my roommate wearing a huge neck brace. "Don't give it a thought," Dick said, waving away my solicitude. "This just wasn't my day. But don't forget that I beat up twenty-five planes before one got even with me."

I wasn't too surprised by Dick's condition, even though I knew he took elaborate precautions before crashing a plane; for one thing, he built a sort of steel cage inside the cockpit and upholstered it with very heavy, resilient padding. However, you don't drop an egg off a ten-story building in a fleece-lined safe unless you're planning an omelet.

"No sweat," I said. "I've come up with a job, so we eat."

Actually, eating was no problem. Our landlady seemed to give a party every night. Roisterers came and went from 8:00 P.M. until dawn. Often the last carload would be shoving off as we somnambulated downstairs for a fast blast of coffee.

We hesitated to squawk about the night-long traffic because the dear old gal was generous with fried chicken, chocolate cake, apple pie, and bottles of homebrew from her well-stocked ice box.

"If she'd take off a hundred pounds, have her teeth fixed, and learn to play piano, you and I would be set here for a couple of years," mused Dick.

The Hal Roach lot was situated on Washington Boulevard in Culver City, about a mile east of MGM, which was then Goldwyn Studios. This area has never been noted for beauty, but within the studio gates there were scenic tidbits on all sides such as Mildred Davis, Edwina Booth, Sally Rand, Marie Mosconi and Jobyna Ralston.

I met Jobyna in a rather unusual way. She accosted me.

Plus Fours were the uniform of the day for upcoming junior executives; playing all the angles, I wore Plus Eights. And tassels on my golf brogues.

As I strode to lunch one day, a husky feminine voice dripping magnolia hailed me respectfully, saying, "Hi, Goofy Pants."

The controlled admiration of this greeting was to key our entire relationship.

Naturally I invited her to have luncheon with me.

A few days later, Hal Roach's partner, Harold Lloyd—one of the comedic immortals—married his leading woman, Mildred Davis. Jobyna succeeded to Mildred's old job, which did little for Joby's humility.

She lived with her parents and brother on Holly Drive above Franklin Avenue. Usually she was brought to the studio by her brother or her father. The Ralstons were a one-car family, but that one car was a Willys-Knight with a sleeve valve engine, the Excalibur of the era.

On one occasion, when our romance was new and the Willys was momentarily laid up to have a sleeve shortened, I volunteered to drive Jobyna home in my Hupmobile. This magnanimous gesture was made at noon, halfway between the cream of tomato and the abalone a la bonne femme. Jobyna said, "See you at six then."

With full heart and stomach, I was called to Beanie Walker's office because of a title emergency.

In those days, comedies ran for one, two, or three reels—a three-reeler being a spectacular. A reel held a thousand feet of film, which was projected at ninety feet per minute.

Nowadays, motion pictures aren't discussed in terms of "reels." They are said to run ninety minutes, one hundred and twenty minutes, or a tail-torturing one hundred and eighty minutes.

There are few things in this world as serious as comedy writing. Nearly everyone is capable of authentic humor—conscious or unconscious—once or twice in a lifetime. Some highly gifted people can be genuinely funny once a week, and an occasional comic genius such as Bob Hope can be funny every day.

A title writer in those silent film days had to *try* to be funny about sixty to seventy times every forty-eight hours. The average one-reeler was interspersed with about thirty-five titles which came in three delicious flavors: *dialogue titles in quotes* (pre-talking picture communication between players), *editorial or time lapse titles* ("Came the dawn"), and *introductory titles.* An example of an introductory title is the following, which I wrote for a Stan Laurel comedy.

The fadein showed eight bounteously endowed Amazons charging toward Stan with the obvious intention of separating him from his virtue. Stan was shown fleeing backward in terror; backward, backward until he fell off the Santa Monica Palisades. Trick photography hurtled him to the beach four hundred feet below. Hitting the sand, he bounced lightly to his feet and went into a parody adagio along the surf line.

An introductory title was needed. In desperation, I came up with, "The lure of the sea was strong in Penrod—he'd been struck by an oar as a child."

Kids thought it was funny and hip adults guffawed at the double entendre.

A title writer soon learned to establish joke patterns. One of the most useful was the "as" joke. That is, to describe a weakling, which a comic always had to be: "He was as tough as wet tissue paper." To tab a stingy man: "He was as close as nine and ten." Or, and this dates the humor, "He was as tight as a Pullman window." To describe the courage of General Pershing: "He was as brave as Douglas Fairbanks."

When the rough cut of a comedy was shown, the film editor inserted a piece of leader (blank film) wherever he felt a title was needed. We title writers carried clipboards to the projection room, made notes, and retired to our cells to scrape our funnybones. If even *one* title failed to get a laugh when the comedy was previewed before a miscellaneous audience, back we went to the studio where we worked all night, if necessary, to come up with a feather husky enough to tickle the rib of that last guy in the balcony when we previewed again the following night.

I became entangled in some such snafu the day I was supposed to drive Jobyna home. I forgot her. Totally.

She called herself to my attention the following morning, tossing off a description of me beginning with "inconsiderate and thoughtless," and progressing through "rude and fatheaded."

At least I stood out from the crowd. Naturally, we began to go steady.

Going with Joby had fringe benefits. Her dad was the prize in a Cracker-Jack box. He had been a foundry worker in South Pittsburgh, Tennessee, and in his spare time he had farmed a couple of acres surrounding his home on Main Street.

According to one of his stories, he barely missed being elected mayor on the Reform ticket. He still believed, years afterward, that his early rising habits brought about his defeat.

By the time the local rooster sounded reveille on election day (according to Dad Ralston), he was in the barn, feeding his horse and cows. Among them was a highly energetic heifer.

As Dad was responding to a call of nature, the wind blew open the barn door, and the calf streaked for freedom. With his unoccupied hand, Dad grabbed the calf's tail, a restraining technique that merely threw the calf into high gear.

And so it was that Candidate Ralston, clinging to the calf with one hand and to himself with the other, shot past the polls bellowing, "Wait a goddam minute. Whoa, goddamit!"

In every community there are bigots; those of South Pittsburgh, Tennessee, terminated the Reform candidate's political career.

Personally, I think they should have sent him to Congress where it has always been an asset to be ambidextrous.

One Sunday afternoon Joby and I drove up a small canyon off Laurel Canyon Boulevard to a scenic prominence; aside from enough level space to park my Hup, the property consisted of three vertical acres. Its price was ridiculously low, because the agent was convinced that no one could possibly build anything larger than a cuckoo's nest on the site. His calculation had failed to allow for the existence of a love-sick comedy title writer from the Hal Roach Studios.

I bought the parcel—five lots for $125.00—and hit Dick Grace for the $20.00 down payment.

The following week, one of Hollywood's periodic menopauses set in. Along with twenty or thirty others, I was let out of the Roach Studio.

6

I trudged home that night to find Dick Grace sporting his second neck brace.

"Going formal again?" I asked.

"Yup. But this is my last engagement with the high life. I got to thinking, while the Doc was working on me, that a guy could get killed, losing altitude that fast without an elevator. After fifty-four crackups, I'm going straight. From now on, nothing but kiwi stunts."

While Dick convalesced, I dug into my trunk again. I rewrote rewrites and sold enough to reimburse Dick for the down payment on my lots, and to keep up the monthly installments. I also invested in a set of retreads for the Hupmobile which was running barefooted, chasing jobs for me.

The dime in my pocket was solo when I got a call from Roach.

Rob Wagner (later the publisher of the brilliant but short-lived "Beverly Hills Script") was working on a three-reel comedy entitled *Don't Park Here,* starring Will Rogers. I was to work with Wagner and Rogers on some sight gags to spark the action.

Rogers was a towering public figure. His name was a household word, so I was agog over the prospect of dreaming up comedy sequences with this kindly, quick-witted humorist.

Wagner took me onto the set to meet Mr. Rogers, saying, "Tay has written a lot of comedy stuff for some of the biggest people in the business. He's going to be our gag man."

At that point Rob was called to the telephone, leaving me alone with the rope-twirler from Oklahoma. He seemed cold and saturnine instead of warm and witty. A silence persisted between us, while I—tongue-tied with admiration—tried to think of something to say.

Just as I was clearing the awe from my throat, Rogers' stubby finger thumped firmly against my chest and he said in his careful drawl, "Don't make any mistakes, Kid. *I'M* the funny man on this picture."

"Yes sir," I said, looking squarely into a pair of icy eyes, then backing out of the royal presence.

When I reported the conversation to Rob Wagner, he said, "What's a title? From now on you're my codirector. Let Rogers *be* the funny man."

Rogers, however, was not content to be star and gag man; he was constrained to be the director as well. Rob Wagner resigned, telling Roach, "Let Garnett finish the job."

Which I did without bloodshed. But barely.

At liberty again.

As I drove up in front of our boarding house that evening, I noted Dick Grace in his native dress (bandages) sitting on the top step, only his red-rimmed eyes and cracked lips showing amid the gauze. "I got myself grilled," he announced ruefully. "I told them rare, but I'm damned near well done."

Doubling for a film's heroine, he had been dressed in a blonde wig and a flowing chiffon negligee. As per script, the villain set fire to the heroine's home. To escape, she (Dick in drag) was to jump from a second-story window onto a green-dyed raffia lawn.

As Dick landed, aflame, a prop man with a fire extingusher was to put out the fire. Unfortunately, no one had checked the condition of the extinguisher in advance of need. It was empty.

Dick saved his own life by rolling in the artificial grass to smother the blaze.

"You shouldn't be sitting here," I protested. "You should be in bed."

"No bed."

"Whatta ya mean 'no bed'? Our rent's paid until the end of the month."

"We've been took, my friend. But good. There isn't even a toothbrush left in this house. Not even a paper clip. Our house mother has gone over the hill."

A moment later the law arrived. So their trip wouldn't be a total loss, they took us to the pokey. Our enterprising landlady, it seemed, had been supervising a thriving bootleg operation, as well as running a successful call house.

Dick and I had served as window dressing for the enterprise. The dummies in the window.

I told the officers, "There's one thing I'd like to salvage, if possible: my Navy Colt .45."

The sympathetic cops said they'd do what they could, but chances were excellent that our former hostess had set up light housekeeping across the border.

The Chinese have a proverb that can be translated, "All roads cross twice." Eventually I recaptured my artillery from the hairy mitt of Clark Gable—but I'm getting ahead of my story.

After the officers had dropped Dick and me on our forlorn doorstep, we agreed to check into the Christy Hotel for one night. The following morning I drove Dick to the Union Pacific station and put him aboard a Chicago-bound train. He had decided to go home and write a book about stunt flying for films. He thought audiences had a right to know that it was dangerous.

He needed no crystal ball to foretell the flying disasters of the future that would take the lives of Omar Locklear, Viola Dana's fiancé; Bernard Durning, a fine director of air action films; and Harry Sweet, a Sennett comedian who dived a plane into Big Bear lake; neither plane nor pilot was ever recovered. Mary Astor's first husband, Kenneth Hawks, was to die with half a dozen others when two planes collided in midair; Will Rogers and Wiley Post were to crash at Point Barrow, Alaska, and the greatest stunt flier of all, Paul Mantz, was to die in the midst of the 1966 filming of *Flight of the Phoenix.*

After waving goodbye to Dick, thankful to see him traveling by train for a change, I drove very, very slowly to the Ralston residence to explain why Jobyna and I would have to postpone our plans—again.

"The hell with it," shrugged Dad Ralston. "We'll build your house while you're between jokes. Got any cash stowed away?"

Cash was in short supply, but I still had—in my footlocker at my mother's house—a small inventory of wartime fiction that I'd never stopped to polish. I rented a typewriter and polished until my elbows ached; I got lucky. I sold quite a few as film originals to Poverty Row producers. With that loot I bought a tent and staked it on my lot beside the Hup.

Dad Ralston borrowed a pickup truck so we could patronize a wrecking company where we bought doors, windows and some framing lumber that had been snatched from the jaws of termites.

My self-architected plans called for one big utility room, plus kitchen and bath. Later we would add a bedroom. Still later—according to my Mitty imaginings—the house would increase by additional bedrooms and De Mille bathrooms, a bar, a projection room, a butler's pantry, a music room, and a formal entry with several suits of armor standing beside the grand horseshoe stairway.

The first job was, of course, to get started by building a flight of permanent steps from the road to the building site. I used concrete, contouring treads and risers to ascend in easy switchbacks. They turned out to be beautiful steps. ALL EIGHTY-FIVE of them.

I hate to remember how many hundred-pound bags of cement I lugged up that stairway to pour the foundation for the house and to install a septic tank.

By the time Dad Ralston and I had completed the foundations and started framing, I was broke again. The last of my speculative manuscripts was rejected, so I had to think up a new source of grocery money.

I reported to a casting office at Universal and was asked if I could swim. I said I was born with gills. Next question: could I ride a horse? "Why, shore," I drawled, standing as bowlegged as possible.

I was sent to a castle set on the back lot where a moat filled with water the color and consistency of pea soup was crossed by a drawbridge. The idea was for me to gallop a horse off the open end of the drawbridge and SPLASH! into the goop. The fact that I was to be wearing armor didn't seem to worry anyone but me. Stunt men are expendable.

At that time my knowledge of the horse as a species consisted of two facts: He was a hayburner with a speed of maybe ten miles per hour, and if mated to a donkey, he sired a mule who refused to continue the genetic experiment.

Thanks to my stunt I picked up a fresh bit of equine lore.

The moment the horse and I hit the water, I went into an easy dive and came up blowing out algae and a tadpole. The nag followed standard horse procedure and tried to climb aboard the first solid object touched by his forefeet: me. He nearly drowned me before I read him accurately, dived deep, and swam underwater far and fast.

I'm still morose about the financial arrangement: The horse was paid thirty bucks for the stunt. I got ten.

Yet my next job made a sissy of that horse. I was hired to double the "heavy" in a barroom fight with a famous Western star. He's long gone, so I'll skip his name. He had once been a professional pug and certainly knew how to do a picture fight.

Currently there is much criticism of the brutality of American films, but the truth is that a properly staged movie donnybrook is as programmed and as carefully timed as a ballet, and no more deadly.

The most photogenic punch is a wide, barndoor swing that misses the chin of the apparent recipient by several inches, just as that recipient snaps his head back to indicate instant of impact. The legitimate ring punch, good for the ten count, photographs like "throw Mama from the train a kiss."

The star, Mr. White Hat, and I worked out an action routine in rehearsal, but when the cameras began to grind, he went to work— wearing a fixed grin—and beat the hell out of me. I knew that if I hit back, I'd lose my stunt check; he knew it, too. I wound up with a pulpy face, two black eyes, half a dozen loose teeth, and a couple of cracked ribs.

When the director finally caught on and yelled, "Cut," Mr. White Hat strolled away from my soggy form, wagging his head and observing to the world in general, "The kid had an inch reach on me and probably ten years, but, by God, I'm still a pretty good man."

I figured he was a sadistic exception to film rule, but a few days later I was hanging around a set where a professional fighter, George Godfrey, was cast as a stoker in a sea saga called *Hell's Cargo,* starring George Bancroft.

Godfrey was a magnificent ebony Apollo, and an artist at pulling his punches.

According to the script, the stoker (Godfrey) led a mutiny that was put down by Bancroft in a fight to outbloody the celebrated battle in *The Spoilers.* Ordinarily the star would be doubled, but Bancroft did his own fights.

As the last phase of the choreographed fight was played out and the director called, "Cut and print it," Bancroft obviously said to himself, "I'm going to deck this big blackbird—but good." Reaching back to North Dakota, he smashed Godfrey squarely on the chin. Godfrey didn't move a muscle. Very gently he said, "Man, you oughtn't to do that. You liable to hurt somebody that way."

Since I lacked that brand of stamina, I decided to take myself and my natural nose into another division of the picture business.

However, I've never forgotten that stunting had roofed my house and installed the windows. I was able to take up residence without gas, electricity, or a telephone. I boiled coffee over canned heat in a "granite iron" pot lent me by Pop Ralston, and ate canned pork and beans with a spoon "borrowed" from the Roach Commissary.

On Christmas Eve I had just enough scratch to buy a five-pound box of candy for Jobyna and five gallons of gas for the Hupmobile. I drove with outthrust chin to the Ralston home, determined to keep Christmas merry. My determination was shored up by anticipation of Ma Ralston's cooking.

I parked in my usual spot on the dead-end street, and had opened the car door when the Hup was struck broadside. Jobyna's chocolates merged with the threadbare pattern of my sports coat, and my legs buckled under me.

The driver of the assaulting car struggled from behind his steering wheel and staggered toward me as Dad Ralston stormed out of the house, yelling, "Ya goddam crazy drunk, ya might've killed Tay!"

The drunk began to sob, "You're picking on me because you're so old I don't dare hit you."

"So old" was fight talk to Pop. I had to step between the juvenile and the senior citizen to keep them from clobbering one another. That explained the subsequent black and blue marks on me, both fore and aft.

The police arrived and trundled the drunk off to the soak tank. It was determined that he had no insurance and had been driving a

[61]

friend's car without a license. Both cars were towed away, shedding parts.

My skinned shins and bruised ribs gave me a little trouble, but my big trouble was provided by Jobyna. Something was wrong between us, and I couldn't figure out exactly what. Sure, I hadn't been able to take her out much for many, many weeks, but there was going to come a day when life would be all Montmartre, Henry's, the Del Mar Club.

When she drove me up Laurel Canyon that night she said, "It's been a million laughs, Tay. See you around," and left me standing at the foot of my eighty-five steps. Steps up which I had planned to carry her as a bride.

I was surprised to find a special delivery letter in my mail box— from my mother. It was a Christmas card "To My Dear Son," and a note of thanks for the initialed scarf I had sent her. She added, "I have a large doctor bill that I would like to pay before the end of the year. Could you possibly send me my regular check a few days early this month, and if a little more than usual could be added, I'd appreciate it."

Merry Christmas!

Light your torches and pull up your tights.

On December 26th, a Monday, I walked three miles to Schwab's Drugstore on Sunset Boulevard, to telephone each studio in which I had a contact, mentioning casually that I was at liberty. I emerged from the telephone booth totally tapped out, and still at liberty.

I had known, of course, that Hollywood closes up around December 15th, and stays that way until around January 10th. No matter what some people may think, Hollywood is a hard-working town, so it takes Christmas holidays seriously. It is also an emotional town, so Christmas permits it to rejoice and spread vast layers of goodwill.

Someone had given me a box of cigars which I turned in at Schwab's for cash. With that I bought chow for a week.

On my despondent way back up the canyon I noticed that the gas company was digging a trench to install a main. I approached the foreman for a job.

"Glad to get you," he said. "Most guys won't work this week."

The following morning the hotshot writer, the sidesplitting gag man, went to work with pick and shovel. When cars passed, I averted my face; I didn't want to be recognized by my erstwhile studio friends.

Ditchdigging is hard and hungry work, so that first week's pay looked awfully good. I sent half of it to my mother, and with the other half I bought groceries and signed up for gas service; I felt I owed the company that much.

I was setting one trembling foot after the other at the end of my shift one twilight, when a car drew alongside and a sweet voice called out, "Hi, Goofy Pants."

I fell into the Willys, making like a newly adopted puppy.

Jobyna said, "Ralph Ceder's been trying to reach you. He's working at Sennett's and the gag spot's wide open. It's all yours if you want it."

"IF I WANT IT! Jesus H. K. Ryst!" When I started breathing again I said, "How about a celebration? By Saturday night I'll be able to spring for dinner at Musso-Frank's."

She looked up. She looked down. She said, "I'm awfully sorry, Tay; I hate to tell you this—right now especially when things have been so rough for you. Well, I'm engaged to Richard Arlen. We're going to be married soon."

Richard Arlen was one of Paramount's top stars, handsome and talented; to make matters even worse, he was a helluva nice guy.

He still is.

This will give you some idea: When Arlen was at the pinnacle at Paramount, he noticed the behavior of a newcomer from Georgia, a messenger boy who was courteous, hard-working, and competent. Top stars seldom pay much attention to messengers and mail room clerks, because they come and they go, giving up the long climb to Hollywood success in favor of returning to college, courtesy of dear old dad.

However, A. C. Lyles was different. His quiet proficiency impressed Arlen, who told him, "You're going to be a top producer in this town some day. I want you to promise me that, when you've made it, you'll cast me in every picture you make."

"I promise," said A. C., smiling in his unassuming way and nodding his appreciation.

A. C. Lyles is now one of Hollywood's most respected young producers. Whenever a shooting script for his next picture is completed, he sends a copy to Richard Arlen with a note reading, "Pick your part."

Arlen, now snowy-haired (which makes the scamp handsomer than ever) chooses a role and gives it his best. He regards A. C. as the soundest investment he's ever made.

7

AND SO I WENT TO WORK IN THE OLD SENNETT "TOWER," OTHERWISE known as the Snake Pit, on the third floor of a frame office building that had once been painted white, but was recovering rapidly.

The first floor was occupied by the accounting offices, the general manager's office, Sennett's office and steam room. Additional paper work was relegated to the second floor; the third, originally outfitted as a gymnasium for undermuscled executives, had been converted into a gag room.

Over the years the Sennett Tower came to be regarded as the greatest school for film writers that ever existed in Hollywood.

Incidentally, when the stairway from second to third floor had to be renovated, a trusted carpenter accepted a twenty-dollar token of appreciation, and built one riser about half an inch higher than the others. Sennett, tiptoeing up the flight to catch his brain factory dawdling, inevitably tripped over that high riser, alerting us. Pressure pays off: In the forty seconds between Sennett's stumble and his arrival at our door, some of the greatest nonsense ever put on the screen was conceived.

Within Sennett's little patch of real estate there sprouted such hardy perennials as Charlie Chaplin, Ben Turpin, Chester Conklin, Harry Langdon, Slim Summerville, Bobby Dunn, Ralph Graves, Bill Bevan, Andy Clyde, Harry McCoy (who was also a gag man), and the immortal Stan Laurel, later teamed with Oliver (Babe) Hardy.

These comics were usually menaced by such heavies as Vernon Dent, James Finlayson, and Kala Pasha; they were soothed by such beauties as Marie Prevost, Phyllis Haver, Natalie Kingston, Alice and Marcelline Day, and Gertrude Astor.

Writers in the Snake Pit worked in pairs. I worked with three different men, not one of whom telegraphed, by appearance, the fact that he was a very funny guy.

Hal Conklin was the first, a soft-spoken, gentle master of the English language. He was a gray eminence entwined with ivy, but he managed to disguise that fact to escape the usual gag writer's prejudice against anyone who could define "risibility."

My second partner was Vernon Smith who looked, spoke, and acted like a Superior Court judge. He was stern, grim-visaged, and forceful. Sometimes I thought his humor so individual, and so dependent for punch upon his unripe-persimmon puss, that Harry Langdon should have been writing his lines, and he should have been the actor.

The third highly talented writer with whom I worked off and on, was Frank Capra, a warm-hearted Italian family man, as nice a guy as I've ever known, and as capable.

The Tower could also have been called Babel when ten or twelve teams were "at work" simultaneously, because our "writing" was vocal. We limbered up by discussing loudly and at length the baseball or football standings, as the season provided. Next, we touched upon the previous night's social activities, which reminded us of the gin bottles under the couch cushions. A pint or so later we would have reached the subject of girls, past, present, and future.

At which juncture, my partner—seeing the sun sinking over the yardarm, and hearing Sennett's hearty cussing on the stairway—would remember that we had been assigned a Langdon story. He would say, "Hey, I have an idea. See, Langdon is a Scottish immigrant—kilts, sporran, the works . . ."

I would pick it up. " . . . in steerage on a ship in Liverpool . . ."

" . . . on his way to the U. S."

"He's already seasick, even with the boat still tied up . . ."

". . . so he rolls into his bunk. Did they have bunks in steerage?"

"What the hell. This is *our* ship. He goes to sleep . . ."

". . . and in comes this crook, about the build and beauty of a bull moose . . ."

". . . he is about to conk Langdon, when . . ."

". . . a pellet comes flying through the porthold. The crook catches

[66]

it with a nice underhand, unraps the paper from around the stone . . ."

". . . the stone is an EMERALD about the size of a cough drop . . ."

". . . and the note reads, 'Ditch it. The ship is being boarded by Customs Officers.'"

"He has to find a place to hide the stone. The officers are pounding on the door . . ."

"He looks at Langdon, snoring a cadenza with his mouth wide open . . ."

"With a tea-drinking gesture, he drops the stone into Langdon's maw and Langdon swallows it . . ."

"Now, we're set. Every time Langdon thinks he's going to be seasick, the crook shoves a pistol in his back and says, 'Fight it, Pal . . . or else.'"

We had developed a gag routine. Eventually, with further embellishment, it appeared in a film released under the title, *The Sea Squawk.*

Today there are two kinds of gag routines: visual and verbal. Life was simpler in the days when we had to dream up only the visual.

In order to save time when Sennett was breathing like a flamethrower down our necks, we developed an informal library of gag patterns. A favorite, because of its flexibility, was "The Ghost in the Pawn Shop," a generic term applied to any menace stalking the comedian.

Its origin was an ancient vaudeville act that was adapted to a thousand film situations, and still is. It went like this: a burglar entered a pawn shop and, in the dark, brushed against a skeleton. By some means known only to the prop man, the skeleton adhered to the burglar's back and accompanied him wherever he went.

The gag was advanced by permitting the burglar, a timid thief, to catch a glimpse of his own shadow with its passenger, as cast on the wall by the headlights of a passing car. Once that routine had been thoroughly milked—the burglar reaching up to touch the fleshless hand on his shoulder, his hair standing on end (because of an off-camera static electrical device), etc., etc.—the topper was provided by the burglar turning his flashlight upon a full-length mirror and discovering a whitened skull peering over his shoulder. He would dive, yelling, out the nearest window. Our fadeout would show him running in terror into infinity, Brother Bones still following, knees and ankles flexing in a *danse macabre.*

A switch on the "Ghost in the Pawn Shop" theme was the "Bomb under the Bed" routine.

An establishing shot showed a lighted bomb being planted under the comic's bed. (A comic was invariably the intended victim of these gags, as are Doris Day and Jerry Lewis today.)

The establishing shot was followed by scenes of the comic getting into bed, being called to the telephone, returning to bed, being summoned to answer the door, hitting the mattress again, remembering his prayers and bounding out to kneel with clasped hands beside the bed, his knees almost touching the bomb.

These scenes were intercut by shots showing the sputtering, ominous shortening of the fuse. When suspense could no longer be sustained, the comic went sky-high and usually emerged from black clouds as an unlikely angel.

Forget his politics for a moment and agree with me that Charlie Chaplin was one of the greatest gag men of all time. We "borrowed" one of his routines and adapted it repeatedly.

In the original version Charlie was trying to extract a large, obviously expensive platter from the top of a massive china breakfront. Handicapped by his traditional baggy pants that caught on everything, and flapping shoes that never knew a firm foundation, he managed to hoist himself on hands and knees to the cupboard's midsection counter. From that eminence, he stretched to his fullest reach—teetering uncertainly—and began to tease the platter forward with his fingertips.

In the sneaky manner of all inanimate objects when approached by Chaplin, the platter *seemed* to respond to his coaxing. It inched forward coyly, but just out of full hand grasp, it balked, half on, half off the shelf.

Chaplin's thin shoulders lifted in his characteristic shrug, as he started to climb down, obviously in search of another solution.

At that point the contrary platter jumped off the shelf and perched on Charlie's concave back. Crouching on the counter he tried to grasp the platter over his shoulder; it was just out of reach. With every move Charlie made, the platter inched downward, flirting with the floor.

Charlie's back became immobile, but by manipulating his versatile feet, he was able to open the top drawer of the cabinet, then the next—and to descend on that improvised stairway. As he extended a tentative foot toward the bottom drawer, the platter released its hold on Charlie's coat and crashed to the linoleum.

Charlie registered his own brand of horror: closing his eyes and quivering from top to toe.

Finally, forcing his eyes open, he slowly turned to look behind him. There lay the platter—intact.

Breathing a vast sigh of relief, Charlie hopped from his perch in a burst of self-congratulation—and landed squarely on the platter, demolishing it.

One of my favorite gag sequences was written for Harry Langdon, about five feet two inches of comedy genius, a man with a cherubic face and the wide, incredulous gaze of a child, as many film fans will remember. He weighed about a hundred pounds with lead-soled shoes, and was customarily cast opposite Junoesque Gertrude Astor.

As our gag line would have it, Gertrude's enthusiasm for Harry was commensurate with her size. Harry, in his quietly desperate way, managed to elude encirclement until—ever the gentleman—he was maneuvered into escorting Gertrude home. That is, if "escorting" can be interpreted as cowering in a corner of the taxi, defending himself from amorous advances.

As the taxi halted at the door of Gertrude's apartment building, she pretended to faint. Manfully, Harry accumulated the lady in a pair of trembling arms and staggered from cab to stairway, where he collapsed.

There he rested on the bottom step, Gertie on his lap, while he reviewed his dilemma. Carrying her up that interminable flight of stairs was obviously impossible, so he tried another technique. By rocking back and forth he was able to manufacture enough lift to bump upward one step, cargo included. That done, he caught his breath, dug in his heels and hoisted the seat of his pants onto the next tread. Rock and bump. Rock and bump. Up, up, up.

Leaving Harry bumping, we had the camera swing to a drama on the stairway landing, twenty steps above. A janitor positioned a tall stepladder directly at the head of the flight being negotiated by Harry.

The janitor climbed to the top of the ladder, unscrewed a burnt-out light bulb from the ceiling fixture, climbed down and went in search of a fresh bulb.

When the film was shown in theatres, audiences—catching on—began to anticipate the inevitable, and went into paroxysms of laughter.

Harry failed to realize that he'd reached the last of the formal steps; with courage above and beyond, he continued his ascent from stairway to ladder. Upward, ever upward he was carried by his rocking chair escalation until he ran out of landing strips. Ditching on the corridor carpet, Harry disappeared beneath quantities of Gertrude Astor.

Then, as now, I persisted in ignoring the W. C. Fields' Law No. 1: "Never become involved with a dumb animal or a talking child."

In a slightly earlier era at Roach's, a committee of gag men dreamed up a lion sequence for a Snub Pollard comedy, directed by Hal Roach himself. The story line dealt with a cowardly big game hunter.

The action was to take place in a huge cage camouflaged with jungle greenery. The cameraman was to remain outside with his lens inserted between bars and leaves. Snub was to enter, gun in hand, at stage left, and tiptoe through the jungle.

Meanwhile, a "trained" lion was to enter at stage left, behind Snub, and pad along a path parallel to Snub's course, which would take Kitty between Snub and a line of trees masking the cage.

When Snub reached the chalk mark indicating the middle of the cage, he was to pause, place his hand Indian fashion above his eyes, and peer toward stage right. As the lion neared his own median chalk mark opposite Snub, Snub was to turn slowly and peer stage left. That would make it possible for the lion, unseen by the comic, to exit stage right.

[70]

The timing was tricky, but the trainer said it would work. This gag was based on the timeworn philosophy that you never see the one that gets you.

What we hadn't planned was that Snub, while turning around, would trip over a branch and land flat on his derriere, his back against the trees. The lion, unable to go behind Snub, took an uncertain step across him.

Finding the footing soft and the climate balmy, our lion followed standard cat procedure. He curled up for a nap in Snub's moist lap.

Hal Roach, desperately improvising, yelled, "LOOK SCARED, SNUB! LOOK *SCARED!*"

Snub, not a strong swimmer, could only bleat, "Help! Wardrobe!"

That experience should have warned me, but at Sennett's I had an idea for a pussycat gag. The cat was supposed to stroll along a shelf and kick over a huge vase that was to land on the comic's head, knocking him out. This Rube Goldberg bit was part of a running gag about man's exploitation by his domesticated animals. You know: Your watchdog fawns on the burglar, but bites your rich Aunt Kate.

Our prop man borrowed an alley cat from the pound and experimented. Bits of diced liver were placed at one end of a high, narrow shelf, and the cat was placed at the other. A rubber band was inserted between two of the cat's toes, not tightly, but firmly enough to be an annoyance. As soon as she started to walk, she began to kick backward to get rid of the rubber band.

My idea was that the kick would appear to the camera to be deliberately malevolent, as if the cat *intended* to bop the comic.

I took out insurance: I had a prop man attach one end of a stout black thread to the top of the vase. As the cat kicked backward, whether she upset the vase or not, Props was supposed to pull the thread, thereby achieving our purpose.

We started with a very hungry cat. She kicked backward absently ONCE, then tiptoed past the vase with great care to reach the liver.

We tried again. Again she slid past the vase, more intent on goodies than on tidy toes.

On the fourth or fifth attempt, the cat—filled to the whiskers—jumped off the shelf and raced to the exit.

We went for a second cat, a third, and a fourth. Production cost for liver was ruining our budget. Maybe a gross of cats later we acquired a fastidious Tom who loathed having anything between his toes. He kicked and kicked and kicked, en route to luncheon. He passed the vase, kicking lustily, and whammo! he actually struck it a glancing blow. It rocked precariously. It needed only the slightest yank on the thread to tumble it onto the head of our patient comic.

The excited prop man leapt up, yelling, "He hit it! The bastard honest-to-God KICKED it."

I stared, horrified, as the vase stopped rocking and returned to plumb.

The prop man had forgotten the essential black thread.

At last report he was still running. Here's a message for him, "Come home. All is forgiven. After the second block, I dropped the hammer."

One of my favorite jobs at Sennett's was writing gags for Slim Summerville and Bobby Dunn. Slim was built like a noodle that had forgotten to quit. Bobby was brief and compact. He had been a circus star whose specialty was a high dive through a burning hoop into a teacup of water.

(There came a tragic day when Bobby, sick and destitute, did a perfect swan dive from a downtown hotel's twelfth floor into a dry street, but that is another story.)

In Hollywood's brighter day, Slim and Bobby were the twin nemeses of a Sennett director named Alfred Goulding. Like all travelers, Goulding returned from the Orient with extensive stories about his purchases, particularly the rug he had ordered for his living room.

"It'll be months before I get it," he explained. "It's being woven by hand in colors I chose: a pale creme background with a border of pastel flowers. Eighteen by thirty-six feet. Not another like it in the world."

For weeks he could talk of nothing else.

At last the rug arrived. "You've got to see it tonight," the director told us. "Come over about seven."

I arrived first. The boys reported a little late, and a lot loaded. However, they rhapsodized over the rug; they crawled over it, they bounced upon it, they wallowed in it. In their exuberance, they bumped against a writing desk, upsetting a bottle of green ink in a spatter pattern on the pale rug.

Slim burst into tears, and Bobby, wringing his hands, raced to the door for fear for his life.

As Slim joined the escape he sobbed, "We'll make it up to you, Alf. If it's the last thing we do, we'll make it up to you."

They did, too.

An hour later a messenger delivered a fresh bottle of green ink.

At about that period in history, Vernon Smith and I were accorded a promotion: We were assigned to the bungalow originally built on the Sennett lot for Mabel Normand.

It was generally believed in Hollywood that Mabel, the great comedy star of her day, had been the one true love of Mack's life. He enjoyed many passing fancies, some fancier than others, but he never married. Many of us also believed that Mabel, married to Lew Cody, had been in love with Marshall (Mickey) Nielan, who was married to Blanche Sweet. (In show biz, then as now, the cast changed, but the plot remained the same.)

Why, we wondered, had Vernon and I been moved from the tower to that sacrosanct villa so soon after Mabel's death? Hours were spent conjuring up reasons. Our charm? Our scintillant wit? Our creative genius?

The envious tower slaves, paying us sour visits, theorized that Sennett was so mercenary he couldn't bear to have one square inch of the lot standing idle. We were warned that our quarters would be usurped by the next big-eyed cantaloupe kid to hit Hollywood.

It didn't work that way. The next big-eyed whatever she was, came and went without dislodging us. Personally, I think the Old Man wanted to change the character of the bungalow as quickly as possible; new faces and new reasons for his rages would help him ride out his emotional storm.

We understood his bad temper, but some of the edicts deriving from it were absurd. The most obnoxious was, in our opinion: The premise of all stories must be stated in full in the FIRST TWO MINUTES OF THE FILM.

One morning when we heard Sennett stamping toward our bungalow, Vern said, "Let's kill off the Old Man's premise rule once and for all. Let's lay a wild one on him."

Our assignment was a Ben Turpin story. Vern pulled out all the stops. "We start with a long shot of a train on a trestle crossing a wide river . . . "

I took it up: "Turpin is seated in the diner. He speaks to the waiter. Cut in a spoken title: 'Fish.' "

"The waiter yells to the galley, 'Fish.' "

"Okay . . . the chef drops a line out of the window and hauls in a huge fish . . . "

"The grilled fish is set before Ben. He cuts it open and finds . . . "

"A bottle!"

"And in the bottle there's a will . . . "

We should have known we couldn't con Sennett. He jumped up, waving his arms and yelling, "Ya smart-ass sonsabitches, you're fired. Get out of here and never come onto this lot again. NEVER."

Sennett's rages lasted quick. Less than twenty-four hours had elapsed before he needed us—and for larger numbers than we had been collecting prior to the storm.

On another occasion we were again struggling with a Turpin sequence. When writers hit a dry spot, as we had, the finger-drumming presence of the boss is Milltown country.

"You've got to have SOMETHING for Turpin," he fumed.

I said, "We can always fall back on that old Standard-Sennett-Scene-Plot."

"What the hell is the Standard-Sennett-Scene-Plot?" growled the Old Man around his cigar. It was not a smoking cigar; it was an eating cigar. At $2.00 per copy.

Vern gave me the nod and Don Quixote Garnett set out, astride his good steed Sarcasm: "Well, there's this vine-covered cottage with a white picket fence around it. Inside there's a sergeant's desk in a police station. On the floor above is the firehouse with the inevitable pole descending into the basement where there's a bakery with a huge vat of dough, just waiting for the comic, and the whole goddam mess is located on the end of the Santa Monica pier."

So he fired me again.

And again. And again. But each time I returned, the take was improved.

Nowadays an actor and a director, thanks to television residuals, can eat frequently, but before the establishment of the Guilds, we all worked like Indian elephants—strictly for hay. We checked in at daybreak and were allowed to escape sometime between sunset and sunrise. Regardless of quitting time, we were expected to be back on the job again at dawn.

At Sennett's particularly, a living wage, pay boosts, and financial consistency of any sort were unknown. This was only one area in which all employees made common cause: contriving some way to extract an extra buck from the Old Man.

Cross-eyed Ben Turpin, working an eighteen-hour day, began to shed weight as a Sennett Model-T shed cops. Charlie Chaplin, no slouch at getting and keeping cash, advised Turpin to rebel. "Go tell Mack that, hereafter, you're quitting at five o'clock, and don't let him talk you out of it. After all, you're unique."

Ben studied Chaplin's expression, decided that the word "unique" was not a dirty crack, and nodded in agreement. The following afternoon he presented himself and his five o'clock ultimatum to the Old Man.

Sennett bellowed and blustered, threatened and cajoled.

Finally Ben held up his hands. "Okay, Mack," he said. "OKAY. I'll go on working the same old hours. But from now on, AT FIVE O'CLOCK THE EYES GO STRAIGHT."

Nothing on earth could have straightened Turpin's eyes, but the notion snagged Sennett's sense of humor and he began to grin. Turpin had it made.

Bewhiskered comic star Ford Sterling, hearing of Turpin's minor miracle, also made a trip to the Old Boy's office to demand financial uppage.

Sennett responded by shaking a furious fist under Sterling's string tie and shouting, "If you ever dare come to me again with that kind of an ungrateful, selfish, greedy squawk, I'm going to kick you out of this office, *personally.*"

Sterling knew that Sennett could make good his threat, thanks to his hod-carrying days, so the comic yielded the battle, but not the war.

The next morning Sterling, arrayed as usual in Prince Albert and top hat, strode onto the lot with a rolled mattress on his back. He carried it to Sennett's office and positioned it strategically outside the door.

Marching to the side of the boss's desk, Sterling performed a precise about-face, bent double to present an ample kicking surface, and announced, "Now, I want that raise."

Sennett was a patsy for a sight gag. Sterling got the salary boost. Labor negotiations were fun in those days.

The ad libs were funnier, too. Stan Laurel and I were standing on a set one afternoon, scrutinizing a parade of highly delectable bathing beauties.

With a sigh Stan turned that dead pan to me and observed, "That's the trouble with the picture business; you look at filet mignon all day, then go home at night to cold hash."

Years later, after a good many Keystone Kops had gone to that big Ford in the sky, The Masquers honored Sennett at a testimonial dinner. It was strictly stag, so some of the stories told were not for *McCall's* magazine, but mainly the speeches were much too long and excessively flattering.

According to the speakers, Mr. Sennett walked on water and caused the dead to rise. The superlatives would have brought a blush of embarrassment to the cheek of Cassius Clay.

I was called upon to speak very late in the program. By that time everyone in the audience was fed up to here with it. I arose and said pleasantly, "I have never listened to so much crap in all my life."

I waited several seconds for the boffo yak to subside, then added, "Yes, the Old Man is a genius. What else could you expect from a creature sired by a bulldog and born of a barracuda? True, he opened up a whole new vein of comedy, but to hear him scream when he signed a gag man's check, you'd have thought he'd opened an artery. I can speak with authority, because I was fired more often by this dear old bastard than anyone else who ever worked for him."

From the dais Sennett yelled, as he coughed with laughter, "That's right, Tay. That's right."

Looking back on it, I regard it as my finest after-dinner speech. It had all the elements of postprandial style: shock, humor, and brevity. Or as Sam Goldwyn once said in agreement with a critic who praised a scene for "brevity": "And besides, it was short."

[76]

INEVITABLY THERE CAME A DAY WHEN MY DIVORCE FROM SENNETT WAS final. The standard call for reconciliation never came. I waited twenty-four, forty-eight, seventy-two hours. The suspicion began to dawn that the Old Man had failed to find me funny the last time.

It didn't bother me at first, because I used my unexpected leisure to achieve civilization's ultimate luxury: inside plumbing. I finished the bathroom in Hangover House.

Being unable to come up with sufficient scratch to buy a conventional bathtub, I designed and manufactured a brilliant blue Roman bath out of tile left unguarded at the Beverly Hills building site of an affluent friend of mine. I've often wondered if King Vidor ever figured out what happened to that first delivery of tile.

Despite the sensuous beauty of that bathroom, I discovered—by a process of elimination—that certain items of furniture were essential in a bachelor's pad. My broken-down sofa in the living room provided me with the necessary rest, but it lacked sex appeal.

Nowadays, Mustang makes it happen, but in my day there was no lure like an Ostermoor. Yet, for acquiring that facility, there was no substitute for money.

I wrote a couple of stories for adventure magazines, but the take in those days was a penny a word, with the inescapable result that five thousand words fetched fifty dollars. So much of that went into my Furniture Fund that there were times when the rumbling of my stomach scared my neighbors, the coyotes.

For recreation, I hung around the studios, looking available.

One day a studio electrician, an old Navy buddy of mine, broke the news that a shipmate of ours had augered in. Services were set for that afternoon. We agreed to attend.

At graveside I glanced beyond the coffin, during the sounding of Taps, and for the second time in my life looked across a dead body into the eyes of Joan Marshfield.

The other mourners drifted away; Joan and I met under a blossoming jacaranda tree. I was still trying to catch my breath when she asked softly, "Any chance of your buying an old friend some luncheon?"

"Flannel Cakes?"

"Musso-Frank's!"

The sound of her voice, that intimate, husky chuckle, awakened a medley of moonstruck memories.

Over our cakes and coffee I learned that, several months earlier, Admiral Marshfield had lost a skirmish with pneumonia. His final illness had resulted from an unscheduled athletic event. He had broad-jumped out a lady's bedroom window into a Brooklyn sleet storm, a feat for which he was neither conditioned nor clothed.

I asked about Joan's plans for the future; as soon as European weather improved, she said, she planned to join her younger sister, an art student, in Paris. Meanwhile, there seemed to be a vacant six weeks in her schedule that might as well be invested in California.

With Joan I met several interesting and influential people, among them Louis Goodstat, who hired all the talent used at the De Mille Studio, owned at that time by Producers Distributing Corporation.

The beautiful colonial building on Washington Boulevard in Culver City has had a various history.

The studio was built by Thomas Ince. After his death it was taken over by PDC. Later it became Pathé, and even later it was purchased by David Selznick, and became the birthplace of the film version of Margaret Mitchell's *Gone With The Wind*. As this is written, the plant is known as Desilu-Culver, and is owned by Gulf & Western Corporation, a condition subject to change without notice.

Goodstat invited me to visit the De Mille operation. I toured the handsome executive quarters and the orderly stages, amazed to discover that movies could be made successfully without the confusion and clutter of a junkyard. The Sennett lot always looked like the last battlefield in a conquered country.

God bless Lou Goodstat, wherever he is; he signed me to a SEVEN-YEAR writing contract at important numbers. My first assignment was to concoct a silent screen play (the infant industry hadn't learned to gurgle yet) from the Don Marquis fantasy, *The Cruise of the Jasper B.*

This fragile story dealt with an old sailing ship beached forever on concrete pylons in a stagnant harbor. Plot and characters were delightful—pure Don Marquis—but motion pictures must *move,* and *Cruise* was an exercise in verbal, rather than visual, charm.

Inevitably, the movie entitled *The Cruise of the Jasper B.* was closer to *The Sea Hawk* than to the whimsical Marquis original. Forgive me, Don.

When most people think of Don Marquis, they smile reminiscently over *Archie and Mehitabel,* but I smile in honor of his small daughter even though I've forgotten her name. At age six she had accommodated herself philosophically to the untidy life of a writer.

Don Marquis was, by nature, a predawn worker. He would roll out of bed at an hour when milkmen were still snoring and would start his day with a brisk horseback ride along the Beverly Hills bridle path which bisected Sunset Boulevard in those days.

Cobwebs dispelled, he would return to his desk. Pulling off his boots, he customarily set them neatly nearby, after having installed a fifth of his favorite in his left boot. Don was not an alcoholic; he simply found it useful to tipple when manufacturing dialogue for a typewriting cockroach and an alley cat, *toujours gai.*

One Sunday morning Don returned from his ride to find his daughter sitting in his chair, elbows on either side of the typewriter and chin propped up by fists.

She told her father dourly, "I'm getting out my column."

Don glanced at the blank paper. "Not going too well, I see."

"No," gloomed the six-year-old, scowling at her father's riding boots. "I haven't had any whiskey."

It is the dream of every writer to have a hideaway all his own, secluded, silent, inviolate. At PDC, I was assigned a private office in Writers' Row; I could hear quiet flowing through the room.

Solitude was ideal for daylight hours, but when Joan Marshfield left for Paris, I paced the floor of my lonely pad, night after night, my own footsteps thundering in the emptiness. Why had I let her go?

Abruptly, my isolation was invaded by TWO roommates, one male and one female, but the allocation was fouled up.

Zelda Sears was moved into my office so I could teach her the mechanics of screenplay writing. Handsome, white-haired Zelda had been a theatrical star before becoming a successful Broadway playwright. During her first day on the De Mille lot she attained sainthood in the hearts of her coworkers.

Zelda had come to C. B. De Mille's attention because of the New York success of her tragic melodrama, *Silence,* starring H. B. Warner. *Silence* was an early think-piece; at third act curtain its principal character was executed.

C. B. bought the motion picture rights, and placed Zelda—sight unseen—under a three-year writing contract. Because Zelda was in the midst of a new play, she made arrangements to defer the starting date of her contract for six months.

That delay resulted in Zelda's reaching Hollywood shortly after the screen version of *Silence* was completed; she was invited to preview the film. In the projection room, Zelda learned for the first time that De Mille had given the story a HAPPY ending.

Gray-faced and blazing-eyed, she strode into De Mille's office.

As he arose, bowing and expecting to be overwhelmed by praise, Zelda demanded, "Is it true that you are planning to make a picture of the life of Christ?"

"Why—er—yes," admitted De Mille.

Observed Zelda icily, "I dare you, I JUST DARE YOU, to give *that* script a happy ending."

So much for my girl roommate.

As for my boy roommate: One day Alan Hale, Sr.,—also under contract to PDC—asked me how my house was coming along.

I gave Hale a minute description of my pad.

"How about a roommate?" he asked.

I began to leer, hastening to inquire about her coloring and vital statistics.

"This is a guy . . . " he began.

"Forget it, friend."

"Now just a damn minute. This guy has been a director, a helluva good one. He's just run out of luck; the way the picture business is right now, he can't get a job. He's been locked out of his room and the hotel's holding his clothes for back rent. His name's Tom Buckingham."

"Tell Buckingham he can bunk with me, provided he likes Mexican food. I'm hell with a tortilla," I said.

This Buckingham turned out to be darkly handsome, with curly hair and lively brown eyes. He appealed to women and vice versa. He could fall in love at the drop of a hat, and he always carried a spare hat. When he fell in love, everything went out of focus. He wrote poetry. He sang songs—off-key. He bought flowers, perfume, and jewelry, a real achievement before the invention of the credit card.

It took a certain amount of time and living with Buck to learn of his idiosyncracies. As I dished up our first twosome dinner he said, "After my peanut diet, this is a banquet. I've been sleeping on various bedroom sets at Columbia Studio. I was afraid to leave the lot for fear I couldn't get back on, so I had to live on peanuts from a vending machine. A penny's worth for breakfast and lunch, and two pennies' worth for dinner. Last night I shot the wad. I knew I was coming out here to bunk and eat with you, so I spent my last four cents on one single meal!" He shrugged. "What the hell, it's only money."

Although Buck proved to have few bad habits, he *was* addicted to marriage—a downright matrimonial mainliner. He had been married five times to four wives. Three of the wives were what you would expect of your average beauty contest queen, but the one to whom Buckingham was married twice is worth comment.

When both were sober, she and Tom loathed one another. She was, except with a load of 86-proof aboard, a meticulous lady, chilly, white-gloved, and superior.

After two drinks, the hem came out of her skirt, her hair slid four degrees to port, and she became a helluva laughing, singing, good-time Charlotte. She and Tom found each other irresistible.

In the midst of a moonlit, multidrink evening, they drove to Santa Ana (Hollywood's Gretna Green in those days) and were married. When they regained consciousness the next morning, their consternation was monumental. They separated at once and Charlotte sued for annulment.

Upon the annulment being granted, thanks to polite perjury, Charlotte and Tom met to sign papers and to exchange congratulations. "Now that's over, would you buy a girl a drink?" said Charlotte.

Naturally, Buck ordered champagne. When the third bottle was upended in melted ice, Charlotte and Tom set off for Santa Ana to be remarried.

The following morning Charlotte again sued for annulment.

Buckingham swore off matrimony; except for one subsequent slip, he held to his vow and dedicated himself to saving fellow bachelors whenever possible.

Love was everywhere, but an honest dollar was hard to find. Yet Buck, hitting a lucky streak, made friends with a Dutch furniture dealer who imported rugs from Amsterdam. The association was originally formed because of Buck's vague conviction that he could interest Hollywood celebrities in outfitting their stately mansions with luxury underfoot to match the overhead.

At the rug dealer's suggestion, Buck and I drove—in my new Lincoln coupe—to a selected house on a dead-end Hollywood street. What we saw in the dealer's storage room brought tears to our Prohibition-parched eyes.

Imported rugs are normally packed around a center pole. Ingenious shippers of the day figured a way to tape liquor bottles (filled) together to form a shipping core. At first the rug merchant had intended to use the liquor for his own table, but thanks to Volstead, the rug poles were soon worth more than the rugs. Cannily, he decided to go into the beverage business—without a license. He needed a discreet salesman.

Tom moistened his lips as he volunteered to unload the merchandise (brandies, Dutch gins, Bols Liqueurs, and absinthe) on a fifty-fifty basis.

We streaked home where Buckingham hit the telephone. He sold cases of liquor as if they had been packages of chewing gum. After months of being ignored by studio messenger boys, Buck began to receive calls from command levels. Thirst makes all men equal.

At that point a problem arose: delivery. Tom's car had long since been repossessed, so I volunteered my Lincoln, feeling that the stuff should travel in a style worthy of it. I even lent him the honorary sheriff's badge I'd received in recognition of some favor I had been able to accord the gendarmerie.

"If you happen to get into a minor traffic beef, show this badge. It should square any little mishap along the way," I said.

A galvanized Buckingham, once more captain of his soul, went into the long glide down Laurel Canyon.

An hour later I had a studio call, so I took a taxi. As I returned at seven that evening, I leaned out of the cab in mesmerized horror as we rounded the final curve toward home. The cabby, hardened to ghastly sights, observed laconically, "Some guy in a Lincoln must've tangled with a gravel truck."

The air was thick with the mingled fragrance of rare old brandy, the pungency of gasoline, and the gritty smell of sand and gravel. Broken bottles, twisted metal, and jumbled rocks littered the highway.

I looked around for Buckingham's body.

He was missing, and the accident was too new for an ambulance to have come and gone. I paid the driver and climbed my interminable stairway, looking for evidence of blood and clothing shed in agony.

Nothing.

Sick with apprehension and devastated by the loss of my sole status symbol, my Lincoln, I turned the front door knob with an icy hand.

There on the living room couch lay the pajama-clad body of Buckingham, as beautiful as a marble figure in the Louvre. I checked him over swiftly. There was neither a scratch nor a bruise visible, and his breathing was that of an innocent child who has emptied his father's bar out of mere curiosity.

Relief gave way to fury and fury to laughter; pinned to Buck's lapel was my deputy sheriff's badge, the token guaranteed to square any little mishap that might befall him.

$\mathcal{9}$

A MILLION WORDS HAVE BEEN WRITTEN ABOUT C. B. DE MILLE, BUT AN incident that I caught firsthand tells as much about the *man*— not the legend—as could be told in a three-hour film.

When Mr. De Mille was casting the original version of *The King of Kings,* he announced that he personally would select every individual to be used in the picture. Even the mob scenes were to be peopled by faces appropriate to the Old Testament.

Day after day, three or four hundred extras reported at noon, and, trembling with hope, awaited the inspection of the putteed director.

He stalked down the ranks, his riding quirt flashing like the sword in a knighting ceremony as he said, "You are a foot soldier. You, over there, are a soldier on horseback." His assistants scurried along, keeping score and noting telephone numbers.

Each day for weeks the same elderly extra managed to take a place in the front line for the entire blazing hour of review. The immaculate cuffs and collar of his shirt were frayed, and he had the sharply-honed look of the undernourished, but as De Mille approached, the proud old-timer came to rigid attention, shoulders back, head held high and chest expanded to the limit.

No one could have missed the routine, particularly De Mille. However, the director's broad streak of genius was bordered by a narrow band of sadism. Day after day he passed the valiant man without a glance. He would tap the man to the right of the oldster: "You are a foot soldier." Then the man to the left: "A soldier on horseback."

As De Mille turned away from the old man, the extra would deflate, his spine seemed to go soft, and his lips trembled.

Finally, one torrid afternoon, De Mille wearied of his game. He paused before the perspiring actor and took a long step backward. With head tipped quizzically to one side, the maestro inquired, "And what, sir, are you? A foot soldier or a soldier on horseback?"

Drawing himself to the limit of his frail five feet five, the extra answered with dignity, "I, sir, am an actor FLAT ON HIS ASS."

De Mille, a quick man to pick up a cue, grinned as he responded, "You're good enough for me—as an actor on foot OR on horseback, and as long as this picture goes, you're working.

And work he did; probably he enjoyed the longest uninterrupted run in the annals of Hollywood extras.

Incidentally, I've talked to a lot of youngsters who have been convinced that if they could get extra work, their acting future would be assured. Such an opinion indicates a total lack of understanding of a nebulous Hollywood fact of life best labeled "status." Offhand I can think of only half a dozen actors or actresses who have come out of the "atmosphere" ranks to emerge as "names." Prominence must first be attained in Europe, on Broadway, on television, or in certain Little Theatre groups before Hollywood will start a serious flirtation.

"No" as an answer has been raised to its nth degree by Russia.

"Yes" as an answer has been raised to its nth degree in Hollywood.

Being brash, young and *very* Navy, I put in a lot of studio time before I understood that when a supervisor asked me, "Isn't that great?" the only acceptable response was, "Yes, sir."

On one occasion at De Mille's, I was told by the executive producing head, Bill Sistrom, to report to a certain supervisor whose name was, let's say, Ginzborough.

Ginzy handed me a script, saying, "Be back in an hour with suggestions as to what you, as a writer, can do with it."

In forty minutes I reported, "Nothing."

The supervisor collected his chins from his Sulka tie and demanded, "Have you NO suggestions?"

"Yes. Take it out and bury it before someone finds out what that smell is."

Two hundred and eighty pounds of supervisor quivered upward as he arose to his towering five feet two inches and yelled, "I want

[85]

practical, constructive suggestions. We start shooting that script *to-morrow* morning."

I made what I considered a highly practical and constructive recommendation: "If you've gotta shoot tomorrow, file off the sights so it won't hurt so much when they shove it."

The Ginzy report of my horrendous behavior was rushed to De Mille's desk, but—to everyone's amazement—local seismographs registered no disturbance.

Ginzy finished his picture and sneak-previewed it.

The comment cards would have decked the Notre Dame line. The kindest word written about the opus was, "IMPOSSIBLE."

Ginzy basted his turkey and previewed it again.

It had progressed from "Impossible" to "It stinks."

Ginzy, no quitter he, edited it a third time and again dared a preview. The theatre emptied as if someone had yelled, "Fire!"

The next morning De Mille summoned everyone who had been involved in the catastrophe. In those days he had a spotlight rigged on his desk and aimed at a visitor so he could administer, simultaneously, a tongue-lashing and temporary blindness.

Using masterly diatribe he questioned our talent, our intellect, our masculinity, and our legitimacy, not necessarily in that order, and fired the lot of us, effective as of that instant.

We turned and shuffled toward the door, hands outstretched to avoid intervening obstacles.

"One moment," said C. B. abruptly. "I recall an episode that took place several months ago." He repeated the comments I had made to Ginzy about the script. "As a result of that man's analysis, he was reprimanded for his insolence and vulgarity. Had we filed off the sights, as he recommended, we could have saved thousands of dollars. That young man is still working for Pathé-De Mille. The rest of you are through."

Naturally, the Ginzy script haunted me. I wondered if the picture was actually as bad as I thought, so I had it run off in the studio projection room.

The room had to be fumigated.

It stood to lose the studio around three hundred thousand dollars, large money in those Depression days. When a picture was "put on the shelf" it was doomed to oblivion, and the accounting department bought a gallon of red ink.

The three hundred grand worried me. When I worry, I can't sleep. When I can't sleep, I get ideas.

I went to C.B. and said, "Sir, I've got a hunch that, by spending a little additional money, we can make the film releasable."

He listened while I outlined my notion, which was to turn the melodrama into a comedy, a tightrope I had walked many times even at that early date.

"How much will it cost?" he asked.

I said I'd get some title cards printed, cut in a few transitional scenes, then get an estimate from the production office.

"The sooner, the better," said De Mille. "We've got stockholders yelling themselves hoarse."

The estimate was nominal, so De Mille gave me the go signal.

This suds special was sort of a Graustark-in-Egypt thriller. It dealt with the built-in hazards of the king business. Rudolph Schildkraut played the newly-crowned Pharaoh, and May Robson was cast as the scheming mother-of-the-pretender who planned a fast tomb for Schildkraut.

The opening scene showed Pharaoh's chariot wheeling between two lanes of turbaned, kaftaned subjects, each bowing low and registering enthusiasm.

I introduced a slightly different interpretation. I lined up a dozen extras in the Western Costume Company robes originally used, but I photographed them from the rear. Each bowing, cheering subject was holding a bomb about the size of a grapefruit, its eighteen-inch fuse sputtering ominously. From that point on, it became a Sennett comedy with sand.

The result was a few light years short of being the funniest script ever filmed, but at least the laughter my alterations provoked was intentional. Also, the film's grosses—even in those days of two-bit admissions—cured a gratifying amount of stockholder laryngitis.

I'd like to record the title of my pineapple-upside-down picture, but there may be a print of it lying around in some film library, and I don't want a "friend" to exhume it and show it around the Bel Air circuit. I'm still too young to retire.

Encouraged by my small success with the Cairo turkey, I went through the studio "dead" shelves and resuscitated several films that still registered a slight pulse. Those hours in the projection room also familiarized me with the capabilities of some of the Pathé contract players such as the great Gloria Swanson, Jetta Goudal, Ann Harding, Constance Bennett, Ruth Chatterton, Lina Basquette, Rod La Roque, William Boyd (destined, much later, to become Hopalong Cassidy), Alan Hale, Kenneth Thompson, Clyde Cook, James Gleason, Robert Armstrong, and that very funny and talented Jack Oakie.

I was like the wise virgin—with certain notable exceptions—who burned the midnight oil in readiness for some crucial event. I didn't know what to expect of the future, but I knew that I wanted to direct, and I figured that if I knew what to avoid, and which players to avoid it with, I'd be halfway home.

During that germination period, I learned that a running comedy gag could be turned into a dramatic haymaker. Elliot Clausen and I coauthored a script entitled *Skyscraper.* My good friend Ralph Block produced it, and the stars were Sue Carol (who later married Alan Ladd), Alberta Vaughn, Bill Boyd, and Alan Hale, whose son is his image.

Boyd and Hale were cast as superstud steelworkers. The relationship between them was that described in film parlance as "Quirt and Flagg," a reference to the roles immortalized by Victor McLaglen and Edmund Lowe in the film version of Lawrence Stallings' *What Price Glory?* In brief, Boyd and Hale were buddies who battled endlessly for booze and broads, but who closed ranks against all outsiders.

Clausen and I dreamed up an additional running gag: The character played by Hale had a gold pivot tooth of which he was inordinately proud. The ungrateful tooth was inclined to execute a chandelle into the wild blue yonder whenever Hale got into a fight. The instant that happened, both Hale and Boyd gave up all else to pursue the errant upper central incisor.

We advanced the gag by filming a Saturday night rampage in a beach resort's fun zone. The boys terrorized the feminine population, devoured their gross displacement in hot dogs, and—even though they were high-rise steelworkers—were rendered loop-legged by the roller coaster.

They wound up in a giant rolling barrel, trying to recover Hale's dislodged tooth. Gleaming malevolently, it slid, leaped and danced away from the grasp of the tumbling partners. Its eventual capture and replacement provided the scene's climax.

Parallel to this nonsense, a serious plot line was developed: The building being punched skyward by the steelworkers had been improperly engineered. Under stress, its concrete foundations collapsed in a scream of destruction, followed by an avalanche of timber, steel beams, and helpless men.

Slowly a dreadful silence descended. Here and there hoarse voices began to lift in the dazed questions of catastrophe.

Boyd, staggering to his feet, demanded, "Where's Mike? Anybody seen Mike? MIKE!"

As if in answer, a gold pivot tooth detached itself from a mound of debris and slowly rolled away into the dust.

Top left:
Gad, what mothers did to sons during my formative years. On the photograph's reverse is written "William Taylor Garnett, aged 2 years." If either Wayne or Ford saw this, I'd have to leave town.

Top right and middle:
These pages from the July 15 and August 19, 1915 *Photoplayers' Weekly* are self-explanatory.

Bottom left:
1919—freshly graduated from Pensacola. I took those ensign's shoulder paddles very seriously.

Bottom right:
My father, Dr. William Muldrough Garnett, and I, taken after my intensive examination of the condition of Los Angeles' vaudeville. I stood on tiptoe and wore my hat to be a shade taller than dad.

Top left and right:
Early 20s—from a rank ensign to a ranker civilian, or, Hollywood vs. Navy. Hollywood lost.
Middle:
On June 26, 1927, Vilma Banky married Rod La Roque, never dreaming that a few years later they would freeze with me through S. O. S. ICEBERG. For the 1927 nuptials Cecil B. De Mille served Rod as best man and Samuel Goldwyn gave the bride away without a single slip of the tongue.
Bottom right:
While we were filming the Arthur Miller, multi-award winning script for THE FLYING FOOL, starring William Boyd, our second-plane cameraman, who was supposed to film the antics of the first plane, failed to show up at takeoff time, so Ensign Garnett took over the controls, never having flown that type of plane before. There's no business like show business.
Bottom left:
On the RKO set for PRESTIGE in 1929. Beautiful Patsy Ruth Miller with her husband. The overcoat insulated me from the chill.

Top left:
Same PRESTIGE set. Adolph Menjou, Ann Harding, and Melvyn Douglas about to break Pathé's bread and my head.

Top right:
The handsome devil to the right is Robert Fellows, my colleague, friend, traveling companion, fellow-elbow-bender. I have never met his equal. This shot was taken on the back lot at MGM, during the filming of PRESTIGE.

Bottom left:
Patsy Ruth Miller (the first Mrs. Garnett) and Edward Everett Horton in THE HOTTENTOT (Pathé).

Middle:
Alan Hale, Sue Carol (Mrs. Alan Ladd somewhat later), and William Boyd in POWER (Pathé).

Bottom right:
Helen Twelvetrees and Ricardo Cortez in BAD COMPANY (Pathé).

Left column, top to bottom:
Robert Armstrong as the prizefighting Shakespearian scholar, and his fan, Lina Basquette, in CELEBRITY (Pathé).

James Gleason, Harry Sweet, and Franklin Pangborn in HER MAN (Pathé).

Bill Boyd and Renee Adoree in THE SPIELER—written, produced and directed by T. G. in a hyperthyroid moment (Pathé).

James Gleason and Robert Armstrong—handsome dudes—in OH, YEAH! (Pathé).
Top right:
Marie Prevost and William (Hopalong Cassidy) Boyd in THE FLYING FOOL (Pathé).
Bottom right:
Helen Twelvetrees and Phillips Holmes in HER MAN.

10

MY NEXT CHORE WAS TO MANUFACTURE A SCRIPT FROM A LEGIT BROADWAY bomber entitled *Celebrity,* written by Willard Keefe; in spite of the play's quick demise our studio was quicker—it bought the film rights.

Celebrity was a think-piece about the fight game. Its hero, patterned after Gene Tunney (the first literate leather-pusher in the American ring), was more interested in Shakespeare than in the Marquess of Queensbury.

It was a great idea for the Book of the Month Club, but a plot line not likely to fascinate the Saturday night film fan. When I outlined the problems presented by the original play, my supervisor of the moment had an Instant Remedy: "So YOU write an original. We'll just keep the title. Nobody saw the play, so nobody will know the difference."

In my version, Robert Armstrong played our synthetic celebrity, a nearsighted, punch-drunk, fourth-rater who was being exploited by his greedy manager, Clyde Cook. Our hero's girl was gorgeous Lina Basquette.

I was hanging around Sistrom's office one morning, mother-henning my script, when word came that the director assigned to *Celebrity*—after reading my canvas opera—had taken off for Palm Springs. Possibly forever.

Telling myself that the script wasn't all that bad, I still admitted that I might be comparing it with those I'd seen lately in the turkey tank.

In the midst of my soul-searching, De Mille came striding into the office, followed by his retinue. Upon learning that the original director had thrown in the towel, De Mille glanced around, spotted me and began to wave his riding quirt. "Look. You want to direct. See what you can do with this one," he ordered, then stalked out en masse.

I'll draw a modest curtain over the success(?) of *Celebrity,* but at least, at picture's close, I had directed my first feature film, it avoided the shelf, and theatre patrons refrained from giving a necktie party in my honor.

Robert Fellows, with whom I later studied geography the hard way—on the spot check—came to me courtesy of a pratfall.

When Bob left school he could have gone into the respectable, peaceful boat business with his father, who was the head of the finest boatworks on the Pacific Coast: Fellows & Stewart. However, Bob, in common with many a son of a successful father, was determined to carve out his own career even if he cut his throat in the process.

By a series of maneuvers as complicated as giving a straight answer in Russian, Bob became Madame Alla Nazimova's stage manager, and understudied the juvenile lead in her road company. When Nazimova's health failed, Bob returned to Hollywood in search of a job. Careful scouting turned up a position that, he was assured by the personnel official, would utilize his youth, vigor, and dramatic experience.

He became C. B. De Mille's First Chair Boy, a position without precedent or succession.

De Mille habitually traipsed from one end of his traditionally huge set to the other; exhausted, he wanted to be seated instantly. The Chair Boy's job was to carry a chair in pursuit of C. B., sliding it beneath the great man's posterior the instant De Mille, always without warning, began to fold up.

"I'm developing extrasensory perception," Bob confided to me. "This guy never looks behind him to see if his chair is there. The instant he presents the angle, he ASSUMES that support for same will materialize."

Late one afternoon Bob took refuge in my office. He was sweating profusely, and his skin had the color of ripe Roquefort.

"It's been hell," he gulped. "The Old Man's been giving me a real bad time lately. This morning was a stinker. The actors were blowing their lines, an arc exploded, and the camera buckled in the middle of a big scene. Every time something fouled up, the Old Boy hung it on me heavier. Finally I'd absorbed all I could take, so when his majesty went to sit down—I wasn't there. He liketa fractured his tailbone. As his can hit the deck he yelled, 'You featherbrained idiot, get out! You're fired!!' "

Bob began to grin. "Being intuitive, I resigned."

When I stopped laughing, I said, "Wonderful. I'll take you on as my first assistant."

To hire a man fired by De Mille was tantamount to professional hara-kiri, but I was young and cocky and not too bright.

"You'll be boiled in oil in a De Mille bathtub," predicted Bob happily.

A few days later Mr. De Mille ventured out of bounds: he patronized the common people's washroom.

He was leaving as I entered, providing me with a moment of shock. It had never occurred to me that the local messiah had occasion to use the john.

I stood aside to clear the doorway.

De Mille said affably, "Good morning, Tay. I understand you have a new first assistant."

I thought, "Here it comes," and assumed a boom-ducking stance.

"He's one of the best assistants in the business," said De Mille, "provided you don't let him handle furniture."

So ended l'affaire squat tag.

11

EARLY IN 1928, I WAS ASSIGNED TO PRODUCE AND DIRECT A FILM ENTITLED *Her Man;* Tom Buckingham and I had whipped up the script from one of my original stories.

We came up with one of my all-time favorite comedy routines, and one that has been "originated" by many subsequent writers.

Our principal set was a Havana dive. One of our comic characters, eventually played by Jimmy Gleason, was a hard-luck guy, a sailor with two hangups: alcohol and slot machines. The Havana set pandered to both tastes, with a one-armed bandit lurking at the end of the bar. Every time Gleason passed the slot machine, en route to a shot of plasma, he dropped a quarter into the hungry maw, held his breath, and hit the arm.

Lemons.

In the next sequence he put the *commitha* on the machine, depressing the lever very slowly with his LEFT hand. Closing his eyes, he waited.

Lemons.

Several cuts later he attacked the handle savagely and glared at his adversary in what is known technically as the Pay-Off-or-I'll-Dismember-You Method.

As he walked away, he was frozen in mid-stride by the stubborn metal clank that indicated the machine was still serving lemons.

There has never been a comic to equal Jimmy at pantomiming fury. His sharp-honed Irish pan would writhe, his eyes would take fire, and his sinewy body would draw itself into an exclamation point of rage.

In the windup sequence, Jimmy became embroiled in a barroom

brouhaha and was looped backward into the arms of the iron monster. As he slowly slid downward, his inert right elbow caught the handle and depressed it inch by inch until it reached the extremity of its arc, unloaded Jimmy onto the floor, then snapped back with a triumphant crash.

As Jimmy lay supine, the jackpot—rivers of silver, avalanches of coin—poured over his unconscious form.

So much for the comedy relief. When we were casting the male lead for *Her Man* we wanted a guy who could handle the fight scenes, as well as stir the libido of the femme contingent.

One of the actors tested was a tall, brawny guy from the New York stage. His name was Dean Jagger.

I wanted him for the part, but my boss had cooked up a deal with Paramount-Lasky to borrow one of their contractees, Phillips Holmes, in exchange for one of ours. Thanks to such didoes a studio balance sheet is kept from blushing.

I persisted in my choice however, and told Jagger, "I'm trying to figure an angle. I'll call you in a day or two."

I didn't hit upon a solution, and—for one reason or another—I never placed the promised telephone call.

During the ensuing twenty-five years I saw Dean in many fine film portrayals, but not once in person, a standard situation in Hollywood.

Then, one bloodshot morning, I walked into the steam room at Finlandia Baths and spotted a vaguely familiar face. I studied him. He studied me.

Dean Jagger spoke up: "About that part in *Her Man;* I guess you decided to use somebody else."

In addition to Gleason and Phillips Holmes, our cast for *Her Man* consisted of Helen Twelvetrees, Ricardo Cortez, Slim Summerville, Marjorie Rambeau, and ill-starred Thelma Todd.

All were elated upon discovering that *Her Man*'s background was Havana. They were unelated when they were told it wouldn't be necessary for them to make the location trip. Only a cameraman, Eddie Snyder, and I were to spend a few days in Cuba, picking up background footage for "process" shots.

In regard to "process," it would be almost impossible to explain it

[98]

to the layman, because of its highly technical nature. Suffice to say that physical conditions frequently make it necessary to photograph a film's dramatic action at one time and place, and its background elsewhere and at another time.

Obviously it would be impractical to photograph a dramatic scene on the deck of a sailing ship wallowing through a violent storm. So, for the sake of safety and convenience, a full-scale section of a ship's deck is built in the studio and mounted on a hydraulic platform equipped with mechanisms that will make it roll, pitch, and toss.

The storm is created by releasing tons of water from enormous spill tanks, and unleashing gale force winds from huge four-bladed Pratt and Whitney-powered wind machines.

This tempest can be stilled by a director's yelling "Cut," a civilized arrangement that permits the drenched actors to grab a healing hot toddy.

The scene, to be completed, must have a background of stormy seas and rocky cliffs which supply the dramatic impact and suspense.

Enter process, laughing.

Eddie Snyder and I, in search of backgrounds for our film, sailed to the Caribbean where we photographed some wonderful stuff around Havana by day, and checked the daiquiri scene by night. Reluctantly we finally set out for our parched homeland via New Orleans. From New Orleans and intensive research into the bootleggers' version of the Ramos Fizz, Eddie and I faced two thousand miles of Texas en route to California.

While we were sweltering in the Southern Pacific waiting room, contemplating an echelon of flies power-diving an apple core, my eyes were abruptly refreshed by a lovely view of two gorgeous girls interrupting the heat waves with a collection of cool curves.

Between the two beauties strolled a jaunty guy wearing white trousers, a striped blazer, a bow tie, and a straw hat. That wardrobe did it. I told Eddie Snyder, "They've gotta be show people. Why don't you ooze over and introduce yourself, and say I'd like to meet them?"

Eddie was great at tossing around the word "Hollywood," and when it was dropped in those days it had plenty of bounce. Eddie returned in a few seconds, accompanied by the dolls and Striped Blazer.

Striped Blazer said, "These girls are beauty contest winners from Louisiana. We're going on to the semifinals in Texas. See, I've been teaching them to walk properly. In beauty contests, a girl wins in a walk. Very tricky to learn, but now they walk like mink."

He illustrated the desired ambulation. However, just as tight pants emphasize a girl's femininity, this chap's walkaway accentuated his masculinity. It inspired a boffo yak from us spectators.

The train was called and all five of us went to my drawing room. Snyder, grinning, produced a bottle from under his coat. There are few people more valuable in picture making than a resourceful cameraman.

We had a ball all the way to Houston. Who wouldn't, with tinkling glasses, two beautiful broads, and a guy who couldn't open his mouth without breaking us up?

After he and the girls had left us, Eddie and I sat around chuckling over the guy's wisecracks. I said, "I don't know whether he'd photograph or not, but he's sure as hell funny. Of course, he'd have to have that nose rebuilt."

Eddie amplified, "Valentino he positively ain't. Maybe he better stay in vaudeville. Teaching beauty contestants how to walk isn't a bad deal for a bachelor."

I nodded in agreement. "Yeah—he wouldn't have a prayer in Hollywood What did you say his name was?"

"Bob Hope," said Eddie.

So much for me as a fortune-teller. Smog in the crystal ball.

I'd feel worse about this failure to diagnose top talent if I were the only guy in the picture business with 20/20 hindsight, but I belong to a big club.

While I was finishing *Her Man*, Tom Buckingham was writing a script entitled *The Painted Desert*. Bill Boyd was assigned to star, but Howard Higgins—set to direct—was having trouble finding a satisfactory heavy. Higgins explained his problem to me. "This is a tough part to cast. This guy is a charmer through four-fifths of the picture. Only in the last fifth is he revealed as a double-dealing bastard. Where ya gonna find a guy to fill *that* bill?"

One evening, in accordance with my lifelong practice of keeping up with legit presentations, I went down to catch a performance of

The Last Mile, playing at the old Belasco. Cast as Killer Mears was a big, jug-eared guy with a heavy mop of dark hair, dimples, remarkable gray-green eyes, and a voice that sent ripples down the female spine, according to the blonde chatterbox sitting near me.

I went backstage after final curtain to talk to this stud, and came away convinced that I had located Higgins's heavy.

Buckingham and Higgins caught the next evening's performance and the following morning Higgins talked Bill Sistrom into signing the gentleman at $150 per week. The contract included a series of options to be exercised by the studio after the completion of *The Painted Desert.* In brief, they had a legal lock on the guy from then on.

Sistrom's comment, in regard to the heavy's contract, is Hollywood history: "If this hambone clicks by some crazy chance, we can always change that cornball moniker. Who's going to swoon over a guy named Clark Gable?"

By the time *The Painted Desert* was finished, Buckingham and Higgins were yelling their heads off, making the announcement that Gable had what it takes: an authentic, built-in star personality.

Bill Sistrom resisted the propaganda. After studying the rough cut of the picture, he gnawed his lower lip pensively then decided to DROP Gable's option.

Buckingham, Higgins, and I stormed into Sistrom's office to protest. He listened absently while rearranging the clutter on his desk, then snapped, "'Look—you guys! You run your end of the business and I'll run mine. Heavies like this Gable are a dime a dozen."

I hasten to add that in *many* ways, Sistrom was a very bright guy.

So is Paul Schwegler, erstwhile All-American from Washington State, who was once my second assistant.

When I was shooting *Stand-In,* Schwegler stood by for several days, biting his tongue. I failed to understand his hangup. We had a fine cast (Joan Blondell, Leslie Howard, and a newcomer who had built an early reputation as a heavy). I had decided, before rolling a camera, that *Stand-In* could be spiced by using, in a sympathetic role, a man who usually played meanies. His name was Humphrey Bogart.

After sitting, first on one cheek then the other, during the daily rushes, Schwegler turned to me in the darkroom and demanded,

"Have you lost your cottonpickin' mind? What makes you think you can turn *that* guy into a leading man? The sonabitch LISPS!"

History has vindicated me in regard to Bogart; history made a real patsy of me in a slightly different division of the Rueful Hindsight Sweepstakes.

I was offered the directorial job for a comedy to be titled *The Awful Truth,* starring Irene Dunne and Cary Grant. I read the script and came down with a fit of the witties. I announced, *"The Awful Truth* is about as funny as the seven-year-itch in an iron lung. No thanks."

The script was offered to Leo McCary. I had dinner with him one night and learned that he was in the midst of shooting the film. "How could you take on that turkey?" I wanted to know.

Leo grinned, "To be blunt, I needed the job. Sure, the script was terrible, but I've seen worse. I worked it over for a few weeks, changed this and that. I finally decided I could make something of it."

He did. An Academy Award Oscar.

Duke Wayne has to pick up the tab for the next report.

When radio was the medium with the message, Duke and I produced a pilot for a series entitled *The Lightnin' Kid,* the story of a frontier wanderer who scorned a gun but used a bullwhip with which he could disarm the fastest draw afoot or a-horseback.

I thought the story line had everything—action, an admirable hero, comedy, the magnificent background of America's far horizons, and an idealistic point of view. However, it didn't sell because we were bucking the Private Eye cycle.

Time passed, yet I couldn't forget *The Lightnin' Kid.* I decided, in the spring of 1954, that if Duke didn't want to turn the idea into a television series, I'd buy him out. I met him for luncheon in the Polo Lounge at the Beverly Hills Hotel and outlined my plan.

Looking me squarely in the eye, Duke demanded, "Tay, are you nuts? A TV Western! You've got to be kidding. A year from today, there won't be a Western on television. I won't let you do this to yourself."

Never mind, Duke. Even Nostradamus didn't win 'em all.

12

ONE MORNING BUCKINGHAM SAID, "YOU'VE BEEN GREAT, AND I APPRECIATE all you've done for me, but I've got to make some housing arrangements on my own before I cut my throat while shaving. I *really* hate myself in the mornings."

"Forget it," I advised, "unless you have an offer from something stacked, weak-willed, and well-heeled."

"In case I do, I'll check to see if she has a friend for you," Buck promised, and the subject was dropped.

At the time I was working on a script that was giving me headaches, and a girl ditto, so two or three weeks had passed before I realized that Buckingham was missing. I ran into him in Henry's one noon, and he said, "I'm sharing a house with Paul Franklin. I sure miss your cooking."

I assured him he could always sign on again, but I gathered that he found Beverly Hills more convenient than Laurel Canyon. Suddenly I understood what had been bugging me. Subconsciously, I had been aware of his absence, and I had been lonely.

What, I wondered, was keeping Joan Marshfield in Paris so long? I had heard nothing from her in months, which explained my vague sense of desolation.

I cabled: "WHEN YOU COMING HOME?"

Back came the answer: "AM HOME STOP GOT TIRED OF WAITING STOP ADDRESS COUNTESS HENRI TOULOUSE STOP FORTY ONE RUE PIERRE CHARRON PARIS SIGNED JOAN."

After awhile I was able to pick myself up from the floor.

Some guys in my circumstance would have gotten blind drunk. Not I. I had to have a change of pace. Some guys would have committed suicide, but I had a script to finish. Some would have wallowed in self-pity.

Not a bad idea.

Ultimately, however, you light your torches and you pull up your tights.

With tights fairly taut, I carried my torch to the apartment of my new Australian playmate, John Farrow.

Johnny was my kind of people: Of Irish descent, he was a poet of merit, and had been published in all the top literary magazines of the day. Blondly handsome, with unforgettable blue eyes, he could be capsuled as type casting for the Crown Prince.

We had first met when he was brought to my office at Pathé by a producer who said, "The boss wants you should learn Mr. Farrow how to write screen plays."

We shook hands. Johnny flashed a subtle deadpan wink, I grinned, and it was Instant Friendship.

After the producer had left, John asked, "Is it possible for one to teach a tyro to write screen plays?"

"Not unless he has enough sense to do the job on his own," I answered honestly. "But possibly I can come up with a few handy do's and don'ts."

"All suggestions will be appreciated," grinned Johnny.

"How about dinner tonight?"

"Suggestion received and accepted with gratitude."

Our mutual admiration deepened upon discovering that both of us suffered from sea-itis.

I had always been boat-batty, and this gent dug my passion for anything that would float. He was authentically salty; he had hit the U. S. beach by jumping ship in San Francisco, having arrived on an Australian windjammer. He played the total ignore for Immigration authorities, an omission he had to correct many years later.

Soon after our meeting, Johnny and I pooled our dimes and bought a seagoing pumpkin seed, a no-class sloop with a centerboard, and christened her—for some sensible reason that escapes me now— *The Ida.*

We had full headroom in the cabin if we stayed on our hands and knees, and we had to depend upon a Johnson outboard kicker to get

[104]

in and out of the harbor, but we were as proud of her as if she'd been a Lipton Cup defender.

However, one windless Sunday when our outboard clunker conked in the middle of the Catalina channel, I blurted to Johnny, "I'm dying of sunburn and I have a charley horse in each leg. Furthermore, I'm tired of the Coast Guard whipping out a rosary every time we pass the breakwater. Let's get a ship with full leg room even if it has to be a stinkpot."

What a blue water sailing man thinks of a power boat (stinkpot) skipper cannot be recorded, not even for readers of John Updike.

Let's just say that Johnny became master and sole owner of *The Ida.* Turning up his nose at me, the traitor, he gave extensive orders to a boat builder. *The Ida* was treated to a facial, a permanent, and some badly needed foundation garments.

Weeks passed, Writing jobs piled up and Johnny couldn't get near his ship in drydock. Dreaming of cruises to be, he had *The Ida* towed back to her slip at the yacht anchorage.

Came the day when the bills arrived for the boat's transformation. They were what you might describe as exorbitant, i.e., the entire U.S. 6th Fleet could have been repainted for less. Appalled and infuriated, Johnny refused to remit one penny until he had inspected the work.

The boat builder began to bear down on Johnny. When threatening letters and telephone calls failed to get action, a collection agency sent in a crack relay team that hounded the poor Aussie around the clock.

It was too much. Johnny jettisoned his deep sea fantasies, groaning, "All right, take the boat if you must, but let me alone so I can get on with my work."

Forthwith a deputy, bristling with court orders, arrived at the anchorage in Wilmington and demanded to be directed to *The Ida.*

The anchorage manager, deadpan, pointed. "There. Starboard side of the third float."

The deputy studied the spot as his jaw came unhinged.

Beside the float, about eighteen inches of *The Ida*'s mainmast arose above the water. There she was, the gallant little ship that had carried Johnny and me through many a rough channel crossing; her rejuvenation had sapped the last of the old girl's strength. Alone and deserted, she had sunk at the dock in snug harbor, and there she lay in the mud at the bottom of the bay.

Fade out on the good ship *Ida.*

My second boat was a round-bottomed fishing craft named *The Girl Friend.* Like many girl friends of that era, she is still breasting the waves and vice versa with matronly verve and grace, although I don't have her present address.

However, my first channel crossing on *The Girl Friend* convinced me that I had bought a problem; sweating at every pore, she was unable to wallow from San Pedro light to Avalon (roughly a twenty-mile trip, and I mean roughly) in less than three hours.

I turned her into a houseboat for use at Catalina, and popped for a Gar Wood speedboat for commuting purposes. Naturally, I christened the speedboat *Girl Friend, Too.*

Because I acquired her at a bargain, I had refrained from inquiring too closely into her pedigree, always a mistake with a boat or a woman. Yet she was sleek, steady, easy to handle, and dug out like a .38 on a .45 frame.

I was halfway between Wilmington and the Catalina Isthmus on our maiden voyage when a Coast Guard cutter signaled for me to heave to, then boarded me. I was totally mystified.

The authorities examined my papers and craft in detail, thanked me for my cooperation, and left. The C.G. guys are the greatest, but they're not gabby. I was given no explanation.

A week later the incident was repeated.

And two weeks later.

The repetition began to exasperate me, so I researched the past of *Girl Friend, Too.*

I had rescued her from a dubious life. She had been a rumrunner, one of the most notorious on the Pacific Coast. Which explained all that power.

To free her from her past and give her a new start in life, I had her painted black. However, as long as I owned her, we were stopped and inspected regularly. It shows how tough it is to quit the rackets.

Eventually she passed into hands less loving than mine and was killed, you might say, in an argument over right-of-way with the San Pedro breakwater. She had reverted to her old ways, except that on

[106]

her final run her illicit liquid cargo was in her skipper and not in her bilge.

Girl Friend III, a 65-foot twin-screw cabin cruiser with lots of sex appeal and plenty of drinking room, was succeeded by *Katinka,* a fine diesel cruiser from which I parted reluctantly, but I had spotted her successor, and—at least on the high seas—there is no love like the new love. Poor *Katinka!* Shortly after I sold her, she was skillfully navigated at full speed into a Catalina cliff. The cliff won.

Finally I bought *The Athene,* my fair and lovely 104-foot yawl that appears in a starring role later in this story.

In London, Paris, Rome, or New York, one can usually judge a man's standing in his field of endeavor by his status symbols: the Rolls-Royce, a home on Long Island, a pad in Essex, a racing string at Churchill Downs, a yacht at Portofino, or an invitation to an Earl Blackwell party.

In Hollywood, however, the make of a man's car, the area in which he lives, and the authenticity of his wife's diamonds indicate nothing more than his ability to make a down payment.

The sole status symbol never to be stolen by jewel thieves, junked for lack of a compatible differential, or abandoned because Martians moved into the neighborhood, is an oceangoing vessel.

For years, John Ford's yacht, *Araner,* plied the seas regularly between Los Angeles Harbor and Honolulu.

Jim Arness's trimaran *Sea Smoke*—probably out of Seasick by Gunsmoke—came in first in the 1968 Newport to Honolulu race, but he was beaten by Buddy Ebsen's craft on a handicap basis.

Errol Flynn's *Zaca* was mainly famous for its portholes.

C. B. De Mille's *Seaward* had neither an imaginative name nor a sunken bathtub.

A yacht once owned by Spencer Tracy, then by Dick Powell, was recently hijacked; the pirates failed to stop when the Coast Guard fired a warning shot across their bow, so the Coast Guard came alongside and boarded them. One bearded pirate rushed on deck, brandishing a butcher knife in fine Spanish Main fashion, but was quelled by one quick look down the barrel of a C. G. .45.

Steve Cochran died aboard his yacht in Mexican waters. Knowing

Steve, I'm sure he died happy. The boat was "manned" by an all-girl crew.

A. C. Lyles, ace young producer, tells a good yacht story. He was a weekend guest on a boat tied alongside Jerry Lewis's craft at the Newport Yacht Harbor. As he approached the boat one Sunday morning, three little kids passed him at a dead run, rushing to meet their father.

One of the trio threw himself at his parent and breathlessly announced, "Dad, guess what! Jerry Lewis SPOKE to me. He didn't say a word to Tommy or Bud, but he spoke to ME!"

"Yeah? What did he say?" inquired the father.

The boy reported ecstatically, "He said, 'GET YOUR GRUBBY PAWS OFF MY BOAT!'"

Yes, indeed, to be salty is to be IN. And often to be IN DUTCH with one's current wife, as witness the plight of a topflight Irish producer who bought a boat of boats: about 110 feet of teak deck, stainless steel galley, and indefatigable bar.

He invited a number of his chums, including me, to join him on a cruise to the Hawaiian Islands. In a benign moment he included his long-suffering wife.

"Nothing doing," said that disenchanted lady. "That cruise is just an excuse for a fourteen-day binge."

Her spouse swore that he was on the wagon and intended to take said wagon to sea.

"I'll ride the *Lurline* and meet you in Honolulu," the lady ruled. "If you've weathered the trip in good condition, I'll spend the summer on the boat with you."

To prove that he was sincere, the producer permitted his wife to provision the ship—without liquor.

However, as departure time drew near, the owner of the *Spree* began to contemplate, rebelliously, man's right to a rolling gait at sea.

He telephoned the provisioning wholesaler and made arrangements for the *many* cases of individual cans of tomato juice (previously ordered) to be filled with 100 proof bourbon.

On sailing day the producer broke out the first case of "tomato juice" and stood at the rail, toasting Mrs. Producer, who had used the family speed boat to escort the *Spree* beyond Catalina Island and temptation.

The producer was awakened at an obscene hour the next morning. When he protested, rough hands pummeled his shoulders and a bucket of ice water was sloshed in his face. He was told loudly, "We've sighted Diamond Head."

"You're nuts," raged the dripping producer. "How could you 'sight Diamond Head' twelve hours out of San Pedro?"

I said at the top of my lungs, "We're FOURTEEN days out of Paydro, and there's a Coast Guard cutter bearing down on us. You'd better shape up."

The producer struggled to the mirror and studied his two weeks' growth of beard. Only the instant vitamins of several cans of "tomato juice" made it possible for him to go topside and roar the order, "Man the rail. Pipe the landing party aboard."

Leading the procession of Honolulu socialites and newsmen was Mrs. Producer. She kissed her husband's stubbled cheek, and decked his neck with leis, shook hands with me dubiously, then moved down the line of passengers and crew as graciously as an empress inspecting her flagship.

As soon as she had moved beyond earshot, the producer sagged into my supporting grasp and demanded hoarsely, "Who's the broad?"

One final epic of the sea: Lewis Milestone, a fine director, is a man of many interests, not one of which is the roaring surf. In his opinion, salt water is strictly for sharks, or, to quote him, "I am an 18-carat, full-jeweled landlubber."

One Friday afternoon, Buckingham and I—after a few short beers with old-fashioned chasers—decided to shove off for a weekend at Catalina on *The Girl Friend*. Because there is no evangelism anywhere to equal that of dedicated sailors, it occurred to us that the time had come to convert Milestone.

Eloquent as Buck and I were on the subject of sailing, I doubt that Milestone would have dug the advantages of signing on for the voyage if he too hadn't taken on enough liquid to feel the tide of high adventure surging through his veins.

As we chugged out past the breakwater, heading for Catalina through a black and moonless night, Millie stood beside me, glass in hand as he balanced on the balls of his feet, his cheeks pinked by the rising wind. He was the best-dressed yachtsman I had ever entertained, immaculate from jaunty cap, red scarf, and brass-buttoned blue jacket to white slacks and navy blue topsiders.

We were well out of sight of land when I noted that Buckingham had disappeared. I said to Milestone, "You take the wheel while I find out what Buck's doing. I'll be right back." I added a warning against relaxing his vigilance for an instant, or letting go of the wheel for any reason at all.

Going below, I had no trouble finding Buck. He was stretched out on one of the bunks, fast asleep. I studied his inert form. His breathing was deep and regular; his face wore the softened look of total relaxation.

"That's one helluva good idea," I said, committing myself to the other bunk.

I woke up with sunlight streaming into the cabin. Coming to my feet in a broad jump, I realized that we were turning in a tight circle.

I went topside on the double to find Milestone still standing by, blue with cold and soggy from mist. It was obvious that he had started to panic when he realized I had been detained, but at that point the true genius of Millie had manifested itself. He had reasoned that if he put the wheel hard over, the boat would circle; we would be getting nowhere, but we wouldn't crash into Catalina's rocky shoreline either. He had remained valiantly at the helm through the long night, his only companion the snarling sea.

There are few things on earth as totally unnerving as the clamp-jawed silence of a naturally garrulous man. Millie uttered not one syllable from the time I relieved him at the wheel until we reached Catalina where he leaped to the dock and stalked toward the steamship office, obviously intending to book passage on the excusion boat that made a sedate round trip each day.

Months went by during which I neither saw nor heard from Millie. Then one afternoon we met in the narrow studio hallway. He studied me; I grinned at him. Suddenly we began to laugh.

"Made any trips to Catalina lately?" he asked.

"Nope. I've sold my boat."

"I *thought* you smelled better. Thank God, now we can be friends again," said Millie.

13

IN THE DAYS WHEN I WAS AT PATHE, ONE OF A COMPLICATED LIFE'S COMpensations was that a man could tell the girls from the boys. Among that era's finest examples of Venus Ascending were Lila Lee, Marian Nixon, Virginia Fox (who became Mrs. Darryl Zanuck), Laura La Plante (who married Irving Asher), Radie Harris (now a top columnist on *The Hollywood Reporter*), and a girl I had worshiped from a distance since *The Hunchback of Notre Dame,* Patsy Ruth Miller.

Farrow was dating Lila Lee; Lila's buddy was Patsy Ruth; we made up a foursome with the result that Patsy Ruth was bestowed upon me without malice or premeditation. I hope.

One Saturday afternoon John suggested that I drop in at his apartment on Havenhurst Avenue for a hangover cure; when I arrived, Lila was serving the balm. Casually she reminded us that a friend's birthday was coming up, so why didn't we go shopping for dear old Joe?

"Patsy will join us at the jeweler's," she added, giving the line a reading that was a throwaway masterpiece.

I tossed off my beaker of headache cure, and unsuspectingly went along to the glittering shop on Beverly Drive, where I helped select cufflinks for Joe Whatzisname. That accomplished, the girls began to study diamond rings—as girls will.

For some reason, the logic of which now escapes me, I bought Patsy Ruth an engagement ring.

The studio tried to bail me out by sending me to the Feather River Valley to direct a picture from a script that Jimmy Gleason and I had written. It dealt with the lives of boomer brakemen and was entitled, in a catch phrase of the era, *Oh, YEAH!* Gleason, Robert Armstrong, and Zasu Pitts were the stars.

Patsy came up to the location to visit us. My pals looked her over and whistled. They said, "Lotsa mama, but don't get married. A permanent girl is very expensive, not to mention an enduring headache."

I remembered Joan Marshfield and what a nice investment she would have been on a permanent basis; I remembered the emptiness of my house in the evening. Trapped by reminiscence, I settled for an early wedding.

The ceremony was slated for 4:30 on a sunny Saturday afternoon at Los Angeles' St. James Episcopal Church on Wilshire Boulevard. The bride was exquisite in candelight satin, rose point lace, and a sprinkle of seed pearls. She was attended by a pride of bridesmaids.

The groom wore a hangover, a ghastly pallor, and the traditional cutaway and striped trousers. I should have carried a calla lily in my gray-gloved hand, but the florist insisted upon lilies of the valley in my lapel.

At 4:20 the organ took up my shakes and began to vibrate the pastor's study as if we had spawned an earthquaker of No. 7 magnitude.

Tom Buckingham, who had the role of best man, thrust his head out to case the sanctuary, or—as he said—"to count the house." After a few seconds of horrified scrutiny, he drew back, closed the door, and backed against it, gasping, "I don't know how long I can hold them off, but I think I can give you twenty minutes' head start. Run for your life, man."

I was chicken. I stayed, even though I knew that Buck's was the voice of bitter experience.

During the early days of our engagement, I tried to make it clear to Pat that, basically, I was not a marrying man.

She failed to find that attitude endearing. Inevitably, I suppose, we had our first married quarrel the week *before* we were married. I wanted her to move into my hilltop house in Laurel Canyon, although I had some misgivings about carrying her up those eighty-five steps.

Pat wanted me to move into her house on Crescent Drive in Beverly Hills, which she shared with her father and brother. I suppose I was an introverted bridegroom, but I wanted to be alone with my bride. A psychologist would undoubtedly have deduced that I cherished a phantasy of recapturing, with Patsy Ruth, the world-well-lost companionship I had known with Joan Marshfield.

Patsy thought my desire for privacy absurdly romantic, but consented to a summit talk with her male relatives, who considerately moved out.

After our wedding, Pat and I drove to the Santa Barbara Biltmore for a typical Hollywood film maker's one-day honeymoon. The marriage was still idyllic when we returned to Beverly Hills Sunday evening. I carried my bride across the threshold and straight into the waiting presence of "Daddy," and "Brother."

They had moved back in.

Ratsy Puth (as Bob Fellows always called her) and I sat on the stairway and exchanged views for four long hours. The match ended in a draw; it was decided that I would remain in the house if Ratsy's kin would return to their apartment. No hurry—anytime the next morning would do.

I have described this decision as a draw for the reason that I was sent away on location before I had a chance to defend my title. When I returned, we Millers were again a household of four.

At the end of six months it occurred to me that I had married the wrong Miller, because both the male Millers were great guys.

Oscar Miller ("Daddy") was a baseball fan, and I've always been a football nut, so our dinner table conversations must have been a shade less than enthralling for Pat.

I must say for our marriage that Patsy Ruth elevated me from the ranks of the Hollywood hoi polloi. Because of her youth and loveliness, we were invited to spend a weekend at San Simeon, the sky-hung fief of William Randolph Hearst.

Incidentally, if movies had never become vocal, Patsy Ruth would have been one of the great stars of all time. She was a talented actress and she photographed superbly; however, her voice was high and abrasive, not at all compatible with her patrician beauty, so she was retired by the microphone.

Anyhow, anent San Simeon, Patsy was given our marching orders by an explicit Hearst secretary. Thursday morning at seven we were to be picked up by a chauffeur and driven to the railway station; we would board a special car that would carry us to San Luis Obispo. From there we would be convoyed by limousine to the castle.

Excellent plan, well executed. We were shown to quarters by an equerry who asked, after a deprecating cough, "Sir, do you happen to have any liquor in your luggage?"

I admitted that a sneaky fifth, seal unbroken, happened to have found its way among my shirts during the confusion of packing.

"I should like to suggest that it be turned over to me," said the aide, meeting my eye with an expression that added, "or else."

Although I am usually an independent type, I was awed by my surroundings, so I handed over my survival kit.

The master-at-arms announced, "We shall meet in the Great Hall for cocktails at seven-thirty. Dinner at eight." And he bowed himself out.

Patsy Ruth and I devoted the next fifteen minutes to incredulous scrutiny of our accommodations. We had been assigned to the Doge's Suite—a signal honor, according to P. R.

Its floors were travertine marble and on its walls and ceilings were Old Masters, reputedly punctured here and there by peepholes.

The bed, once employed by a succession of ardent Venetians, was definitely smaller than Catalina Island, but bouncier to the touch. "I won't dare go to sleep," I confided. "If I should awaken during the night, I'd think I was lying in state."

Patsy Ruth shushed me for fear the room was bugged.

We reported to the Great Hall at the prescribed hour and were served ONE pale cocktail, then we were summoned—about 100 of us —to the dining room whose north wall was barely visible from the south. The room's titanic proportions and the stately pageantry of the service reduced the most brazen among us to childish diffidence. I fought an inclination to do the "church and steeple" bit with my hands. P. R. was wearing the fatuous little smile of the best kid in Sunday School.

After a magnificent dinner, we were herded into the music room. There we saw an unreleased Hollywood film, after which the major domo explained that *Taps* at San Simeon was ten-thirty.

Breakfast was served between seven and eight.

[115]

On Friday's agenda was a morning tour of the grounds, luncheon at twelve, an afternoon tour of the grounds, cocktails in the Great Hall at seven-thirty, dinner at eight, movie at nine, lights out at ten-thirty.

On Saturday we were to rough it: a picnic in the wilderness. We were permitted to elect our transportation to the picnic spot, by horseback or by car. I hadn't been on a horse since that stunt nag tried to drown me, so—somewhat sheepishly—I settled for pneumatics.

When we reached the picnic site, I remembered Marie Antoinette and her dairy farm at Fontainebleau. She never had it so good.

A fieldstone barbecue grill, about thirty feet long, had been stocked with charcoal; a dozen white-hatted chefs were standing by, awaiting the arrival of the first fish. Beside each chef was a full deck of porterhouse steaks—just in case.

Beyond the kitchen facilities stretched the picnic area proper, a plot roughly a hundred feet square, totally carpeted by lap rugs and dotted with cushions.

With a few bared navels, it could have doubled for a C. B. De Mille harem set.

A liveried servant, of which there seemed to be about one per guest, stepped up and asked, "Would you care to fish, sir?"

I nodded. If he'd asked me to dive for pearls, I'd have reached for face-mask and basket.

My tour conductor picked up a pole and creel. "This way, Mr. Garnett," he said, leading me along a landscaped path to a fern-bordered deep blue pool.

"This, I fancy, will be as good a spot as any," he murmured. He baited my hook with a salmon egg, cast, and handed me the pole. A split second later a three-pound trout hit the bait. My assistant was instantly at my side, net in hand. He removed the fish from the hook, dropped it into the creel, baited my hook, cast, and again gave me the pole.

I had to wait maybe six seconds before another overweight trout took the bait, was reeled and creeled.

"Would you care to catch another?" my aide inquired.

"Thank you, no," I sighed. "I'm quite exhausted."

It didn't get a tumble.

I cornered Pat and growled, "Let's go home."

"Are you out of your mind?" she demanded without moving her lips. "We leave here when we're graciously permitted. NOT before."

Further conversation was precluded by the arrival of my personal squire who announced that my fish were ready, and asked if I preferred anchovy butter or sauce Mornay.

Sensing that I had passed the point of no return anyhow, I brazenly asked for, and was served, a porterhouse steak, charred and rare.

"Company Dismissed" was sounded after breakfast Sunday morning. An hour later our detachment of limousines started down the hill, signaling the reverse order of march.

To my astonishment, we were invited to play several return dates at San Simeon. To Patsy's exasperated bewilderment, I flatly refused the booking—which may have had something to do with Pat's ultimately dropping my marital option.

14

MY MARRIAGE WAS FOLLOWED BY TWO ADDITIONAL CATASTROPHES: A PAIR of highly forgettable films entitled respectively *Bad Company,* which it was, and *Prestige,* which it wasn't.

At that point my contract expired, to my considerable relief. Mr. Joseph Kennedy had taken over Pathé and was brandishing a very broad new broom.

Over luncheon at the Hollywood Brown Derby one noon, my long-time friend, producer-director Harry Joe Brown, asked me, "What're you going to do next?"

I said I was looking for a sea story, something a little closer to First Cabin than *Moby Dick.*

Brown said thoughtfully, "Hey—I've got an idea. There's a thing called *Transatlantic* kicking around Warners, a terrific idea by Bob Lord. They must've had a dozen scripts written on the theme, but nobody's licked it yet, because essentially it's stark tragedy and that isn't box office. Zanuck's likely to sell it pretty cheap."

I asked what it was all about.

Brown gave me a fast wrapup of the story line: two intrinsically decent people, a handsome man and a beautiful girl, meet on board a transatlantic steamer and fall in love. The kicker is that both are condemned to death, she by heart disease, and he as a convicted murderer.

I capsuled aloud, "Two doomed people meet and fall desperately in love. It's a helluvan idea. Naturally the public isn't buying stark tragedy, but I'll bet not one of the guys who've tried to write it has thought of taking a whirl at it in terms of comedy."

"How in hell can you tell a tragedy in comic terms?" Brown demanded.

"It's just a hunch, Joe, but I believe that the scenes could be treated brightly, even gaily, as direct counterpoint to the somber tone of the underlying plot."

After leaving Joe, I called my agent—the fabulous Myron Selznick—and told him what I'd heard about *Transatlantic,* explaining that I hadn't read it, didn't want to read it, but felt that integrity demanded I pay for the springboard idea. I asked Myron to buy it for me as cheaply and as quickly as possible, explaining that Patsy Ruth and I were leaving the next day with Sol and Faye Lesser. We were taking the S. S. *Virginia* through the Panama Canal to New York.

I took my Corona on board and every morning I worked from eight until noon. By the time we docked in New York, I had a forty-page treatment completed. I was elated because, among other comedy ideas, I had hit upon a running gag in which I had confidence, although the extent of its importance I hadn't yet realized.

As we walked into the lobby of the Warwick Hotel, I was called to the telephone.

Myron Selznick on the horn. He announced jubilantly that on the day we had left Hollywood, he had "leaked" the news that I had solved the *Transatlantic* problem. By the time the leak reached Zanuck at Warner Brothers, it was a tidal wave. Zanuck wanted me to write the script and direct the film.

I started to object, but foxy Myron overrode me with, "I'm talking from Darryl's office and he wants to say 'Hello.' I'll put him on."

Darryl didn't say "Hello"; he said, "How soon can you get back here?"

"I haven't been in New York an hour."

"Have a nice vacation. Be here in ten days with the finished treatment," he said, and hung up.

When I broke the news to Patsy Ruth that we would have five days in New York, followed by five days on the train en route home, she said a number of things that gave me the impression she was annoyed.

Ten days later I unpacked in Beverly Hills and discovered that my precious forty-page manuscript was missing. I checked the Warwick, the Santa Fe Railway, and my memory. Nothing.

I scrutinized Patsy Ruth long and accusingly, but she merely smiled an inscrutable smile and said, "Don't look at me."

I burned rubber out to Burbank to confide in Doc Solomon, Warner Brothers studio manager and a great guy. Explaining that I was committed to having that treatment on Mr. Z's desk the next morning, I asked for two offices and two secretaries.

For fourteen hours I dictated to first one secretary, then the other. They were the greatest, so the treatment was completed on schedule.

As I was leaving the Warner Brothers lot, lightheaded after giving the script to Mr. Z's secretary, I met my friend Wilson Mizner and asked what he was doing.

"Worrying, mainly," he admitted. "My option comes up next week. Usually a guy gets word before this if the answer is affirmative. I've had no word, so . . ."

I told him, "Just hang onto the left one, Bill. I'm seeing Darryl about writers tomorrow morning. I'm going to need a shooting script in one helluva hurry, so you'll be in."

That was not altruism on my part; Mizner was a master at writing crisp and witty dialogue.

A few steps further I met Joe Jackson, who also had the Option Blues. He was one of the finest script mechanics in the business, so I gave him the pitch I'd given Mizner.

Zanuck's reaction to my treatment was, "Jeez, Tay, it's GREAT. How soon can you be ready to shoot?"

I got a fast nod to my request for Mizner and Jackson, so I tested my luck a little further. For leads I wanted Bill Powell and Kay Francis.

"You had Powell before you came in," said Zanuck. "But what about Kay's speech impediment?"

"I can write around that. All I have to do is duck any word beginning with 'r' or 'l'." (I remembered having heard Kay read the line, "It wouldn't be right, even if we are in love," as "It wouldn't be wight, even if we ah in wuv.")

Darryl snapped, "It's *your* problem."

"For the character roles I'd like Aline MacMahon, Frank McHugh, and Warren Hymer."

"Okay."

We were on our way, hats off and hair flying.

I promptly scrapped the *Transatlantic* title. The story line I had developed started in Hong Kong and necessitated a brief sequence ashore at a port of call, midjourney. For the purposes of high romance, how can you beat a stopover in Hawaii? So our ultimate eastbound destination became San Francisco, and our title, *One Way Passage*.

Those who have caught *One Way Passage* on the late, late, late show, are familiar with the running gag involving the Paradise Cocktail.

Our lovers, Kay and Bill, were introduced by the bartender when each—a stranger to the other—ordered a Paradise Cocktail. As the story progressed, the lovers' nightly meetings to dally over a Paradise Cocktail assumed the mystic implications of a love rite.

After finishing their cocktails (served in champagne glasses), Bill and Kay shattered the bowls and placed the stems, carefully crossed, on the bar to complete the ritual.

It was this gag that resolved our seemingly insoluble enigma: a tragedy with a happy ending.

As the ship passed through the Golden Gate, the lovers pledged themselves to meet on New Year's Eve in Tijuana, although each knew secretly that their immediate parting was forever.

A swift dissolve took us to a gilt and velvet night club in Tijuana. Midnight. Orchestra blaring *Auld Lang Syne*. Couples kissing. Balloons bursting. Toy horns tooting. Toasts raised to a bright New Year.

Behind the bar two tired bartenders, their backs to the festivities, were drearily cleaning up.

Suddenly there was an eerie tinkling of breaking glass.

The fat bartender growled, "Watch your elbows with them glasses."

The thin bartender protested, "I never touched nothin'."

They turned to stare at the bar.

Lying on the shiny mahogany were the crossed stems of two champagne glasses.

[121]

The End.

It was a four handkerchief tag.

After the preview, Kay Francis rushed from the theatre weeping wildly. Throwing her arms around me she sobbed, "It's heahtbweaking. It's the most moving film I've eveh seen. It's unfohgettable. But what about yoah cwedit?"

"Beg pardon?"

"Oh, Tay! Youah cwedit! Youah witing cwedit! You wote such lovely speeches foah me. Why isn't youah name given witing cwedit?"

I told her about my conversation with Hal Wallis, the producer, in regard to the credits. (They mean almost nothing to the layman, but they are vital to people in the picture industry.) Hal had asked me, "How do you want to handle the 'Original Story Written for the Screen' credit?"

Like a ceremonial Chinese dinner, *One Way Passage* was a joint effort; the initial idea had been Robert Lord's, I had prepared the treatment, Joe Jackson had engineered some of the story development, and Wilson Mizner had cracked out with scintillant dialogue.

"Let's not get overextended on this thing," said Hal. "Let me remind you of Sam Taylor."

Shuddering, I recalled the preview, several months earlier, of *The Taming of the Shrew,* starring Mary Pickford and Douglas Fairbanks. It had been directed by the talented Taylor, who had also contributed importantly to the script.

Not only had he taken directing credit, but a writing credit that read, "By William Shakespeare, with Additional Dialogue by Sam Taylor."

He was nearly laughed out of Hollywood.

Wanting no part of that treatment, I settled for "Directed by."

One of my life's (and Hollywood's) little ironies was that—the following spring—Robert Lord won an Academy Award for "Best Original Story written for the Screen"—*One Way Passage.*

15

WILSON MIZNER, TO THIS VERY DAY, IS ONE OF THE MOST QUOTED MEN EVER to illuminate the Hollywood scene.

He was six feet three; his big-boned frame and massive shoulders made him appear even taller. His cranium was enormous, and his hair bushed out in an iron-gray mane. He seemed to be in masquerade, as if—when a small boy—he had been given a lion's role in a school play, and had persisted in wearing the headdress through the years, oblivious to its dusty age and unbelievable disarray.

Like many an oddly assembled man, Bill Mizner had one attractive physical attribute: his smile, which widened his face to sudden symmetry.

Nevertheless, he smiled seldom and spoke even less.

While we worked on the dialogue for *One Way Passage,* he would lie back, inert, in a huge upholstered chair, his bulging eyelids closed over his deep-set eyes.

At about the time Joe Jackson and I exchanged irritated glances, sure that the big guy was asleep, Bill would clear his throat gently and murmur what was likely to be the funniest line of the day.

Sometimes, when creativity lagged, Mizner—eyes closed as usual —would refresh us with an outlandish biographical anecdote.

If his recollections were reliable, he had been a sourdough in Alaska, (unsuccessful), the operator of a Fairbanks badger game (successful), a drunkard (addicted to alcohol), a hophead (addicted to opium), a confidence man (addicted to money), and the inevitable summary of all these: a writer.

One of my favorite Mizner yarns dealt with an Alaskan winter during which he found the Arctic weather inclement and the prices ridiculous. An egg was selling for five bucks, and a bowl of thick, greasy bear soup was priced at ten dollars.

Mizner was without visible means of support, but his pal, a waiter, was literally swimming in liquid assets.

This waiter, name of Sid Grauman, had replaced his trouser pockets with wide-necked hot water bottles. Whenever he carried a ten dollar bowl of soup from kitchen to dining room via a conveniently long hallway, he managed to pour several tablespoonsful of steaming liquid into one of his pockets.

As rapidly as he accumulated a bowl of soup, he peddled it in the alley for five dollars. Bill, because he was a friend, was fed on credit.

Yet Bill's pride was piqued; he yearned to sit in the dining room in preference to lurking in the alley. Never one to underestimate human carnality, Bill finally decided there was a fortune to be made in the badger game. Womanhood was a rare and precious commodity in the frigid north where only two types were extant, the Available Annies, and the Virtuous Wives, although you couldn't tell the players without a program.

Bill made a date with a waitress who shared his yearning for steam heat and inside plumbing. She agreed to lure a well-laden miner to her cabin and cooperate fully in an outraged husband drama. The anticipated take was to be split fifty-fifty.

However, women are fickle. This particular chick suffered from tenderness for a bartender. She confided the plot to him, adding a suggestion that they make off with the loot, leaving Mizner to the mercy of the shorn miner.

Men, too, are fickle. The bartender preferred Bill, his best customer (on the cuff) to the dame. He warned Bill, "That swinging door is a two-timer. Look out for her."

Came the night of the drama. All went as planned with one exception. Instead of carrying a gun, Mizner burst in upon his "wife" and her guest, brandishing an object that looked like a miner's cylindrical pack of dynamite wrapped in a newspaper. Actually it was a can of tomatoes.

Mizner played the scene strictly East Lynne.

"My God, my WIFE!" he yelled, "I'll blow you both to hell."

The miner, reaching for his pants and parka, chattered, "A mistake, sir. I didn't know she was married; I swear to God I didn't. I'll make it right. Take my belt. There's fifty thousand worth of dust in it. You can start over somewhere else—a rich man—forget all this . . ."

While Mizner stood transfixed, muttering oaths and obscenities, the miner escaped.

Bill kicked the door shut against a blast of snow, and fastened the money belt about his middle. "I'll be seeing you, Honey," he said, lifting his hat to the lady who was improperly costumed for following him into the bitter night.

"Hey, what about MY share?" she yelled.

Bill tossed the can of tomatoes to her. "That just got me fifty grand. See what it'll do for you."

Her aim was bad. She smashed the can against the door through which Bill had just decamped.

An honorable man, Mizner promptly paid Sid Grauman for many weeks of sustaining soup, and squared his account with the bartender.

Another of Mizner's anecdotes dealt with the period when he was sharing an apartment with William Sydney Porter, celebrated under the nom de plume, "O. Henry."

One morning the two Bills awakened hungover, hungry, and broke.

"Be of good cheer," advised Mizner. "Shave, bathe, and dress in your best. We're going to take on a luncheon fit for Jim Brady."

Porter was practical. "What do we use for money?"

"Let the professor lead the way," suggested his friend.

Looking like Wall Street bankers, the pals sauntered into Sherry's and treated themselves to everything from martinis and steak to Baked Alaska and champagne.

Leaning back with a sigh, Mizner asked the waiter to lend him a fountain pen and one of Sherry's pillow-case sized menus.

Two hours later he summoned the maitre d'. "I imagine we owe you twenty-five or thirty dollars," he said. "I've written a short story on this menu; take it to the magazine at this address. The editor will pay you fifty dollars for it. Please settle our bill and keep the change."

[125]

The maitre d' protested, "But you haven't signed it, sir. Without a signature, they won't pay me."

Mizner lifted an eyebrow at Porter.

"Go ahead," said Porter, grinning.

With a flourish, Mizner signed, "O. Henry."

Mizner swore to me that the menu-back story was to be found in any collection of the works of O. Henry, but he refused to reveal the title.

Literary experts grant that William Sydney Porter did not write everything published under his O. Henry pen name, so I've often wondered how many of the trick-ending sagas were actually written by Wilson Mizner.

One day Bill confided to me that he had applied for a very large life insurance policy for the benefit of his church. "Figure it may get me a better post position in the Big Handicap," he explained.

At the examining physician's office he was given a small bottle and asked to oblige.

Shaken by contemplation of his past, which included a conglomeration of ailments contracted from Alaska to Shanghai, he began to have misgivings as to the efficiency of his irrigation system.

Professing embarrassment, he asked if he might deliver a specimen the next morning. Request granted.

Mizner was strolling thoughtfully down Beverly Drive when he met an actress with whom he had been on extremely friendly terms from time to time. She had never looked more radiant, the epitome of health.

It was Fate.

"Sweetie," Bill said, "I've got a problem," and outlined it. He added, "If you will, let's say, stand in for me, I'll stake you to a trip to Europe—*when I get the insurance policy.*"

"It's a novel way to get to Europe, but the offer couldn't come at a better time. My boy friend has just married my best girl chum. A voyage anywhere would give me a wonderful lift," confided the actress.

The following morning the specimen bottle was transferred from the girl to Mizner, to the insurance company doctor.

A week later, Bill and I were chatting in front of the Brown Derby when the girl in question came tripping along.

"How soon do I leave for Europe?" she wanted to know.

Mizner shook his head regretfully. "Europe! Sweetie, you couldn't tinkle your way to Catalina. According to that laboratory report, I'm pregnant."

Pat O'Brien, himself a fast man with a funny, was an old friend and fervent fan of Mizner's.

One morning before Bill had checked in, Pat stopped at our office to pick up the latest news.

"Stick around," I suggested. "Bill will be along any day now, laden with a report of some ridiculous adventure."

"That figures. Bill is the patron saint of the preposterous," Pat agreed. "Has he ever told you about his being a fight manager? No? Well, that temporary career grew out of his admiration for a middle-weight named Stanley Ketchell. Remember Ketchell?"

I remembered him. His technique had been highly individual; not only could he slug from any position, he could absorb a roundhouse punch, hit the deck, then bounce back in seconds. For Ketchell there seemed to be adrenalin in the ritual sound of a referee's counting; before the ref reached ten, Ketchell would leap to his feet and cream his opponent.

When Ketchell had disposed of all local contenders, he and Mizner hit the exhibition trail. It was rough enough for Mizner to keep Ketchell in training amid the good influences of home; on tour—forget it.

Ketchell had two hobbies: 100-proof and dames—until the irate shotgun-toting father of a pretty redhead permanently separated the fighter's head from his body.

Mizner stood beside O'Brien at graveside, tears streaming down his cheeks.

The priest began to chant in Latin. To Mizner's horror, the sound assumed a cadence.

Out of the corner of his mouth Mizner muttered to O'Brien, "That priest had better not start to count, or the kid'll come up fighting."

16

STILL DIZZY FROM THE SUCCESS OF *One Way Passage,* I CHECKED INTO Universal Studios to direct *O. K. America,* starring my good friends Lew Ayres and Maureen O'Sullivan, and written by William Anthony McGuire.

The film's title was borrowed from Walter Winchell's stirring radio greeting of the era, "O. K., Mr. and Mrs. America, let's go to press."

Incidentally, just to butter my ego, I want to record that both *One Way Passage* and *O. K. America* received verbal orchids from Mr. Winchell.

In addition to the star roles, the script called for an improbable heavy, a ruthless but polished gang leader—sort of an erudite Al Capone. This role, incidentally, established a pattern for forty years of suave, oak-paneled mobsters.

We had leafed fruitlessly through the Casting Directory before I remembered a guy I had seen on Broadway in the legit comedy, *Whistling in the Dark,* a gent with a deep, infectious laugh and an impeccable Boston accent. His name was Edward Arnold.

I finally located him in the national company of *Whistling* in San Francisco, and signed him. I've always been pleased that mine was the luck to introduce Eddie to Hollywood, because—laughter being contagious—he was a carrier. Although he wasn't a comedian in the baggy-pants sense, whenever he began to boom with merriment, everyone within hearing distance instinctively joined in.

At that time I needed all the laughs I could get, because the storm signals were up on Crescent Drive at Chez Miller, Miller, Miller and Garnett.

It started on that old battleground, our clay tennis court.

Patsy and Oscar played tennis seven days a week, and talked tennis over dinner six nights a week, effectively ending our old football seminars.

On Sundays (my only leisure day) the Millers held Open House. Free booze and a buffet brunch attracted every handsome tennis bum between the Pacific Ocean and the Texas Panhandle.

As a result, our domestic game had become an unvarying love set: Miller–6; Garnett–0.

So, while Pat volleyed, I dollied—aboard *The Girl Friend III*.

When Pat finally suggested a solo holiday for herself in Tahiti ("to give us both a chance to think things over"), I agreed.

Thinking must take place in slow-motion in the South Pacific, because Pat was gone for three months.

Meanwhile, "Daddy" moved to his own apartment, and "Brother" went back to Princeton—each having gotten The Word. I planted tomatoes in the tennis court and listened to them grow. Occasionally I hummed an old cowhand chorus:

> "Being a bachelor ain't so rough!
> Being a bachelor ain't so bad!
> The wonderful chow I cook myself
> Is the best I ever had."

One peaceful Sunday night I wrote to Patsy Ruth, describing our areas of conflict and suggesting a permanent cessation of hostilities. I mentioned Reno as the ideal scene for the ceremony.

Having become morally a free man, I wrote to Joan Marshfield, the Countess Henri Toulouse in Paris, bringing her up to date.

In due time I received a one-line answer: "Would love to hear from you when you sober up."

I carried that sympathetic, understanding note in my wallet until the words had faded beyond legibility.

The impact of *One Way Passage* had been such that it sent every Hollywood writer mooning to his typewriter in an attempt to conjure up a mystical fantasy.

Tom Buckingham, then under contract to Universal, came up

with an ecto-plasmic thing entitled, *Destination Unknown,* and insisted that I was the only man he would trust to direct it.

Good old loyal Tom. He never failed to cut me in for my full share of his troubles.

I accepted the assignment with reluctance. I felt then and feel now that Hollywood's dedication to aping anything successful must end inevitably in mediocre films and emasculated writers.

In spite of an excellent script and a brilliant cast consisting of Pat O'Brien, Ralph Bellamy, Betty Compson, and Alan Hale, Sr., *Destination Unknown* should have been titled *Destination Oblivion.* It sank without a trace.

Put that one on my tab.

It may have been coincidence, but by the time the reviews of *Destination Unknown* had described it as less than my magnum opus, Patsy Ruth had returned from the tropics and agreed that "Destination Reno" was her scene.

She reminded me that it would be cold in Nevada at that time of year, and a fur coat would represent an appropriate goodbye gift. I believe the incident marked the first historical occasion on which a goat was taken for a mink.

As though on cue, Uncle Carl Laemmle summoned me to his office. He had a problem he thought I could solve, which was a switch.

A German unit had been sent to Greenland to film the calving of glaciers and icebergs for a picture to be titled *S. O. S. Iceberg.* Six months, 350,000 feet of film, and $350,000 later, the expedition had returned to Berlin, loaded with pictures of white scenery, but lacking as much plot as you could get out of the ice compartment of your refrigerator.

Uncle Carl wanted me to shuffle off to Berlin, review ALL the exposed film (roughly fifty-eight hours of actual projection time), select whatever was usable, write a story and script around it, *then* direct the filming of the necessary connective tissue. That was all.

News travels fast in Hollywood. An hour after I had left Uncle Carl's office, I met Bob Fellows jogging across the lot. He waved a large parcel at me, yelling, "My longies. Just bought them for Berlin." He refused to tell who had tipped him off.

Neither of us had been to Europe, so *S. O. S. Iceberg* was a big deal.

Jubilantly we boarded Santa Fe's crack Super Chief, bound for Chicago, where we were to have an eight-hour layover before catching the 20th Century Limited to New York. (Yes, children, that's the way we did it when stagecoaches were discontinued.) After two days in Manhattan, we were to sail on the *Bremen*. What more could two parched refugees from prohibition ask?

S. O. S. Iceberg had been given tremendous publicity. As a result, every city newspaper had carried advance stories about our "repair mission." It was a Hollywood snow job saying, in effect, "When better pictures are made, they'll be simulated on our back lots."

Whenever the Super Chief paused, which was seldom, we were interviewed by the resident newsmen. Bob Fellows and I were gratified. We knew that Uncle Carl would be gloating over our space grab. It didn't occur to us that it might interest other readers—planning to go into business for themselves.

We reached Chicago in the midst of a sleet storm. A snaggle-toothed taxi driver, shoving several of his colleagues aside, rushed to help us with our luggage. "Where to?" he asked.

"Could you take us somewhere to get a decent drink?"

"Yes sir, Mr. Garnett."

That use of my name, since I had never before been in Chicago, should have alerted me. We should have lap-dissolved out of that cab instantly, but I leaned back, gave Bob the big eye, and contented myself with feeling important.

We wound up in a tailor's shop, which proved to be a front for a gin mill. I asked the barkeep what was available. "Anything you like, Mr. Garnett," he responded amiably. "It's all from Canada—and, for you, the drinks are on the house."

Fame and free drinks. Who could ask for more?

After several rounds, Bob suggested that we move on to the Blackstone for a shower and a hot breakfast.

We thanked the bartender and aimed for the exit. Our progress was halted by a gentleman having Mack truck shoulders. He said with a pinned-on smile, "Mr. Garnett, we would like it real good if you guys would not make no attempt to leave."

The man was obviously sincere. His right hand remained beneath his left armpit inside his jacket.

I would have directed the scene differently (less menace), but Bob and I—without critical comment—returned to our warm barstools.

We were served another fine free drink as it dawned on us that we had been snatched, and probably were being held for ransom. Gloom settled as, knowing Uncle Carl's instinctive choice between human welfare and a worn quarter, we estimated our future.

We sipped meditatively, wasting good liquor, because the more we drank, the soberer we grew. When the bartender left his post for a few minutes, a Negro moved in and began to polish glasses. As an elevated roared overhead and rumbled away in the distance, he asked with averted eyes, his lips scarcely moving, "You gentlemen know anybody in Chi?"

I thought of one man: Spike O'Donnell. I had met him in Hollywood, to which successful and personable members of his profession often gravitated in those days. He had visited our set several times during the shooting, if you'll excuse the expression, of *Her Man,* and I had spent time with him at Warner Brothers when we were making *One Way Passage.*

I had been tipped that Spike had muscle on the mob circuit.

The Negro continued to polish glasses for several minutes, then collected some trash and disappeared. The bartender came back to refill our glasses.

I was torn between demanding an explanation and passing out. There were sound arguments for either. I was still deciding when a telephone on the side wall began to ring. Loungers leapt to their feet, their hands going to their sidearms.

One of the hoods answered, then asked the room in general, "Anybody here named Garnett?" I memorized his expression of spurious innocence for future use.

I said, "I'm Garnett," and marveled that my voice didn't break.

Picking up the receiver, I cleared my throat and managed, "Garnett speaking."

"Glad you're in town, kiddo," roared a hearty voice. "Just heard the news. Don't go away; I'll be right over."

"Great. Fellows and I are just having a couple of drinks with five or six of the boys," I said, wishing that, instead of having to ad lib them, my lines had been written by Mizner—faster and funnier.

What happened a few minutes later was theatrical to the extent that I would have been tossed out of Hollywood if I'd dared use the scene in a picture.

An inconspicuous side door was kicked open and there stood a bareheaded, brawny guy wearing an open-necked sport shirt and a sloppy tweed suit—in that temperature! He was flanked by two short, snappy guys wearing black derby hats and black Chesterfields. Each escort kept his right hand inside his topcoat pocket.

O'Donnell strode to the bar while his gunsels, backs to the wall on either side of the door, swiveled their eyes around the room.

"Hello, kiddo," O'Donnell boomed, pounding my shoulder. "How are ya, anyhow?"

He told the bartender, "Get a fresh bottle." He inspected the bottle's closure, decided it had not been tampered with, and watched the bartender as the drinks were poured. We gulped the liquor; O'Donnell said to the room in general, "Thanks for the hospitality," and—flanked by the bodyguards—we got the hell out of there.

Three long black Cadillac limousines were parked at the curb. Three black-shirted types sat stiffly in the forward car; the outline of the man in the rear seat suggested that he might be cradling a Tommy gun.

A similar platoon occupied the rear car.

We were ushered into the middle limo; at a sign from O'Donnell, the convoy squealed away. "Better you're on a train instead of hanging around Chi," O'Donnell stated.

I mentioned the Negro and said I'd like to show my gratitude. O'Connell gave me a long, hard look and snapped, "I heard about you from the Coast. If anybody ever asks you, I HEARD IT FROM THE COAST."

We had missed the 20th Century Limited, so we took the next eastbound rattler which turned out to be, literally, a milk run. From the conductor I learned that we could be dropped in Detroit around 3 A.M. and that there was "a sort of landing field just out of town if you're fool enough to go up in an airy-plane."

Our Detroit taxi driver thought us crazy too, but he studied the night sky and ventured, "Gonna be clear tomorra; maybe Jimmy'll fly you to New York if you're lucky."

We awaited daybreak in a farmer's barn that had been converted into a hangar. The farmer served us several drinks of reasonably fine home brew, and sold us a survival kit to take aboard the aircraft. I've always felt we invented "in-flight" cocktails.

As the sun came up, "Jimmy" arrived, decked out in puttees, goggles, and a leather helmet. I thought, "Shades of Dick Grace."

Incidentally, I want to be credited with having said not one word about Pensacola or the H-boat during this entire episode.

It was roughly a four-quart flight from Detroit to New York. The pilot kept insisting that ceiling and visibility were unlimited, but Bob and I were immersed in an impenetrable fog.

Even the lobby of the Warwick Hotel was socked in. Out of the mists, a covey of newsmen materialized. It seemed that Spike had tipped off his favorite Chicago reporter. (Every gang figure had one in those days.) Our kidnaping had made scare-headlines across the country, so the media wanted our version.

En masse we adjourned to a suite with bar, thoughtfully provided by the studio. Bob and I had to make up for breakfast, lunch, and dinner (missed in Chicago), breakfast (missed in Detroit), and luncheon (missed while airborne). In order to get enough fruit to ease our hunger pangs, we were obliged to take on several old-fashioneds.

Our section of New York was nearly blind when we bade the press goodbye and boarded the *Bremen.* I was walking arm and arm up the gangplank with Bob, until I noticed that he was wearing a diamond bracelet on his slender wrist.

Drawing myself to full height, I stared down at my companion and accused, "YOU are not Mr. Robert Fellows."

She only smiled secretly and shook her head. Aha! Intrigue—the mobs were still after us?

Determined to find Bob, I followed the girl to her stateroom. He wasn't there either.

But someone had sent us a Methuselah of champagne, plus a gross of long-stemmed red roses. The card read, "With much love—Seymour."

Good old Seymour. How thoughtful of him to remember me. Touched by the nobility of mankind, I dissolved. As I brushed away my tears, I had an idea: Who in hell was this Seymour? I told the girl, "I don't even know the sonafabitch, and he's got me in tears."

Yet, ever the gentleman, I controlled myself and opened the wine.

It was horrible to be jolted out of a sound sleep by the crash of wilted rose petals onto the thick stateroom carpet. It was even more shocking to squint across at the opposite bunk and discover that Bob Fellows had bleached his hair.

Or was still missing.

I was momentarily shaken by the possibility of his having fallen overboard, but quickly recalled there was nothing to worry about. He was a strong swimmer.

As we were docking in Bremen, Bob joined me at the rail. I said sternly, "It's about time!"

"Look, Pal, I kept a light in the window all the way across. Gosh, you look AWFUL!"

"I, too, am accustomed to a better view," I retorted.

Our dialogue was interrupted by an excited girlish voice calling, "Yoo-hoo, SEYMOUR! *Here,* Seymour!"

Looking down we saw a short, dapper man, waving and throwing kisses. He was wearing a mink-collared coat, a homburg hat, and on the little finger of his left hand glittered the older sister of the Hope diamond.

I told Bob Fellows, "My God, there's Seymour."

"Who, exactly, *is* Seymour?"

I responded with some asperity, "How the hell should I know? He's just a guy who sent me champagne and roses."

17

In 1933 I imagine the average American shared my own preconceived image of Berlin. I expected to see a hearty, well-dressed people filled with schnapps, sausage, and song.

Instead, as we tried to cross the sidewalk from our taxi to the Adlon Hotel, we were almost overwhelmed by beggars; not professional panhandlers, but tattered, starving citizens, the flotsam left by the backwash of World War I and the Great Depression.

We were too stunned to take it in at once, but before we left Berlin we were brought to realize that the vast majority of Germans were ready to embrace any leader who would promise food, warmth, and a future exempt from the wretched threat of communism. We were neither diplomats nor politicians; we didn't understand the ramifications of the Versailles Treaty, but as compassionate human beings, we knew that millions of the hungry and the desperate were crying out for a deliverer. They thought they had found him in the person of a housepainter named Adolf Hitler.

One whirl of the hotel's revolving door that first morning transported us beyond the reek of poverty and into the magnificent Adlon lobby. It was as if the luxury of the *Bremen* and the opulence of the Adlon were the reality, the anguish in the streets only an hallucination.

An "all's well with the world" mood was restored for us by the presence of Paul Kohner, our producer, standing knee-deep in the lobby's Oriental carpeting. He wore an all-weather grin, because he had just married the lovely Mexican actress, Lupita Tovar. (Thirty-seven years later, the grin remains unchanged.)

The next morning, in an effort to shake off the traveler's typical sense of being isolated, I placed a telephone call to Joan Marshfield in Paris. This entailed using an English–German dictionary, a German–French dictionary, and a French–English dictionary.

The line was busy.

After breakfast, Paul took us to the home of Dr. Arnold Fanck, who had headed the *S. O. S. Iceberg* expedition to Greenland; inescapably he was the man responsible for about ten miles of snow-stacked celluloid.

Dr. Fanck suggested that he run the film for us in what he designated as his "salon," a walk-in deep-freeze that would have frappéd a polar bear. Day after day for several weeks, we sat bundled in our overcoats, hats, mufflers, and fleece-lined gloves, watching glaciers give birth to icebergs. It was spectacular film, but how many audiences are fascinated by iceberg obstetrics?

We ended each frostbitten day by staggering stiffly from Fanck's salon into a blizzard to thaw out. I was learning a new way to acquire bloodshot eyes; although efficient, the process—like artificial insemination—left much to be desired.

I was ecstatic when we had selected everything we could use— about three reels. (Our next step would be to shoot four more reels so as to inject, here and there, a story line.)

"What we need," I stiff-lipped to Bob Fellows, "is a highly talented writer who understands ice *outside* a glass."

"I've heard a rumor that Edwin Knopf is in Germany. Think he could do us some good?"

I jumped to the telephone and alerted Paul Kohner, who located Knopf and set a deal.

Talk about a man's life story being a novel! In the early film days, Eddie Knopf worked in Germany as an *Italian* film star; during the Thirties he did well in Hollywood as a writer; later he became a top-flight producer for MGM; as this is written he is teaching at U.C.L.A.

He is a handsome man; his Barrymore profile is dramatized by eloquent brown eyes. He always shakes hands with his left hand, because his right arm ends at the wrist.

His empty right glove is a badge of honor. Shortly after the end of World War I, Eddie was starring in a film on location at a small

German village. Between scenes, he wandered into a souvenir shop in which battlefield mementos were being sold.

While he was studying a display of faded insignia, he heard an unmistakable and terrifying sound. A child, left unattended, had pulled the firing pin from a live hand grenade. Eddie grabbed the grenade and ran from the shop; he had to pause for a moment so as to hurl the explosive away from clusters of people on the busy street.

No one else was injured, but Eddie's hand went with the grenade, and his face and body were gouged by shrapnel. He nearly bled to death before he could be rushed to a hospital.

A career ended by catastrophe has made many a man bitter; Eddie simply thanked God for his life and turned to another profession.

In the instance of *S. O. S. Iceberg,* he tailored a semidocumentary out of what we already had, and what we could get. His story line dealt with a Greenland scientific expedition plagued by misfortune. When the group's supporting ship was ground to pieces by icebergs, the survivors took refuge on a huge ice floe. Attrition of various types eliminated all but three persons, a woman and two men.

The expedition's pilot, flying from base camp, was able to save two of the company, the woman and one man, but the second man drowned as the floe—in true iceberg malevolence—rolled over.

Altogether, Eddie's script gave us a fine frostbitten potpourri of comedy, tragedy, romance, and travelogue, crowned by a happy ending. Make that "reasonably" happy.

The night before we were to leave Berlin for Switzerland (where the narrative scenes for *S. O. S. Iceberg* were to be filmed), we lounged as usual in the Adlon Bar, the informal Press Club where English-speaking reporters gathered to bitch about the home office.

That day President von Hindenburg had elevated Adolf Hitler to the Chancellorship of the Third Reich. We, and most of the men in the room, couldn't have cared less.

There was one sour face in the crowd: that of Red Knickerbocker, dean of the American foreign correspondents.

Somebody said, "Come on, Red. Drink up. What's *your* beef?"

"You imbeciles! You laughing hyenas," Red growled. "Don't you realize that TODAY you witnessed the beginning of World War II?"

His vehemence sent a chill down my spine. Not because I agreed with him; emotionally, like everyone else, I refused to take his prophecy seriously. Nevertheless, there is something electric in each of us that tingles in response to clairvoyance.

That same evening Bob Fellows and I were invited to a party attended by members of our cast and their friends. It was a lively affair, yet burdened by an undercurrent of gloom. Finally Bob said to Ernst Udet, "I don't understand. Can you explain—in American terms—why you're concerned over the Hitler business?"

Answered Udet, "We feel as you would if Huey Long had been elected President of the United States."

In the midst of packing for Switzerland, it occurred to me that I was a free man; although I hadn't heard from Patsy Ruth, it was reasonable to assume—thanks to the passage of well over the traditional six weeks—that she was on her honeymoon with one of her tennis addicts.

Naturally that reminded me of Joan Marshfield. Everything reminded me of Joan Marshfield.

Once again I tackled the telephone. The call went through without delay. "Oui?" said the voice that had launched a thousand flips.

I swallowed hard. Being a born meeter-of-great-moments with eloquence, I blurted, "Joan, this is Tay. How are you?"

"Oh, Tay-ee!" There was a special way in which she pronounced my name. "Hello-oo," was the velvety added greeting.

The amenities concluded, I got down to the nitty-gritty. "Howja like to meet me in Switzerland and spend a few weeks while I'm finishing a picture?"

Deep sigh. "Oh, Tay-ee. Dear Tay-ee. I can't. I really can't"

"Why not? Tell the dear old count you're going to visit a cousin."

"It's difficult for me to talk at this time."

I said to myself, "Oh, another guy—while the count is at his office, no doubt. I guess all dames are fickle. Well, if she thinks she's going to push ME around."

I laid it on the line: "Okay, Joan. Give me a ring sometime when it's not too difficult to talk."

I hung up with great dignity.

I felt awful.

[139]

18

SWITZERLAND IS HIGH COUNTRY.

I learned why as soon as we started filming *S. O. S. Iceberg*. The Swiss have a beverage composed one-half of boiling tea, one-half red wine. Whenever the Swiss set out across their frigid topography, they carry a thermos of this restorative in their rucksacks. They call it "gluhwein," pronounced gluevine. A carelessly incautious sip of the stuff may also explain jodeling, pronounced yodeling.

Without gluhwein, I should never have learned to ski. If I did.

Our production company was domiciled at the Bernina Hospice, situated at the head of the Engadine Pass; altitude, about 6,800 feet. In a long gone century, the Hospice had been built by dedicated monks to last forever; the stone walls were three feet thick which made it possible to maintain an interior winter temperature of twenty degrees Fahrenheit.

For many years the Hospice had been famous for its brandy-equipped St. Bernard dogs, but by the time we arrived that was a convenience long abandoned, and so was plumbing.

Our first morning in Switzerland, Bob Fellows and I joined our group for a predawn breakfast, only to learn that: (1) our crew consisted in part of a German Olympic slalom champion, an Austrian jump champ, and an all-European langlauf champ; (2) our location was a frozen lake seven miles downhill from the Hospice.

The hiking trail was iced over, so we had our choice between making the downhill trip on skis or awaiting the invention of the helicopter. To save time, we chose skis.

We took off in a burst of American confidence.

Then we got up.

Then we got up again.

And again, and again, and again.

This humpty-dumpty routine continued until midafternoon, when we reached the location, automatically transferring large sums of betting money from the pessimists to the optimists. Our arrival was cheered, but I didn't care for all that muffled choking into scarves.

By that time, unfortunately, our "shooting light" was gone, so there was nothing to do but return to the Hospice. Sadistic companions refused to let me stretch out on the ice and quietly freeze to death. *All* I had to do, they said, was to herringbone back up that hill.

When Bob and I finally reached the Hospice, everyone else had finished dinner and gathered around an accordion player. They cut their caterwauling long enough to break the good news: the following day was a holiday. There was to be a ski competition at Pontresina, so our crew wanted to descend to the resort and knock off a few cash prizes.

"By all means, do," I urged wanly. "I shall work on the script." English translation: I shall sleep until noon.

Nevertheless, the red-eyed dawn was made hideous by the ringing cries of athletes preparing to ski twenty kilometers BEFORE entering the skiing competition.

Schneeberger (our first cameraman and three-time slalom champion, twin talents that had no right to occupy the same body) burst into my room, clapped my black and blue shoulder, and cried jovially, "Mr. Garnett, the competitions you must watch. So beautiful they are. Downhill for you, to coast all the way is possible."

"Too much work on the script," I protested.

"Have the gluhwein," advised Schneeberger. "The head it clears, the stomach it warms, the strength it gives."

After a double shot of that elixir my head cleared, my stomach took fire, and my spirit bubbled with optimism. I dressed quickly and strode to the launching pad. "What a morning!" I started to say; the twenty below zero temperature froze my teeth, tongue and tonsils.

Fellows asked me, "What d'ya think? Shall we give it a whirl?"

I uttered a strangled cry that Fellows took to mean, "Yes." He buckled on his skis.

I lifted my hands in piteous appeal. Too late. My devoted associates missed the gesture of protest; they were busy clamping me into leg irons.

We moved out. At the end of twenty kilometers I had left so many sitz marks that Fellows said thoughtfully, "If they ever ask you to immortalize your prints in the forecourt of Grauman's Chinese, I have a suggestion."

We reached Pontresina in time to watch the last heat of the slalom. Schneeberger won.

"For celebration we now to St. Moritz go," chortled Schneeberger, not even winded.

"I shall commit hara-kiri with one of my own skis before I will splatter myself over one more inch of this landscape," I announced with dignity despite the icicles hanging from my chin.

"Who skis?" demanded Schneeberger. "We now by electric train go, and I think the Palace Hotel you find Fabelhoff."

Oh, Fabelhoff, my Fabelhoff. I could have kissed the registration desk. The Palace's carpets were wooly and warm; the bedrooms were commodious and warm; the bath towels were massive and warm. I sat in a tub of steaming water until I began to crinkle, then fell into a warm feather bed and dreamed of Fabelhoff and warm blondes.

I was awakened by a crash of sunlight and Bob Fellows' ghastly imitation of a rooster. "It's a terrific day," he crowed. "Everybody's going to ride the funicular to the top of Corvilla Run. They say the view is magnificent."

I submerged beneath four feet of feathers.

Craftily Fellows raised his voice to suggest, "Maybe we ought to take some background shots up there."

A sense of duty is my curse. There I was, standing at the summit of Corvilla Run, defenseless, when Schneeberger—having taken the necessary shots—thrust my skis into my arms and announced, "Down from here you start. Out there St. Moritz is."

"Never again," I squeaked. "Never, never, never." (There's a helluvan echo up there.)

Over his shoulder Schneeberger grinned at me. "To get down is no other way." A gross untruth, which I discovered too late to save me.

I turned to Bob Fellows who shrugged and asked a silly question, "What can we lose?"

If I remember correctly, it takes the average skier about twenty-six minutes to make that run. Bob and I did it in two hours and forty minutes, but I maintain we should have been given credit for emergencies such as crossed skis, end-over-ends, and pauses for essential profanity.

When we finally joined our hilarious crew, we, too, were in a benign mood. I was shaping up. Before leaving the Palace Hotel that morning I had taken the precaution of equipping myself with half-a-gallon of gluhwein.

The mark of the civilized man is his ability to alter conditions to suit his individual purpose. It came to me that gluhwein need not be taken exclusively outdoors. I tested the theory in my Palace Hotel suite, in the dining room before a roaring fire, and at the Bernina Hospice during an evening's songfest. Indoors, gluhwein lost none of its authority.

So, when you go to Switzerland, make yourself comfortable before a picture window, regard the view, and enjoy the local grog.

It's the only way to ski.

Top left:
Aboard the *Gloria Dalton,* chartered for THE MAD MARRIAGE starring Helen Twelvetrees— 1931.

Right column, top to bottom:
My CHINA SEAS set the morning my book, *Man Laughs Back,* hit the stands. The pranksters (seated, left to right): Ray June (Cameraman), C. Aubrey Smith, Rosalind Russell, Wallace Beery, Jean Harlow, and Clark Gable.

Bombay, 1935—the TRADE WINDS script called for a scene involving a cobra at close quarters. Our cameraman refused to meet a cobra socially, so I did the honors. Years later I photographed another cobra in a catch-as-catch-can bout with a mongoose for SEVEN WONDERS OF THE WORLD.

I'm the third camel on the left in—you guessed it—Egypt, during the *Athene's* voyage for TRADE WINDS. G.I.s will note that the medium of exchange hasn't changed much in decades.

Top left:
Foreground: Cannon never fired in anger. In second row: Douglas Fairbanks, Jr., Old Dad in muffler, and Harold French. I had completed the script for THE BARBARIANS (all about the Scottish border wars) which Doug is here reading. Little did we dream that we were about to be Scottish mist-ed right out of production.

Top right:
The author, Fredric March, Joan Bennett, Ralph Bellamy, Ann Sothern and our cameraman, Rudy Maté, on the set for TRADE WINDS (United Artists).

Middle:
James Shackleford and I working up some native dialect for TRADE WINDS in the midst of the Sahara. The original caption added that "The desert expedition has been fraught with danger, desert sand storms, a shortage of water, and once a camel bolted with Mrs. Garnett (Helga Moray) hanging on for dear life" (United Artists).

Bottom right:
Ralph Bellamy, T.G., and Rudy Maté (ace cameraman) on lunch break in Bellamy's dressing room on the set for TRADE WINDS.

Bottom left:
You can't get more candid than this, taken on the TRADE WINDS set: Fredric March is wearing a handkerchief to keep makeup off his collar, Ralph Bellamy is tucking the picture into his pocket, and Joan Bennett is getting the handcuff treatment.

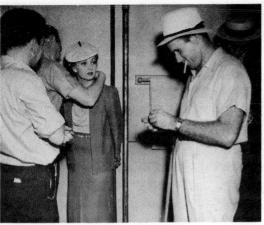

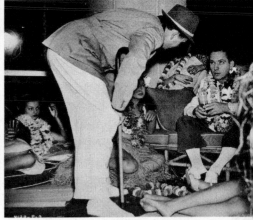

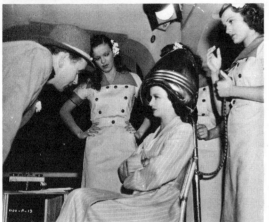

Top left:
Ann Sothern being fitted to a diamond necklace on the set for TRADE WINDS. Her role in T.W. led to her MAISIE film series, and Annie-Pie was off and running.

Top right:
Joan Bennett, left; unidentified hula beauty, center; and Freddie March, right, register boundless enthusiasm over my suggestion for a scene in TRADE WINDS.

Bottom left:
Director in man's most untenable position: within studio beauty parlor. Blazingly blonde Joan Bennett, for plot reasons in TRADE WINDS, was supposed to disguise herself by turning brunette. Her expression in this candid shot indicates a certain ladylike antagonism, but she remained brunette in private life for many, many years.

Middle:
The half-pint hogging the camera in the center is Pete, the penguin, an important character in 1937's STAND-IN. Leslie Howard and his daughter, Leslie Ruth, help Peter with his lines.

Bottom right:
Fortified with gluwein on the locations site for S. O. S. ICEBERG. Gibson Gowland—brought to silent stardom by Von Stroheim in GREED—is my hirsute companion. *(Vogel-Sandau.)*

Left column, top to bottom:
My sweet *Athene*. her surname was "Insolvency." (1935.)

Note, veterans of Vietnam: Kilroy was here—on the Saigon River in the spring of 1936.

Script problems on the streets of Colombo, Ceylon, in 1936. *(Helga Moray.)*

This shot illustrates why a set impresses visitors as being confused. It is. Included is only *part* of the equipment needed to photograph a traveling shot for STAND-IN. Leslie Howard, to the right, is wearing an impressive pair of galluses.
Top right:
My "Composing Room" aboard the *Athene.* What a life! I had autographed photos of every star I had directed, plus some from friends on the various picture lots where I had worked. Most of them were lost when my ranch house burned.
Bottom right:
Best portrait extant of my handsome pith helmet, about to shed rain in a Singapore jungle.

Top left:
The work is arduous and the hours are long, but there are compensations, like how Leslie Howard, Jack Carson, and I learned why girls in bathing suits never freeze to death in blizzards.

Top right:
This set still indicates why film love scenes are more traumatic than torrid. Usually there is enough equipment and personnel present to unsex Don Juan. Marla Shelton and Humphrey Bogart (in his first sympathetic role—STAND-IN) made the job look awfully pleasant.

Bottom left:
Another candid from STAND-IN, showing Bogart in the uncharacteristic role of director, operating a moviola machine. Leslie Howard, obviously en route to the opera, is critical of the entire operation.

Middle:
In addition to making a film, actors and directors are expected to publicize it, so Joan Blondell, Leslie Howard, and I are here giving forth with the mellow vowels on a CBS radio broadcast.

Bottom right:
See, a director has to know *everything*. At this point I'm conferring with Irene Dunne and designer Edward Stevenson as to what Irene is going to wear in JOY OF LIVING—1937.

19

WHILE I WAS MAKING THE ENGLISH VERSION OF *S. O. S. Iceberg,* MY cherished chilblain chum, Dr. Fanck, was turning out a German version. The only points of resemblance between his script and mine were Leni Riefenstahl, Ernst Udet, and count 'em—a thousand beautiful icebergs—count 'em.

Duplicate filming was possible for two reasons. Fanck had shot enough documentary footage to have made *Nanook of the North, Son of Nanook,* and *Nanook Strikes Again;* also, we were able to build, on a frozen Swiss lake, an igloo of ice cakes, and an iceberg in which there was a cave. These satisfactorily simulated the originals photographed in Greenland and—according to the script—used as a refuge by the principals.

For those interested in the technical side of the operation, the iceberg was manufactured by covering a bamboo framework with taut burlap, then soaking the fabric repeatedly until enough ice had been amassed to accommodate Arctic light housekeeping.

Because I was "guest" director, I would shoot my scenes first, taking three or four days to complete a sequence, then Bob Fellows and I would go to St. Moritz "to work on the script."

Dr. Fanck would take over and complete his filming of a segment, after which he and *his* assistant would schlussen to St. Moritz.

This enabled us to keep two Palace Hotel barstools warm all winter.

At the end of one of these happy periods, I went to the hotel desk to pay my bill with an American Express Cheque. The cashier, in somber tones, informed me that Mr. Badrutt (the owner) would appreciate it if I would be so kind as to step into his office.

Formality makes me nervous.

A fast mental resumé assured me that there were no new burns on the furniture, no wine stains on the rug, and that no one had seen the Baroness leaving my suite that morning.

Obviously he had the wrong guy.

Mr. Badrutt, a tall man with flowing white hair, told me sympathetically, "I fear I am the bearer of bad news, Mr. Garnett. Zurich informs me that your President Roosevelt has declared a bank holiday throughout the United States."

I was relieved. I said, "Well, bankers work hard; probably they need a vacation."

Mr. Badrutt's eyebrows lifted. "I'm afraid I haven't made the situation clear to you. This action will have worldwide repercussions, because there is now no exchange quotation for the dollar."

"But there are still *dollars,*" I protested, waving my American Express Cheques.

"Dollars which are, unfortunately, valueless at the moment."

Before I could pass out completely, Mr. Badrutt rested a fatherly hand on my shoulder and said, "It is not altogether tragic, Mr. Garnett. We know the dollar is basically sound. Meanwhile, if you—personally—will sign chits for your expenditures and those of your company, I shall be happy to carry you until the emergency is over."

"Thank you," I managed to say, summoning what heartiness is possible in coma. I was seven thousand miles from home, responsible for a film company, and broke.

Not until I was on the electric train halfway back to the Hospice did the full import of what had happened get through to me.

I, a foreigner in deep financial trouble, had been treated with consideration and courtesy. I shuddered to think of the treatment likely to have been accorded a European by almost any American hotel manager under similar circumstances.

20

I'VE ALWAYS HAD AN IMAGE OF MYSELF AS A BIG DOG MAN. YOU KNOW THE type: bluff, hearty, tweedy, smelling of moors and peat bogs, with leather patches on his elbows, and a briar clenched between his teeth.

When I met Nickynack, I knew he and I would get along, because he fitted my fantasy. Nickynack was the lead dog for the sled team of Huskies we had imported from Greenland for *Iceberg*. He weighed around two hundred pounds, mostly heart and muscle, and when he rested his forepaws on a man's shoulders in comradely greeting, he was about six feet tall.

He was a people dog; he loved human beings, and with them he was gentle, but he distrusted canines, and that went for the fellow members of his team. One of the dogs was a hell-raiser who started arguments in the ranks. After a particularly miserable day with the outlaw, Nickynack killed him. Nickynack worked with soundless efficiency, so that no one knew—except approving witnesses—what had happened until the next morning. We had to order a replacement which was expensive in both time and money.

I told Nickynack, "That was a horrible thing to do."

He stared straight into my eyes with an expression that said, "You run your part of the business, and I'll run mine. You don't understand these things."

I was the one who finally looked away; I was the one who apologized with a steak after Nickynack had ignored me, pointedly, for several days.

When we wrapped up our filming at the Bernina Hospice, the rest of the Husky team was sent back to Greenland, but I kept Nickynack.

He was going to inspire massive problems of housing and transportation, but we had reached a dog-to-man agreement that we would make a fine team. Also, I was nuts about the big guy.

In Berlin we were a smash—especially in restaurants when waiters spied him without previous warning. Furthermore, the aristocracy—always intrigued by an unlikely toy—were gracious to me, and beautiful women stopped me on the street to run their hands through Nickynack's magnificent pelt.

At first Nickynack throve; he was a ham and relished attention. However, as the days went by he grew listless, and his panting became an agony. He tried to adjust; he forced himself to eat, and he accompanied me even when his big frame was shaken by every breath. Berlin was simply too warm for him.

A Swiss friend of mine said, "I have a lodge at 6,800 feet. There, Nickynack could live a good life. If he's not taken to a colder climate, he'll surely die."

I was heartsick. I realized that, next to Joan Marshfield, I was going to miss him more than I had ever missed anything in my life. Anyhow, I explained the problem to Nickynack, we shook hands, and I never saw him again.

However, by Christmas-card pipeline, I learned that, in time, he became a great-great-grandaddy, and as crusty an old codger as ever cuffed successive litters of pups into line.

We had shot *Iceberg* M.O.S. (Mitt Out Sound) because our cast, excepting Rod La Roque, spoke heavily accented English or none at all. Our plan was to dub Leni Riefenstahl and Ernst Udet with the voices of English actors.

I was packing for London when a long distance call came through from Paris.

"Joan!" I thought. "Perfect timing, Baby."

A familiar voice came over the wire—not Joan's.

"Surprise! Surprise!!" said Patsy Ruth.

"How was Reno?" I subtled.

"Who? . . . Oh, *Reno!* I wouldn't know; I've never been there. I thought we ought to talk things over. I could be in Berlin tomorrow."

"Where are you staying in Paris?"

"At the *Rond Point.*"

"Stay there. I'm leaving for Paris tomorrow. I'll call you when I arrive."

"Oh, ALL RIGHT!" she snapped, and hung up.

I glowered at the telephone thinking that just because a dame happens to be a man's wife, she thinks she has a right to louse up his love life.

I called Paul Kohner and, being very cagey, asked how a friend of mine, caught in a jam, could get a quick divorce in Paris.

Paul said, "Tay, you don't want to divorce Pat in Paris. American divorce has become a big money racket there. Talk to Joe Pasternak. He knows the ropes in Budapest."

Over luncheon, Joe explained that Hungarian law required at least one of the principals in a divorce action to reside in Budapest for a minimum of three weeks. I said that would have to be Pat; I had a picture to finish.

Joe was leaving for Budapest that night, so he suggested that I have Pat get in touch with him on her arrival at the St. Gilleart Hotel; in that way proof of her residency could be established. At the end of three weeks, I would be obliged to spend a few days in Budapest to complete my emancipation.

Joe said it wouldn't cost a fortune—aside from severance pay—but . . . "What makes you think Pat will go to Budapest, Tay?"

"She'll go," I stated. The "or else" was clearly implied.

In Paris, en route from the *Rond Point* to a farewell dinner at Maxim's, Pat agreed to go to Budapest. There was neither a bruise nor an abrasion on her body at the close of our discussion.

I escaped with a crimson "Mark Cross" from an alligator purse imprinted on my left cheek.

21

After putting Patsy Ruth on the Simplon-Orient Express, and standing by to make certain she didn't decamp, I telephoned Joan Marshfield.

"Oh, Tay-ee!" she said, and it was spring in San Diego.

She had some errands to run, would be quite busy, but would meet me at a restaurant in the Bois de Boulogne for luncheon.

Like all lovers long separated, we were shy. We talked of the weather, the delicious food, taxi noise, French wines, and are there any good shows in Paris.

Finally I said, "Joan, this is ridiculous. I want to talk about YOU."

"And how is Mrs. G?" she asked, turning up her nose and grinning.

"She's fine; in Budapest getting a divorce."

"Oh. From whom?"

"From meem—that's from whom." It was the best I could do at the moment.

She was nice enough to smile; abruptly explanations began to pour forth. She had been unable to talk candidly on the telephone when I first called, en route to Berlin, because she had been sitting in her husband's sickroom; a nurse and a doctor had been present.

The count, she said with genuine sadness, had been seriously ill, but he was much improved. "Enough improved to make a business trip to Rome. That's where he is now."

She went on, "He's a fine man, Tay-ee, and I'm fond of him, but our marriage was a mistake from the beginning. I'm not French, and I can't become French. I just don't think in French."

She turned her wine glass on the tablecloth, making a design of circles. "Another problem has come between us: I've found that I'm a one-man girl. I should have returned to California when you cabled. I've cried a river over that mistake."

"Why don't we go back to California together?" I found that my voice caught in my throat; I felt seventeen years old.

"Proposal accepted," she said, her face glowing with the look of having swallowed sunshine.

"I have a picture to finish and some divorce odds and ends to pick up, then we can be on our way."

"Thanks for reminding me. I have a few bits and pieces of my own to adjust."

I reached for her hand. "Will it be painful?"

"Not too. Henri is sophisticated, and infinitely wise. As a matter of fact, you two would get on together."

"I don't want to 'get on' with a guy who deliberately stole my gal while my back was turned."

Joan looked at me askance. "No comment," she said.

We had three unlikely days together, getting reacquainted. We walked along the Champs Élysées, we took an excursion boat down the Seine, we had aperitifs at Fouquet's; we bridged half a dozen years.

The evening before I was to go to London, I said, "Just out of curiosity, have you ever seen the suites at the Crillon? They're lovely —when decorated with champagne, caviar, and roses."

"Tay-ee, maybe I'm playing little-girl games, but—if you don't mind too much, I'd like to keep it right this time."

"Oh, Joan! Come on, now."

"Please, Tay-ee. We have the rest of our lives to spend together. I want to do this by the book."

"I'm a dangerous man to let off the leash," I started to say, but her eyes filled with tears. I couldn't take that. *"Don't,* darling. You're right, of course. Absolutely right."

Drawing a long breath, Joan said, "You're a great guy, Tay-ee. Always were. Always will be. I love you."

"I thought you'd never get around to admitting it."

"But proposition declined for the time being."

We both began to laugh. I not only loved this dame, I *liked* her from the top of her screwy little gourd to the soles of her number threes.

We kissed goodbye at the boat train, and I went on to London, congratulating myself on having so gallantly defended Joan's honor.

22

I DIDN'T EXPECT MUCH OF LONDON. FOR OPENERS, A GUY WHOSE FOREBEARS came out of Dublin HAS to be suspicious of any place overrun with Englishmen.

I turned out to be a disappointment to myself. I LOVED London. And (forgive me, Dad), I LOVED the English.

Even so, I was desperately anxious to get back to Paris and Joan.

I was glad to be busy during the day, auditioning voices, and busy in the evening, attending the theatre.

After my ear become accustomed to it, I enjoyed the clipped British diction, but I realized that it would be incomprehensible to the majority of American moviegoers. For that reason, I decided to choose all voices sight unseen, in order to avoid being influenced by personal appearance. Intelligibility had to be the governing factor.

Actors and actresses were required to work to a P. A. microphone in a projection booth at Universal's London offices in Wardour Street. The loudspeakers were set up in the viewing room where I sat, cultivating an earache.

After having cast the Udet voice and those of the other male speaking parts, I set about trying to find a female voice with a libido lilt to dub Leni Riefenstahl.

For some obscure reason, I had chosen Lady Macbeth's "Out, damned spot" speech as the feminine test. Take a tip from me: if you're ever in that kind of trouble, send it to a cleaner.

Late on the third day, I sat up straight and told the operator, "Once more with that last voice, please."

The voice I had just heard combined smoky provocation with

impeccable diction. I steeled myself. With a voice like that, she was bound to look like Dracula's daughter.

Then I met her. So ended my career as a conclusion jumper.

She was about five feet five inches tall, and entirely free of visible architectural errors. She had a strawberries-in-snow complexion, enormous blue-gray eyes, and appropriate silver-blonde hair. I reminded myself that I was interested only in her vocal cords.

In the course of our conversation, I learned that she had recently completed a season with *Charlot's Revue,* starring Bea Lillie and Jack Buchanan.

Her theatrical name was Helga Moray, but she had been born Eileen Atherton, of Irish parents in South Africa.

We made arrangements for her to come to Berlin for the dubbing, giving her an "on or about" starting date.

A hop, skip, and jump later, I was en route to Berlin via Paris.

I telephoned Joan from the Crillon. She answered the first ring. "Oh, Tay-ee. Why don't you come to the house? We have so many things to talk about."

I thought, "What a gal! She's already broken the news to the old boy, and it's hats off and hair flying."

By the time I had paid off the taxi and scaled the chateau steps three at a time, I had planned our honeymoon—in Tahiti—bought and furnished a house in Beverly Hills, and named our first daughter.

The butler let me in and ushered me upstairs. Joan was waiting in the upper hallway.

I held out my arms.

She remained motionless.

I was completely baffled. The tragedy in Joan's eyes, the despair in her sagging shoulders, and the odor of illness that I had been trying to ignore—none of it made any sense. Or any sense that I intended to accept.

"I wish I could have warned you," Joan murmured, "but I took the call in Henri's room. He's desperately ill. The doctor says he could go in ten minutes, or he might live ten years. The point is: He must be kept quiet. No problems. No excitement, no emotional disturbance of any kind."

She attempted a smile. "I want you to meet him. He's really quite a person."

The man propped up on pillows in an enormous fourposter bed could have passed as Spencer Tracy's father. His hair was sandy, but beginning to whiten at the temples. He had the broad, square face of the Tracy clan, and the deep laugh lines about the mouth. His eyes were wide-set, clever, and perceptive.

He said, "Forgive me for not rising to greet you, Mr. Garnett. Garnett—an Irish name, yes? I have the distinction of being the son of an Irish mother, born in County Cork."

He waved me to a bedside chair, adding, "It comes to me, Mr. Garnett, that you are a man who would join me in a glass of wine, yes? My friend, the doctor, has given an ultimatum: no more wine. I have given an ultimatum to my friend, the doctor: go to hell."

He filled three glasses from a bedside carafe. "This, you will find to your taste, I think."

I found it to my taste, and complimented the count.

He went on, "You have come recently from Berlin, I am told by the countess. What do you make of the political situation?"

I repeated Ernst Udet's explanation of German politics in American terms, and the count laughed so heartily that he began to cough. I had heard that sort of cough before. I realized what Joan had meant by "no problems, no excitement, no emotional disturbance."

As soon as possible, I apologized for staying so long, adding, "But I've enjoyed talking to you," and meaning it. Under different circumstances, he and I could have been friends.

"We'll plan to see you on your next trip to Paris," the count said. He added to the butler who had brought in a tray of medication, "Attend to the windows, please. The countess will see Mr. Garnett to the door."

We walked wordlessly down the curving stairway. In the entry I drew myself to attention and saluted my gallant lady. "You're right. He's a helluva guy."

"Will you be in Paris again?"

I shook my head. "But if you ever need me, telephone or cable. I'll come a-runnin'."

I walked out into the marrow-chilling drizzle of a Paris twilight.

After slogging to Fouquet's for a double belt of cognac, I splashed on to the Crillon.

Two hours later I was kalockety-kalocketing eastward across the fields of France. To the unending rhythm of the rails I kept telling myself, "Come on, you stupid bastard. Light your torches and pull up your tights.

"Light your torches and pull up your tights."

23

By THE TIME I RETURNED TO BERLIN, VILMA and ROD LA ROQUE, PAUL and Lupe Kohner, as well as Bob Fellows, had deserted me via tramp steamer through the Canal. I was deeply offended by their defection when I needed them; I was obliged to go to Hungary solo.

In Budapest I registered at the Continental Hotel on the Pest side of the Danube, because Patsy Ruth was living—naturally—at the swank St. Gilleart on the Buda side.

Pasternak had warned me that Hungarian law required a judge, hearing a divorce petition, to attempt to reconcile husband and wife. That was the bad part; the good part was that the judge spoke no English and I spoke no Hungarian.

It reminded me of the story Bob Mitchum tells about my friend, John Farrow. Johnny had missed very little of life, good or bad, but he suffered no guilt feelings whatsoever. Mitchum said to him one day, "Man, you bug me. I've known some rough cats in my time, but you're—without exception—the toughest. How can you profess to being a good Catholic? D'ya ever DARE go to Confession?"

Johnny said piously, "Sure. To one of the oldest churches in California. You know that old Spanish mission on the Plaza in downtown L.A.? I go down there about every week or so and tell everything."

"Everything?"

"Everything. Sometimes I'm in the Confessional as long as an hour."

Mitchum's chin dropped. "My God! What does the priest say?"

Johnny grinned. "Nothing. He just gives me absolution. The poor bastard doesn't understand, or speak, a word of English."

Meanwhile, back in Hungary, our attorney explained that we would be asked many questions which must be answered "nem" (no) or "eganne" (yes). He said we needn't worry; he could cue us with slight head movements. I felt like a Hungarian Charlie McCarthy.

While the judge delivered his lecture, I studied Patsy Ruth. She was as beautiful as ever; I had been enamoured of her since teenage days; she had come joyously into my arms as a bride. I wondered how it could happen that two people who had felt they were all the world to one another, suddenly found they had nothing in common.

Later in my life I suppose there was an ex-wife here and there who could have explained the mystery to me.

My philosophizing was interrupted by a stirring in the courtroom. Our attorney arose. We dummies imitated him. The judge made a brief, stern pronouncement and thumped his gavel. No interpretation was necessary. I bowed to Patsy Ruth; she grinned lop-sidedly and shrugged. She left by one exit; I chose another.

I am, in many ways, a conventional man. I feel that milestones should be marked, so I sent Buckingham a cable: "Congratulations in order. Open can of quail bait."

Back in Berlin, the trees were white with blossom along Unter Den Linden. (During World War II it made me sick to think of the street's destruction, as it now makes me sick to think of the Wall.)

In any case, spring and Helga Moray arrived simultaneously, Helga to dub Riefenstahl, and spring to call my thoughts to Paris.

Inevitably, Helga and I spent a great deal of time together. At first I was half-listening for a telephone call from Joan, but more and more I found Helga an interesting companion. There was a sweetness and quiet rationality about her that is unusual in an actress; particularly a beautiful actress.

As a child she had worked in the theatre in her native South Africa; later Helga, her widowed mother, and an elder sister shared an apartment while Helga tried for a theatrical career, and worked as a fabric buyer to pay the rent.

In Paris, Helga had eventually been signed by Alex Korda, who decided to change her name. "Eileen Atherton," the designation on her birth certificate, was not—according to Sir Alex—"boxoffice." He dubbed her "Helga Moray" and changed her nationality from Irish to Swedish—a stunt possible only for a Hungarian, knighted by a British queen.

In addition to being lovely, Helga was the most compassionate woman I've ever known. She couldn't refuse a beggar on the street.

I protested one day, "Most of those guys are phonies, Helga."

"I know," she admitted. "But I'd rather donate to fifteen phonies than pass up one hard-luck guy."

If I hadn't been torching for Joan Marshfield, I might have realized that I was falling in love with Helga. However, I offhandedly told her goodbye, adding that I'd probably see her in Hollywood some day. That prophecy tossed off, I boarded the westbound *Berengaria*.

As proof of my emotional vacuum at that time, I want the record to show that gorgeous Sally Blaine (sister of equally gorgeous Loretta Young) was a fellow passenger. I gave her absolutely no trouble all across the Atlantic. I hate myself whenever I think of it.

Because my business manager had leased my Laurel Canyon love, Hangover House, to strangers—I would have camped on the doorstep of friends—I rented an apartment. I told myself it was just as well, because every room would have been eloquent of Joan Marshfield.

My agent had lined up a job for me at Metro the minute I could go to work: directing *China Seas* to be produced by Irving Thalberg. It had been written to star Clark Gable, Jean Harlow, Rosalind Russell, Wallace Beery, Lewis Stone, Robert Benchley, and Dudley Digges. You can't get much more voltage than that.

However, at that moment Gable was working in *Mutiny on the Bounty*; Harlow was starring in *Red-Headed Woman*; Roz was in a play on Broadway; Beery was appearing in one of his endless chain of characterizations; Benchley was writing in New York; Digges was in Dublin with the Abbey Players, and Lewis Stone was Judging an *Andy Hardy*.

Speaking of *Andy Hardy* reminds me of another of Bob Mitchum's wry observations. Once upon an Irish summer I was directing a film starring Bob, Richard Harris, and a blonde beauty, at Ardmore Studios in the outskirts of Dublin.

During the early sequences, our schedule called for only the male cast. Those scenes completed, I sent for our dazzling leading lady. "Why don't YOU meet her at the airport?" I asked Mitchum. "Set up your subsequent scenes together, huh?"

"My wife's waiting for me at the hotel, remember?" he drawled.

A paunchy, middle-aged, thoroughly-married Irish friend of mine, toujours the gent, volunteered to be the welcoming committee. He left the set around noon and was missing for seventy-two hours. So was our exquisite actress.

It is that sort of thing that fractures a film budget and drives a director nuts.

When my greeter finally strolled in, looking as if he had swallowed a thousand-watt neon tube, I yelled, "Where in hell have you been?"

Mitchum lounged over to kibitz.

In a hushed tone, the emissary explained, "This is the most remarkable thing that's ever happened to me. It's Fate. I was standing in the airport, just one guy in hundreds, when this beautiful girl came out of the plane and paused at the top of the debarking stairway. Her eyes met mine. I felt as if I'd been hit by lightning. She came down the steps and straight to me as if she'd known me all her life. D'ya know what she said? Can you believe it? 'You're Romeo.'

"I said, 'Yes, Juliet,' and took her hand.

" 'This is it—the divine spark—isn't it?' she went on.

"I said, 'Yes, Juliet.' It was the tenderest, most solemn moment of my life. I drove her to the hotel. She left her luggage, and we started to walk. We've been walking and talking ever since."

He sighed deeply; his paunch and his chins quivered.

I'm a spoilsport. I asked, "What does your wife think about this?"

Totally involved in an inner ecstasy, Romeo failed to answer—failed even to hear my question—as he turned away dreamily and trudged toward the sound stage exit.

Mitchum, his heavy-lidded eyes at halfmast, drawled, "Love Finds Andy Hardy."

(Footnote: It must have been Fate, because—after essential divorces—Romeo and Juliet have now been married for over ten years.)

But, to get back to *China Seas;* no one was worried about our widely dispersed cast, because preparation on an Irving Thalberg picture inevitably went forever plus ten weeks.

Thalberg was the ultraperfectionist; he would throw out fifty good, strong ideas, because—of course—we could get ANOTHER fifty *stronger* ideas. Besides, if he entertained the very best possible plot twist idea for very long, it died of anemia. If Shakespeare had indulged in that method of preparation, *Romeo and Juliet* would have been finished just in time for Laurel and Hardy.

After six or seven months of this preparation, I was wild for action. I had to do *something* to escape my exquisite boredom.

Helga came to Hollywood in response to something I had written about marriage. The ceremony was performed at sea by the skipper of my boat *Girl Friend, Too.*

Later we had the marriage firmed up by a Las Vegas Justice of the Peace, who concluded the ritual by reminding us that he was also legally qualified to represent either of us in the event of divorce!

China Seas continued to wallow in the doldrums, so I was lent to Paramount. The script on which I was to work with Louis (Bud) Leighton and Vincent Lawrence was *Honor Bright,* tailored to star Carole Lombard, Gary Cooper, and a kid named Shirley Temple.

Leighton was, if possible, even more meticulous and less aware of passing time than Thalberg. I had gone from molasses in January to the Mendenhall Glacier.

By the time Bud declared us ready to shoot, my loanout had expired. Thalberg refused to extend it, so Henry Hathaway took over as director and did a whale of a job.

Back I went to *China Seas* and another seven months of preparation during which I wrote a novel in my spare time: *Man Laughs Back.* The title was derived from an ancient Inca proverb that I made up: "The Jungle Laughs, and Man Laughs Back."

The genesis of the story was a dinner party conversation in the midst of which one of the guests told a yarn about a party of young engineers attempting to survey a rugged section of South American jungle. Of the original party, only one lived to tell what happened.

Man Laughs Back was brought out in hard covers by Macauley, a publishing house that went broke shortly thereafter; I have never claimed solo credit for that catastrophe.

Out of the several thousand copies published, one fell into the hands of Merritt Hulbard, an ex-editor of the *Saturday Evening Post,* who had been recruited as Sam Goldwyn's story editor.

Hulbard, liking *Man Laughs Back,* got in touch with my agent and firmed a deal. On the morning we were to sign the contracts, we were told by a Goldwyn receptionist, "Mr. Hulbard is no longer with us."

On closer inquiry we learned that Hulbard and Mr. Goldwyn had met headon and debris was still falling, a routine Goldwyn affair in those days.

When Hulbard went out the door, his projects went out the window, according to standard Hollywood practice. By that time, I had blown an Eddie Small offer, much to my regret, and there were no other takers for the book.

Come to think of it, I may still make it into a film. *Man Laughs Back* had everything, even in today's market: strong characters, a fascinating background, drama, suspense, violence, nudies—de woiks.

It also survived a sea voyage. When I was in Paris a few years ago, I was browsing among the *Rive gauche* bookstalls when a familiar title caught my eye. I picked up *Man Laughs Back* and turned to the flyleaf. The inscription read, "To my friend and fellow writer, Phil Sheuer—Best Always—Tay Garnett."

Until a few years ago, when Phil retired, he was one of the most respected of Hollywood columnists. (But, Phil, in Paris the book would have lost much in translation!)

In addition to writing a book during the gestation period of *China Seas,* I slipped out one Sunday morning and bought the 104-foot clipper *Talayha* from Lazzard Lipman. I had her converted into a yawl, and rechristened *Athene.* More about that later.

Another dividend of this period was meeting a talented writer named Harry Ruskin. He had come to MGM from Ziegfeld Follies where many years of experience had honed his ability to judge story line, comedy tag line, and feminine outline, not necessarily in that order.

We formed the agreeable practice of having luncheon together at the Director's Table in the studio commissary, along with Bob Taylor, Clark Gable, and Spencer Tracy. A sixth member of the group was a guy named Dick Noonan, a struggling, underpaid laughsmith who lived his best gags.

In one of those inexplicable happenstances that could have taken place only in the feudal days of Hollywood, Dick was placed under six-month contract for "a special assignment" with Irving Thalberg without ever having met Mr. Thalberg.

Dick was assigned a lush office and told to make himself available six days per week from 10 A.M. until 6 P.M. He requisitioned the necessary writing supplies from the stationery stockroom, sharpened his pencils, fetched his Thesaurus from home—and waited for assignment. And waited. And waited.

A month passed. Three months. Upon arriving each morning Dick had to pass Harry Ruskin's office. One day when Harry, Spence and I were batting the breeze, Dick went by very slowly, so Harry called out, "Come in—you aren't interrupting a thing. How are things going for you?"

Dick Noonan poured out his troubles. "I'm a nervous wreck. Signing me must have been a fluke—like sending Custer to the Little Big Horn. What am I DOING here? Where's that ASSIGNMENT? Every time someone passes my office, my hands shake until I can't even hold a pencil."

"Take it easy," Spence advised. "Any day they'll want a script yesterday."

"But what do I do in the meantime to duck St. Vitus?"

I understood his quandary; idleness for a prolific writer is unendurable. "Isn't there anything you've always wanted to master—like taking up chess, or learning French?"

"Or masturbating?" added Spence.

Noonan brightened. "I've always wanted to play mandolin. Could I practice quietly if I didn't disturb anybody?"

We approved the suggestion, so Noonan plunked diligently for several weeks.

One late afternoon Spence, Harry and I called on Noonan and asked for a concert—nothing Carnegie Hall, just any familiar tune.

In the midst of *Cielito Lindo* the door burst open, a harried face was thrust into the room, then a soft voice said, "Sorry, boys—wrong office . . ." and the face was withdrawn.

"Who was . . ." Noonan started to ask.

[167]

I said, "Irving Thalberg," adding, "excuse us a minute." To Harry I announced, "Now's our chance to get that answer from Mr. T." As we raced down the corridor, we heard the unmistakable wail of a mandolin crashing to the floor.

Thalberg gave us a fast "Maybe," so we returned to Dick's office to find Spence's face an apoplectic purple from suppressed hilarity, and Noonan quaking in shock and humiliation.

"My God, Dick," I blurted. "What's wrong?"

Noonan gasped, "I was so scared when you said 'Thalberg'—I did it in my pants."

Ruskin gestured total disbelief, saying, "You've got to be kidding."

Furious, Noonan yelled, "Okay, I'LL SHOW YOU!"

He lowered his pants, and at that moment Thalberg once again burst into the office.

Looking only slightly bewildered, he said, "Oh, excuse me," and closed the door softly.

At last, after nineteen months, we were ready to shoot *China Seas*.

Our first scenes were to be shot in the midst of a "typhoon." Preparation consisted of building a set representing a ship's promenade deck that was mounted on hydraulic rockers on the MGM back lot. Alongside the set was a row of towering dump tanks, each holding tons of water that, when turned loose, roared down chutes and tidal-waved onto the deck.

The action called for Wallace Beery, in oilskins and rubber boots, to carry Jean Harlow down the surging promenade, calf-deep in water. Reaching the door of the main salon, he was to kick open the door and step over the high bulkhead into what purported to be safety from the elements. It was a hazardous stunt because of the rocking of the mockup, plus the carefully timed dumping of the tanks.

In view of the danger, we used doubles; a stuntman named Chick Collins doubled Beery, and carried a stunt girl (Loretta Rush) who wore a blonde wig, to duplicate Harlow.

Collins managed to make his way down the promenade and kick open the salon door, but before he could exit, somebody tripped the dump tanks prematurely. Collins, one foot in the air and two arms full of girl, was hit in the fantail with fifty tons of water. Taking off

[168]

like a goosed gull, Collins attained a maximum altitude in split seconds.

There were two possibilities: He and Loretta might land on the mockup platform in a maze of high tension cables, or, missing the platform, they could end their careers on the concrete floor, twenty feet below.

They lucked out, landing on water-soaked cables without being electrocuted. However, at the height of their uncertain trajectory—stunned, waterlogged and without landing clearance—Chick made ad lib history by yelling to Loretta, still clutched in his arms, "Hang on, Honey. We're just passengers."

And so, on to the next cardiac arrester.

On the same hydraulic rockers we built the foredeck of our ship. One sequence concerned a five-ton steamroller that broke its moorings during the typhoon, and, crashing against bulkheads, threatened to scuttle the ship. Gable, as captain, was supposed to rally a volunteer suicide squad to bulldog the monster. (Some readers may find, in this episode, an echo of Conrad's *Nigger of the "Narcissus."* However, in the frenzied words of a television writer who was hailed into court on a plagiarism charge, "We have to get our ideas SOMEWHERE!!" That was the excuse of our *China Seas* writing staff.)

I vigorously protested this stunt to the front office, to wit: "If you think I'm going to work stunt men on a slick deck with a FIVE-TON steam roller running wild, you're nuts."

Cedric Gibbons, the art director, soothed me with assurances that he planned to build a lightweight replica that would be harmless.

The "harmless lightweight replica" proved to weigh a mere TWO tons.

I was stuck with it. I said to my stunt man, "Well, Chick, here we go again."

Gable, standing beside me, shook his head. "No dice. I'm doing this one myself." Grinning, he added to Chick, "Sit this one out. You're still on salary, and we'll need you again tomorrow—especially if I louse this one up."

Chick said, "You won't."

Of course I squawked; I needed the star for the rest of the picture,

[169]

but when Gable decided to risk his neck, his neck got risked. As it worked out, we all came up winners: The stunt man received his check, Gable retained his health, and I receipted for a spectacular stunt executed by The King himself.

At about this time, firearms from the studio's prop department were issued to actors requiring them in subsequent scenes.

Gable was handed a .45 Colt automatic which he studied carefully, then whistled and said, "My God, look at this! It's got so many notches in the grip that it would make hamburger of a guy's hand if he tried to fire it."

I did a jack-in-the-box out of my canvas chair and said, "Lemme see THAT!"

Sure enough, it was mine.

Gable, characteristically lifting an eyebrow, asked, "What in hell IS it?"

"My score card from my Navy days. I wore out several nail files making those notches," I explained. "Among other things."

"You've got to be kidding," Gable said.

Shaking my head, I gave him a rundown on losing the .45 to an absconding Madame Landlady in the long ago.

Jean Harlow, standing by, began to giggle as she kidded Gable, "If this is the way you guys keep score, Clarkie, I'd love to see the stock of *your* hunting rifle."

The gallant Gable came back with, "I'm not issuing any Annie Oakleys, dear, but if you'd like to add a notch, it can be arranged."

When a picture begins to give off the sweet smell of success, it attracts every bee and son of a bee in the studio.

In this case, Mr. Bumble Bee himself.

A director is presumed by motion picture protocol to be autonomous on his own set. A producer, having suggestions to make in regard to any phase of an actor's performance, or a director's directing, is obligated by courtesy to make those suggestions to the director in private.

Bob Thomas, in his definitive biography of Thalberg (published by Doubleday under the title *Thalberg*), has told of my battle with the gentleman very well. I might as well quote Thomas's accurate report, beginning on Page 257:

During the filming of *China Seas*, Thalberg displayed an anxiety he had never shown before. His visits to sets had always been perfunctory, and he had never interfered with shooting unless the director or actors sought his consultation. But he visited the set of *China Seas* every day, and he often engaged in lengthy conversations with members of the cast.

One day Garnett noticed a businesslike conference between Thalberg and one of the actors. When the director ran through a rehearsal of the scene, the actor protested, "That's not the way Irving wants it done."

"Irving is not the director," Garnett snapped, and he continued to direct in his own manner.

Before filming started, Garnett had reached an agreement with Thalberg that he (Garnett), as director, would have the privilege of assembling the first cut of *China Seas*. But when he ran some of the early sequences one evening, Garnett noticed something awry. "That's not the way I shot it," he said.

"Mr. Thalberg ordered it that way," explained the cutter.

On the following day, Garnett noticed another serious discussion between Thalberg and an actor. After Thalberg left the stage, the director asked the performer if he had been coached in how to play the scene. "Yes," the actor admitted.

The next day was Sunday, and Garnett telephoned Thalberg at his Santa Monica home. "I've got to see you," said the director.

"But, Tay—I've got a very busy schedule," Thalberg protested.

"There's nothing more important than this," said Garnett.

Thalberg paused. "All right, come on down."

When Garnett arrived at the beach house, he made a bold beginning: "I've heard stories that you were a son of a bitch where directors were concerned."

Thalberg was astonished. "Jesus. Tay—what did I do?" he asked.

Garnett spilled out his complaints about Thalberg's coaching of the actors. He concluded with, "You hired me as director and gave me the best stars in the business and spent a million dollars for production, and then you wouldn't let me direct the picture. I didn't come to MGM to be put in there as a stooge."

Thalberg listened to the tirade and then said quietly, "Is that all?"

"No, that isn't all," Garnett continued hotly. "You countermanded my instructions about the cutting. That was in violation of our agreement."

"Yes, that's right," Thalberg admitted. "What do you want to do?"

"I'll help you find another director."

"No, wait a minute, Tay," Thalberg said. "You're absolutely right. I *have* behaved like a son of a bitch. But I'll make a deal with you. Henceforth I will come on the set only for social purposes—I think I should visit the company now and then for morale. But I promise I won't interfere in the playing of scenes. As to the cutting, I'll not only let you assemble scenes, but you can prepare the rough cut as well. And I'll make no changes in the film without consulting you."

Garnett's anger was assuaged, and the two men parted with an agreement on future conduct of the filming. Thalberg remained true to his word.

Contrary to all Hollywood predictions, the last scene for *China Seas* was finally in the can.

As customary, I gave the film editor a fistful of assembly notes. Several days would be required for him to make the cuts as indicated, so I was on my own for the weekend. Naturally, I went to work on a story that had been nesting in the back of my mind for months.

I had just rolled the first piece of paper into the Corona and typed the title, *Trade Winds,* when the telephone rang.

Alan Hale boomed, "How about a trip to Tijuana? We're here deliberating over a snort."

"Who's 'we'?" I inquired cagily.

"There's Frank the Morgan, Louis of Calhern, Mr. Dublin O'Brien, *et moi.*"

"Nothing good can come of that," I predicted with accuracy.

"Au contraire. We're red hot and pointed toward the nearest crap table." (Legalized gambling was not available in California in those days, and Nevada was a sleeper jump by train.)

"So goodbye, all ready," I said. "I have work to do. Stay sober and you may stay solvent."

"There's just one thing," demurred Mr. Hale. "We need a car which the four of us haven't got among us."

I sighed. "So I'm elected?"

"By an overwhelming majority."

"Look, Alan. I've got work to do."

"Bring it along. We'll stake you to a beautiful room, with or without."

I uttered one final, feeble protest: "I have to be in the cutting room at nine Monday morning."

"No bind. We all have to be back in town Sunday night."

I unloaded my pals at the Tijuana casino, leaving them with the stern warning, "I mean this: At noon tomorrow I'm leaving for Los

Angeles. If you plan to ride with me, you'd better be here at 11:30 A.M.
—SOBER.

O'Brien studied me closely, then demanded of his colleagues, "Whatever became of Tay Garnett?"

Not unexpectedly, Sunday noon arrived on schedule, but not the Hale–Calhern–Morgan–O'Brien combo. It took two hours to round them up and stow them, all apparently conscious, but obviously insensitive to pain.

I stopped the car short of the border crossing, got out and leaned over the left rear door to deliver a sermon: "Look, you guys. We're going to be questioned at the border by an immigration officer and I don't want any comedy routines or we'll be stuck here all night. I'm going to rehearse each of you, and you'd better be up in your parts. When you're asked if you're an American citizen, Morgan, just nod."

Morgan, in the right, front seat, nodded.

"Hale, are you an American citizen?"

Hale, in the right rear, focused his eyes with a noble effort and nodded.

"O'Brien, are you an American citizen?"

"That I am."

"Calhern?"

"Indeed I am," said Calhern in his best Bond Street manner.

"Just nod, you guys," I ordered. "No ad libs."

At the border the guard was letter perfect in *his* part. He asked to see my driver's license, then turned to Morgan in the front seat and asked, "Are you an American citizen?"

Morgan scored with a silent and dignified nod.

The officer glanced into the back seat and stabbed the air with an index finger aimed at Hale.

Hale nodded with a charming smile.

Passing over O'Brien as if he were invisible, the officer jerked a thumb toward Calhern.

"I am, indeed," purred that worthy.

O'Brien had been cheated, his part cut cold. You don't upstage Knute Rockne. Leaning out of the car he yelled, "I'M AN ALIEN."

It was two A.M. the following morning before my exasperated business manager arrived from Beverly Hills with identification papers that freed us.

China Seas was a tremendous hit. Its success, added to the earlier triumph of *One Way Passage,* convinced me that I couldn't miss with a sea picture.

My hunch was reinforced by my possession of the stalwart sailing ship, *Athene,* and a story entitled *Trade Winds.* It was practically a mandate from Fate for me to make a world cruise. Not that I'm superstitious.

Besides, how often do you get a chance to take your own boat around the world, tax deductible?

My imagination was dragged back from the far horizon by a summons from Thalberg. He wanted me to direct a thing entitled *Riff-Raff,* to star Spencer Tracy, Franchot Tone, and Jean Harlow. The implicit purpose behind the film, stated in today's terms, was to change the Harlow image.

I knew Jean Harlow very well. In person she was just a happy-go-lucky actress whose morals would have stood up against those of any devastatingly pretty girl in any large American city.

(One thing that has always bugged me is that all the vicious stories written about Jean, her personality and behavior, appeared AFTER Harlow and everyone else involved in the lurid anecdotes was *dead.* There was no one left to bring suit.)

Much as I admired Jean Harlow, it must be admitted that, theatrically, she was identified—in the public mind—with lovable tramp characters. Later, Marilyn Monroe was cast in the same hooker-with-a-heart-of-gold mold.

I told Irving, in refusing to direct *Riff-Raff,* "The part written for Harlow is basically wrong. Here you've got the most famous and alluring courtesan in the world, yet this script tries to transform her into a madonna. The public isn't going to buy it."

Thalberg replied coldly, "If you want to play on my team, you've got to get in and DIG."

To which I (*très* young and cocky) responded, "I'll dig my head off if there's gold in them thar hills, but I'm not about to dig holes in my backyard for exercise."

It wasn't funny, but it made my point.

Irving, now at thirty degrees below zero, said, "Well, Tay, I guess that's the end of the line."

I was at liberty. Again.

Except that I had already agreed to a three-picture deal at 20th-Century Fox. Only the contracts waited to be signed.

While the *Athene* was being rerigged and provisioned for a globe-girdling cruise, I made a film entitled *Professional Soldier,* adapted from a Damon Runyon story, and starring Victor McLaglen and Freddie Bartholomew.

This was a Graustarkian adventure about an American gangster (McLaglen) who was hired to snatch a young prince whose life was endangered by the regent. Some variation of the story has been told annually in poetry, prose, or film at least once a year since the year 1150. "Trite" might be the correct technical term.

McLaglen's natural accent was unmistakably middle-British. He complained to me, " 'Ow am *I* to sound like a blinkin' Hamerican 'oodlum?"

"Play Jimmy Durante," I told him.

We went to bat against Graustark with McLaglen's Durante decibels and Bartholomew's veddy, veddy Oxford accent.

The best we got out of the match was something to use as the bottom half of a bill featuring *Laddie, Brother of Lassie.*

24

THIS IS AS GOOD A SPOT AS ANY IN WHICH TO COMMENT ON ONE OF THE oddities of life in Hollywood. One can be as close to a pal as the white and yolk of an egg. (I don't want to be accused of bigotry in this instance, but honestly, I've never heard of the *black* and yolk of an egg.)

As I say, pals can be very close; then, separated by the demands of our cuckoo business, may not see or hear from one another directly for years at a time. When they meet, however, the conversation usually starts exactly where it left off.

Buckingham and I were no exception. After many months of no contact, we met unexpectedly one afternoon at Lucy's. (Not the workshop of a collection of girl entertainers, but a bar-restaurant and film hangout that has fallen on evil days. It now houses the offices and storage area of a nursery.)

Our simultaneous opening remark was "Vodka martini on the rocks."

"Just a minute, Buck," I remonstrated. "The word's around that a medic ordered you to stop drinking."

"True. But I got rid of the bum."

He went into detail. His original doctor had diagnosed his painful ailment as kidney stones and said there were three possible cures: sobriety, surgery, or suicide.

Naturally, Buck went to several succeeding doctors. At length he located a genial osteopath who prescribed a strict diet, but who agreed that two martinis before dinner could only put a high polish on Buck's kidney stones.

Buck concluded, "What the hell. If I never have another gal or another drink or another laugh, I'm still twenty-five years ahead of the game right now."

We drank to that, then went our separate ways.

One Sunday, returning under power to Lighthouse Mooring, I spotted Buckingham standing on the deck of a small yawl as it was heading out the channel. He was too far away to hail, but it suddenly struck me as ridiculous to plan a trip around the world without the Bucking Horse, who was as salt water daffy as I was.

That evening I tried to reach him by telephone. No answer.

I called every night for a week without success, so decided to check with some of our chums.

I caught up with Buck in the hospital. Mentally he was in good condition, because somebody had slipped him a martini in a bud vase. Physically, he looked like a negative of himself; his eyes were sunken in shadows and his cheek bones shone white in the stark illumination of the room.

I felt as if I'd been kicked in the stomach, but I chattered on, "As soon as you can blow this firetrap, I want you to join me in a trip around the world on the *Athene.* We have a helluva script, but we'll have a lot of improvising to do, so I'll really need you."

He let me talk until I ran out of spurious plans. At the door I turned back to look at him. I thought, "What does a guy say in a spot like this?"

Buck said it for me: "Any message for your dad?"

It is generally believed that the liquid flowing through human veins is blood; show people know better. They realize that the life-support fluid is printer's ink.

As soon as the *Athene* was properly provisioned, we granted a press conference on board with food and drink. I announced a sailing date, answered reporters' questions in depth, and generally gave the impression that Magellan had been Mr. Amateur Night.

A few days later an ungrateful reporter expressed some doubt about the validity of my plans. The way he put it was, "The *Athene* is as likely to circumnavigate the globe as it is to sail to Denver."

I was hurt. For once in my show biz life I'd played it absolutely legit. I promised myself to send that reporter a topless broad from Bali. Collect.

A day before the widely publicized sailing date, Darryl Zanuck called me back to 20th for added scenes on *Professional Soldier*. I realized the job would take the better part of a week, but I dared not postpone the sailing.

Never underestimating the power of the press, and being unwilling to provide them with further jokes, I took Helga and boarded the *Athene*. I was one vast grin, and even Helga managed a few tears, as we waved ceremoniously to the small Bon Voyage group on the dock (including Mr. Snide Reporter himself) and put to sea.

Just outside the harbor, screened by the breakwater, we transferred to a prechartered speedboat that took us to Balboa where Bob Fellows met us and drove us to Lighthouse Mooring. Meanwhile, away went the *Athene*, breasting the Pacific on our dream voyage.

As we—exhausted from this ploy—climbed into our car, foolishly left in the parking lot, we were greeted by a cheery voice from the adjacent car.

Sang out Mr. Snide, "I thought you'd NEVER get here."

Once 20th's added scenes had been shot, my longtime pal (and fellow hero of the *Silverado* escapade) Bob Stephens drove Helga and me to the Glendale station to catch Southern Pacific's "Owl" for San Francisco. We had been able to book passage on the S. S. *President Wilson*, bound for Honolulu, where we would rendezvous with the *Athene*.

We were preparing for bed in our compartment when I became aware of Helga's flashing eyes. "Where," she demanded, "is our luggage?"

I answered quietly, "In the trunk of Bob Stephens' car."

Dropping the comedy, Helga asked, "Would it be in order to wire him, mentioning theft? Or maybe, murder?" Her tone was convincing. (Trunk murders were very big in those days.)

Fortunately the luggage arrived twenty-four hours later, just in time for us to board the *President Wilson*.

That's how it happened that, at midnight on December 7, 1935 (happily lacking precognition that six years later, on that date, the Japanese would bomb Pearl Harbor), Helga and I stood at the *President Wilson*'s rail and watched San Francisco and the Golden Gate bridge dissolve in mist.

It's been rumored that the human species, originating in the ocean, waded through the breakers one day and set up housekeeping ashore. I can't vouch for it: I was with Mack Sennett at the time.

In any case, the salty heritage of our species must explain man's unceasing urge to return to the sea, preferably first class, i.e., with indoor plumbing.

Although the S. S. *President Wilson* was comfortable, the people interesting, the room service obsequious (our Chinese room boy, Kong, spoke three words of English: "Yis," "Yis," and "Yis"), I was fit to be tied every time I thought of the *Athene,* under full canvas, pushing her stubborn little nose against those big blue ones all across the Pacific.

I said as much to Jeanette Loff our first night at sea. She and her new husband, Bert Friedlob, were assigned with us to the captain's table. Jeanette was a superstar at Universal, having just finished *King of Jazz* with Paul Whiteman and his band. She was a lovely girl, and we had been friends during the Pathé days, when she had costarred in several pictures with Rod La Roque. Jeanette had been signed by De Mille with three other girls. Their names indicate the clarity of De Mille's foresight: Ginger Rogers, Carole Lombard, and Lina Basquette.

As for Bert Friedlob, his future held a modicum of film-making success, the tragic death of Jeanette Loff, and marriage to Eleanor Parker; however, in 1935, he had lammed out of Hollywood 1½ jumps ahead of the collectors for a gambling syndicate. Bert admitted blithely that he was a sucker for trying to fill an inside straight.

In other respects he was a dedicated—er—romanticist. Any wild yarn that he happened to try on for size promptly became unimpeachable scripture.

Nevertheless, he and Jeanette were "picture people." The picture business is not only a professional way of life, but sire of a heterogeneous race with a language all its own. One of the identifying characteristics of "picture people" is that they are completely at ease only with other "picture people"

For that absurd reason, I was insisting — before we were a fifth of Scotch out of San Francisco — that Jeanette and Bert leave the Dollar Line in Honolulu and join us on the *Athene* for the rest of the trip around the world.

Helga, not given to profanity, remained deafeningly silent throughout my invitation to the Friedlobs.

Later, in the privacy of our cabin, she asked' "Do you really like them all that much?" She brushed her hair thoughtfully for several moments. "I mean, to live with, day in, day out for months? Is the *Athene* really that roomy?"

"Now, just a minute," I bristled. "There are VERY few sailing vessels as commodious and seaworthy afloat today. You'll see: That ship will take all of us around the world with space to spare."

We made radio contact with the *Athene* the following morning. The news was bad: A few nights earlier, her hull had been raked full-length and her propeller shaft broken by a floating object, probably a heavy timber fallen from a lumber vessel. Her lookout, posted to prevent such accidents, had taken blanket and pillows to the foredeck in order to stand his watch in snoring position.

The captain assumed he would be able to get a new propeller and shaft in Honolulu; meanwhile, the *Athene* was making good time under sail and would reach port two days ahead of us.

Anyone who has never wanted to visit Honolulu might as well skip the next few pages; all others drop your ukulele, grab a mai-tai, and read on.

We docked beside the Aloha Tower at 7:30 A.M. on Friday, December 13th amid a fine warm drizzle. Three additional liners were sliding into berths at the same time: *Malolo* from the Orient; *Empress of Canada* from Vancouver, and the *President Coolidge* from Manila.

A white-uniformed band sat dockside playing *Song of the Islands* while a magnificent Hawaiian woman sang and danced a stately hula. I stood at the rail, feeling my face pleat into a permanent grin.

Leis (garlands of pikaki, carnations, yellow ginger, tube roses, frangipani, and flowers I couldn't have identified even if I'd been a milliner) were brought aboard for all passengers. Paul Schwegler and the Royal Hawaiian Hotel did the honors for us.

En route to the hotel I came down with camera fever. I panned my head from one montage to another: fruit vendors selling huge pineapples, stalks of bananas, papayas, and alligator pears; palms and flowering vines everywhere; wahinis squatting on curbs, making leis.

We swung into the circular drive of the Royal, almost lost in the midst of a coconut and lehua forest, and half-drowned in the fragrance of flowers. Our second-floor suite, shared with Jeanette and Bert, consisted of a sitting room, two bedrooms, three baths, and two "lanais" overlooking the open-air dance floor and most of Waikiki.

We had our first Hawaiian dinner at Lau Yee Chai's, billed then as "the largest Chinese restaurant in the world." My fortune cookie read, "Tomorrow not your day."

Who, except the inscrutable Chinese, would teach clairvoyants to be bakers?

The next morning I taxied to the dry dock to check on the *Athene*. Captain Harris, without a fortune cookie, broke the news: There was no proper propellor and shaft available in The Islands. Replacements would have to be shipped by freighter from San Pedro.

"It will take WEEKS!" I groaned.

Joining the *Athene* for the trip to Japan was out. To maintain our locked-in schedule, we had to board the Yokohama-bound *President Cleveland* (taking along our ace cameraman, James B. Shackleford), and send the *Athene* to Hong Kong. We planned to rendezvous with it while the *Athene* was picking up supplies.

I could hear that Los Angeles newspaperman laughing over 2,200 miles of water. I was beginning to hate the guy.

The following day had to be shape-up time. I couldn't stall in Paradise any longer. With Shack I went to work shooting backgrounds for *Trade Winds*. I was as excited as any tourist with a two-buck Brownie.

Among other shots, we set up the camera in an outrigger canoe and photographed the breakers at right angles, with surfers in the background. (A year later, at United Artists' Studios, we used process to put Freddie March upright on a surfboard in close foreground with a beautiful Hawaiian babe in his arms.

(Today's hot-doggers could learn a lot from watching Freddie, hanging ten, in his surf shot in process. At the end of the scene he stepped off the board, bone-dry.)

Inspired by the ease with which the Polynesians handled the seagoing ironing boards, Bert and I decided to try it.

Nobody is going to believe this, but on first try we both reached shore upright.

I quit winners. Bert — still trying to fill an inside straight — made a deal to go surfing again the next day. It took him a month to replace all that skin.

You can't fault the Hawaiian days, but oh! those Hawaiian nights.

One evening we had dinner with the famous composer, Rudolph Friml, an unlikely man to be listening to the thrumming of an ukulele or the whining of a steel guitar.

On another evening Duke Kahanamoku, young and powerful, taught us how to make "Royal Hawaiians" (pineapple juice, eggwhite, and gin). That done, he sat quietly drinking straight pineapple juice while the rest of us went coconuts on his recipe.

Yet another night Hugh Beatty (from U.S.C. and my mother's former driver) came to our suite with his group, "Four Spades and a Club" (a hot version of the Mills Brothers), and treated us to a pitless luau. The pig had already been roasted.

Time stood still for us, but not for the calendar; suddenly there came a day when we waved, dockside, as the *Athene* shoved off for Hong Kong.

As I dried my eyes, Helga uttered a sound that an uncharitable observer could have interpreted as a chortle of grateful glee. Helga had more than her share of virtues, but love of billowing canvas was not among them.

We, the Freidlobs, and Shack left the next morning on the *President Cleveland.* That departure from Honolulu was a heart-stopper I'll never forget. All the beach boys (Chick, Sam Colgate, Flash, Tubby, young Kahanamoku, even the Duke himself) showed up with leis for the girls. There were also leis from Hugh Beatty and his gang — leis from the *Athene* crew in absentia — everybody in our stateroom singing and tipping a bottle of Oke — then "All Ashore" . . . Throat-lump time.

Off Diamond Head we dropped our leis into the sea in tribute to a Hawaiian god who was thereupon obliged to bring us back to the Islands one day. I did a thumbs-up toward the palm-green land and the ultramarine sea to let the Old Boy know that I held him to his legend.

Bert and I recovered from the Bon Voyage party in less than three days, jolted into sobriety by discovering that Christmas comes on December 25th at sea, as well as ashore.

The coincidence was called to our attention by the purser who said, "The captain has reserved a private dining room for the five of you and authorized me to plan a special Christmas dinner."

Bert, modestly broadcasting word that his uncle was Fred Harvey's general manager, had chummed up the purser. At mention of the Harvey name, the purser knelt and bowed to the east; thereafter the larder consisted of goodies that not even the captain knew were aboard.

The traditional turkey dinner set, our next problem was satisfying the feminine need to open packages. The ship's store provided a number of "Isn't that sweet" things, but not one single, "Oh, you shouldn't have done it" item. However, promises of pearls to be selected in Japan made visions of sugarplums dance in their heads.

Any sane man would have hated to pilot that ship into Yokohama Harbor; visibility was zero-zero as we nudged through schools of small craft. It was eerie to catch sight of passing fleets of fishing junks, or sampans with split bamboo sails, that loomed abruptly out of the fog and disappeared just as swiftly.

When we were finally moored, we noticed that docks and warehouses were modern concrete structures seething with men in kimonos and wooden sandals. Thousands of bicycles were parked on the dock along with rickshaws MUCH smaller than the "authentic" two-passenger vehicles the MGM prop department had led me to expect.

Even so, there was an exotic shot wherever I looked — but no light to shoot it. My troubles were only beginning.

Customs refused to release our brand-new, ultra-advanced Mitchell camera on which I had been depending for process plates. Even Bert's soapy pidgin won us nothing except release of our old Eyemo, which had been okayed in the first place. The Eyemo was an excellent hand-held job, but impractical for process plates.

Why would Customs release the Eyemo, but not the Mitchell? We were caught between the unfathomable Oriental mind and the complicated Japanese language.

Placated by the promise that the Mitchell would be returned to us when we left Japan, we taxied to Tokyo — thirty miles over excellent roads — and checked into the Imperial Hotel.

As many people will remember, the old Imperial (since replaced) rode out the 1923 earthquake, but only because it had a center of gravity so low it couldn't figure which way to fall. Proof of its equilibrious struggle remained in the undulant corridors and room doors under which a rickshaw boy could have klop-klopped with a full load. A midget rickshaw boy, that is.

Shack, Bert, and I explored the incredible Frank Lloyd Wright building while the girls rested. We found the basement bar almost immediately and were about to order a drink when the bartender brought us a bottle of iced champagne. "Gift of genterman," he explained, nodding toward the other end of the bar.

A fan of Hollywood, we thought, as we turned to greet the wide-toothed smile of a bespectacled Japanese in kimono who lifted *his* glass of champagne and bowed ceremoniously without spilling a drop.

We, too, raised our glasses, saluting him, then sipped ruminatively. What was his pitch? A screen test? Surely not with that mass of molars. A guide job? In that elegant kimono? Never.

"This is ridiculous," I asided to Bert.

"Your taste buds have been blunted. This is as fine a champagne as I've ever clapped a lip on," answered Bert, untroubled by any emotion except gratitude for the free ride.

Our champagne finished, we bowed again to our host, who out-bowed us without effort. Checking at the front desk for mail, we were astonished to learn that — thanks to our careful planning — we had reached Japan on the eve of a holiday called "Matsunou-chi," that lasted until January 7th.

A further discovery was that police permits were required before anyone could film street scenes.

We contacted the Foreign Office and were treated with the greatest consideration. Not only were we supplied with the necessary documents but with an official guide, a Mr. Kibe, a college student working his way through the diplomatic service. He spoke flawless English with which he asked innumerable questions about the U. S.

Answers to our questions about Japan were avoided with exquisite courtesy. We took advantage of that courtesy to ask how we could extract our Mitchell from Customs.

"Customs? I do not understand," he said.

Bert, ever helpful, went into his pidgin, explaining that "those stupid Japs down at the dock" — he pantomimed a harbor crammed with ships — "latched onto MY camera." He gestured a crank camera on a tripod.

Mr. Kibe reacted with total facial immobility, but the quivering at his waistline indicated that he was about to bust a gut. When articulation became possible, Mr. Kibe said, "I have relatives in Customs. I shall see what may be done for you."

Meanwhile, after a bowing bout that left both Mr. Kibe and Champagne Charlie pink and breathless, our friend of the Imperial bar joined our party. Among other things, he arranged to stage a "Lion Dance" for us on the lawn of Kiyomizu Park. That frenetic footage, plus publicity stuff of famous geishas in rickshaws at the Buddhist temple, used up about four quarts in one afternoon.

What we failed to photograph was the party given in our honor on our last night in Tokyo. We were invited to the Emperor's Geisha House, a private club whose members were drawn entirely from the nobility. Our host was head of the Foreign Office. Incidentally, he had been a Harvard classmate of President Franklin Roosevelt.

Twelve of us, including Shack, Helga, Jeanette, Bert, and me, were relieved of our shoes and seated on the floor at navel-high tables. Each was served hot saki and oysters, two to a plate; each oyster contained a flawless white pearl. (Months later Helga had the pearls mounted in handsome cufflinks for me. Some time after that, with Helga's blessing, I gave the links to my friend, Broderick Crawford.)

Thirty or forty sakis later, about midnight, Jeanette and Helga were told that a cavalcade of private rickshaws was waiting to take the girls — convoyed by half a dozen geishas — back to our hotel. Behind that suggestion was a note of pride in Japanese national hospitality for male guests.

Those bluenoses, Helga and Jeanette, refused to leave, thereby cramping the action for the rest of the evening.

Our host saved the situation by saying, "Excuse me for a moment, please, while I explain to my colleagues the eccentricities of American wives."

Naturally, we were unable to understand the Japanese monologue, but his tagline — whatever it was — got a helluva laugh.

Throughout the rest of the evening we were regarded with a pitying perplexity that completed our emasculation.

And so — on to Miyanoshita.

To our astonishment, Mr. Kibe actually managed to extract our Mitchell from Customs without our having to leave Japan.

Shack, promptly testing it, found that it was inoperable.

He was furious. Just before we left Honolulu, Shack had disassembled the Mitchell and greased every part against salt air corrosion; after reassembling it, he had tested it to make sure it was functioning perfectly.

In our room at the Fujiya Hotel, Shack again took the Mitchell apart, finding several loose pieces rattling around the interior. It was obvious that the lens louse who had taken possession of the camera from Customs had made patterns of every part, but had been unable to reassemble them properly.

Somehow I've always had a feeling that the difficulty was soon corrected.

Miyanoshita is a cinematographer's dream sequence. Jubilantly, Shack and I set up to photograph the gardens of the hotel with white-crowned Fujiyama standing boldly against a dazzling blue sky in the distance — and, to our amazement, Champagne Charlie in the foreground, complete with identifying glass.

He waved hospitably to indicate a waiter approaching with a bottle for us.

I asked Shack, "Do you get the feeling we're being followed?"

"He'd make a nice pet, but you'll never get him out of Japan. Somebody's bound to claim him," Shack opined.

Next stop: Kyoto and the Miyako Hotel. We fell in love with the city on sight. "It's so authentic," Bert said with his unfailing knack for the bon mot.

Kyoto has never suffered a major earthquake, so it had never been rebuilt; the architectural masterpieces of the dynasties stood intact (and still do). Shack and I were drooling, but even in those days there were penalties for runaway production. Before we could get our Mitchell set up, the weather began to enshroud the scenery in goose down.

One of the troubles with foreign travel, business or pleasure, is that there's nothing to do when it snows. I always feel guilty if I simply sit in a hotel room and read, and locationing in the bar is rough on the liver.

However, while the girls left on a shopping tour by taxi, Bert, Shack and I sought out the resident gin mill. We were tossing around the problem of ordering a Ramos Fizz in Japanese when a waiter hove to with a bottle of champagne.

A ripple ran through us. First we stared at one another, then we slowly swiveled to case the room. There he was, arising from a darkened corner, lifting his glass and bowing.

We sat in silence, concentrating on our drinking. By the time the second bottle arrived, we were well rehearsed in the bowing routine.

Finally Shack ventured, "But we haven't DONE anything."

"That we know of," I added. I've always been fascinated by a script in which somebody blameless, like Cary Grant, is mistaken for the guy with the Hope diamond and is pursued through cornfields and across the face of Mount Rushmore. Any face.

Bert ended our speculation by saying modestly, "Probably the people at Immigration, knowing who I am, have assigned him as bodyguard."

We made one precious purchase in Kyoto, feeling that no home is complete without a papier-mache lion's head. We figured we could always stage a dance on the back lot at 20th-Century Fox, using maybe the Tiller Girls.

Because of the continuing blizzard, we had no choice but to go by train to Kobe, and there to board the *President Coolidge* bound for

Shanghai. Shack had to be left behind to get our absolutely essential process plates. "You won't be lonely," I encouraged him. "You'll have Champagne Charlie all to yourself."

Shack said, "Hell, no. He's Bert's bodyguard — remember? You'll have him straight through to Los Angeles Harbor."

We learned later that our Charlie made Shack's life bearable during the five-day blizzard and even helped carry equipment when good weather sent Shack from one end of Kyoto to the other on a shutter spree. Finally, it was good old Charlie who — as water widened between hull and wharf — stood dockside, lifting a farewell toast to Shack at the rail with a magnum under each arm.

Who was he? Why was he? Shack explained him as Alcoholic 007 with an unlimited Foreign Office expense account.

While Shack was mystifying Charlie by photographing girls, temples, gardens, and Buddhist priests in preference to trying for military installations, we were having our own troubles.

The *President Coolidge* dropped anchor in the river at Shanghai at five in the afternoon of a bitterly cold, rainy Monday, January 13. Chinese Customs refused to permit us to take our cans of film into Shanghai, where international photography was forbidden. When we explained, with appropriate regret, that we were en route to Bangkok and wouldn't have enough footage to photograph China, the officials relented. However, to keep us honest, they bound the cans with wire and sealed the wire to the cans with wax.

Ashore, we climbed into rickshaws, bound for the Cathay Hotel, and were beset every inch of the way by beggars, foul odors, and filth. We were appalled by the contrast between poverty-ridden China and tidy, clean Japan.

As soon as we were established in our Cathay room, we went to work with a penknife, heated over a candle, and gently eased the Customs' sealing wax from the film cans. (When preparing to leave Shanghai, we resealed the film expertly enough to pass Customs without question.)

Having melted our way through the first barrier, we were eyeball to eyeball with another quandary: how to photograph the streets of Shanghai without getting arrested and tossed into the jug — tantamount, in those days, to a death sentence the hard way. The easy way was via beheading.

During the time I spent freeing the film, gregarious Bert was making friends in the Cathay Bar with a governor of the Shanghai Stock Exchange. I've always wondered how many million shares of Paramount Pictures Bert admitted owning, but that's beside the point.

Bert's new friend (an Englishman born in Shanghai's British Concession) apparently wanted to ingratiate himself with the cinema tycoon. He made arrangements to rent a moving van for us, and had it delivered — with a bilingual driver — to the Cathay's underground garage. We barricaded ourselves in the van behind a load of furniture covered by a tarp. The camera lens protruded through a hole in the canvas.

We elected to photograph the French Concession first at Bert's suggestion, but he abandoned us after ten uneventful minutes. The enterprise was too arctic and dirty for a mogul accustomed to making deals across a mahogany bar.

That night we adhered to U. S. tradition by reporting to "Jimmie's" for dinner. Amazingly, we saw no one we knew in spite of the restaurant's being more familiar to Americans than our Embassy.

Shack arrived the following morning, jubilant over his Japanese footage. He was eager to get rolling in Shanghai but cringed at sight of our moving van. Ridiculing our chickening out for fear of the law, he rented a sedan, hung blankets over the side windows, and removed a rear window so as to shoot through another tattered blanket. He even agreed to take the rap in case we were caught.

With this setup we were able to shoot the ten-foot-wide streets in China City and Chapai across Soo Chow Creek from the International Concession, both forbidden to tourists.

Note: There were hospitals in Chapai where, for a reasonable down payment, plus a fat percentage of the take for the rest of the patient's life, a beggar could be maimed so as to increase his financial success (a horribly twisted back, or an open facial sore warranted not to heal). Some women even rented sick or dead babies to add to their daily income .

We had heard much about Chinese tailors, so whenever we lost our light for the day, we reported to Mr. Wong to be fitted for suits — finest British woolens, silk-lined — at $22 per suit. No wonder there was hunger in Shanghai.

Mr. Wong, a retired general, was candid about the Japanese invasion of Manchuria, saying, "The Japanese is a bad robber, very strong and greedy. He can steal what he likes and eat it. China is a needle. The Japanese can swallow the needle, but when he does, it will surely puncture his stomach and he will die."

In addition to philosophy and fine clothes, Mr. Wong designed a new name for Bert, who had introduced himself as *"Captain* Friedlob."

General Wong's tongue balked at the pronunciation of Bert's surname, so my traveling companion was dubbed "Captain Flob."

There are two things in the world I've never had enough of: time and money. Both were running out when we reached Hong Kong, where the *Athene* was taking on supplies. To stretch a shrinking bank account, we sent the *Athene* to Saigon while we tried to cram three weeks' shooting into six or eight days.

After Shanghai, Hong Kong seemed very spit and polish. Even before the British Crown Colony became the decorated sweater capital of the world, it intrigued Americans.

January 30, 1936 was a banner day. Shack, Helga, and I hired a junk from which to record life in the Typhoon Shelter. Our power consisted of six people: two men who took turns steering while a woman, a girl of about six, and two little boys manned the oars.

The sights were terrific: a baby tied to an inflated fish bladder, an effective life preserver; farther along a child needing a bathroom, simply held overboard by his mother; the marriage junk, a bright spot where couples spent their honeymoon; streamers flying off all junks for luck in the New Year.

Our conversation was desultory: "Isn't THAT something," or "Get that with the Eyemo," or "There's local color for you!" This was counterpointed by the tinkling laughter of Asia, and conversation from the boats sounded like, "See the funny clothes. See the faces white like fishes' bellies."

I permitted myself a moment of uncharacteristic analysis: The

[190]

Hong Kong Chinese appeared to be happy in the business of staying one jump ahead of famine.

The thought of happiness, as always, reminded me of Joan Marshfield. On impulse, I mailed her a gold bracelet set with pearls. Helga helped me pick it out — for my "cousin" in Paris. She didn't even say, "You've never mentioned a relative in France."

Wonderful girl, that Helga.

At the risk of sounding like a news broadcast, I'm going to tell something about our trip through French Indochina (now North and South Vietnam, Laos, and Cambodia, of course) because, today, that part of the world has intruded its woes into the very heartland of America.

On Saturday, February 1st, we boarded the 800-ton coastal steamer *Canton,* bound for Haiphong. No travel folder could do the craft justice: a deckload of live sheep forward and a pack of steerage coolies aft. First class consisted of a German, traveling for Bayer Aspirin, three Jesuit priests, and the five of us (Helga, Jeanette, Shack, Bert, and me).

Thirty-six awful hours later we reached Haiphong, a place I never longed to be, and still don't.

Only one good thing came of it. I bought a cork helmet, a lightweight chalk-white topper that satisfied a dream cherished since my boyhood service with Kipling. At last I was pukka sahib and, by God, let the Riffs watch out.

In those days, no matter where you wanted to go in Indochina, "you couldn't get there from here." In an attempt to foul up that ancient wheeze, we hired an open car to drive to Hanoi, about 2½ hours away. Shooting from the car, we recorded a primitive womanpower irrigation system. Swinging a cone-shaped basket between them, two women dipped it into a pond at the bottom of the swing, filling the basket. At the peak of their swing they emptied it into a newly planted rice paddy.

The roads were lined with black-pajama-clad people carrying loads to market; mostly women sweating under shoulder poles; a small girl, almost invisible under two large bales; a tiny Manchurian pony (the only breed able to endure the heat) hitched to a cart loaded six feet high with produce, five girls helping the horse by simultaneously pushing him and propping him up.

Hanoi proved to be a large French provincial town — no tourists, and no French spoken. We checked into the Grand Hotel Metropole — $5.00 per person, bathroom with bidet but no W. C. Verrry interesting, those French.

The month was February; even so, the heat was beyond the scope of the English language or the Fahrenheit thermometer. We slept under netting that simply notified mosquitos that dinner was ready; the enormous revolving ceiling fan above our bed operated with enough cursing and moaning to have kept Rip van Winkle AWAKE for a hundred years.

The next morning we almost ran to the train in eager anticipation of a twenty-one hour trip to Hué, now known as Bob Hope Country.

Promptly we walked through the train in search of a faint breeze and/or local color. Camera at the ready, we'd spot a lovely young girl, often suckling a child at her beautiful bronze breast. Thinking artistic thoughts, we would call to her. Turning a matchless profile past our camera, she would smile — playing hell with both our film and our libidos. The women of Indochina (now as then?) painted their teeth with some sort of shiny black enamel. Later we learned the reason: to hide the loathesome stains caused by chewing betelnut.

The train paused briefly at a water tank; instantly there were five or six urchins peddling coconut half-shells filled with milk. Bert took one and added brandy; I held out for ice, of which there was none.

I rambled about the platform, unfortunately leaving the Eyemo with Helga on the train. Rounding the corner of the grass shack that served as stationmaster's headquarters, I caught sight of the world's most unorthodox automat: about a dozen Annamite women milking themselves into coconut shells.

I didn't tell Bert.

Another exotic charm that eluded capture by camera was the odor of that train. It was one vast ferment of packed humanity. Unhousebroken babies vied for space with chickens in wicker pens; betelnut-chewing patriarchs expectorated at random; sweat steamed from bodies that had never known soap, and clouds of dust and insects settled on the scene like animated itch powder.

In addition to sweat, dust, bugs, and fetor, the passengers had one other possession in common: bananas. Adults were eating them and children were mashing them in their hair. There were banana skins hanging over window sills, crushed on seats, and rotting in the aisles.

Scientists say that the olfactory nerves tire rapidly. By the time we reached Hué — at four in the morning — my sense of smell had been unconscious for hours.

Our train and dawn arrived simultaneously in Hué's totally deserted station. No band. No mayor. No key to the city.

Eventually, in the steaming half-light, a collection of "pouse-pouse" (rickshaws) chattered up, and took us to the Grand Hotel, a misnomer. Beds small, mouldy and granite-hard.

I groaned out at eight and pouse-poused to the Bureau of Tourism, where — thanks to the magic word "Hollywood" — an army car was placed at our disposal. I've always wondered if that favor were granted in the hope that our film would shock Paris out of colonialism, with the corollary result that homesick French officials would be summoned home.

Hué, in any case, was a cameraman's bonanza. The nearby river was the social center. In it water buffaloes bathed, kids swam, and mothers did their laundry. Arching over the stream was a footbridge on which oldsters gathered to observe the water follies.

We were photographing the scene when I heard a peculiar squishing and felt brief impact against my elegant cork helmet. I glanced up to see four or five Indochinese ancients howling and congratulating one of their number on his marksmanship. I had served as a peg in a Southeast Asian betelnut version of horseshoes.

Our pouse-pouse boy did his best to wash my headgear, but by Gad, sir, the Riffs had won. I was a disgrace to the British Empire.

As I strode along the street, I paused at the first betelnut tree, shook my fist and hissed a bitter curse, "May all your customers switch to bubblegum."

My morale picked up considerably, along with a high incidence of amusement from the natives, when I located another helmet. Unfortunately, it was pith, much bulkier and heavier than my cork beauty. "Let them laugh," I told myself. "Little do they dream that I am the thin white line between them and the Riffs. And getting thinner."

I don't want this to sound like a conducted tour, but all traveling Americans will empathize with our adventure of that evening. We sought out an attractive hotel (in comparison with the rest of Hué) with a clean-looking dining room.

The menu was written, unfortunately, in Indochinese French — as distant from Helga's French as Brooklyn English is from London — and the waiters spoke no English.

We went the view route, scanning the plates of nearby diners. One popular dish appeared to be an Asian version of beef stew, so we ordered it by gesture.

When it was served, we approached it cautiously, although its aroma was delicious. We conferred. It wasn't beef — or lamb — or pork.

The *maitre d'* bounced over about that time — a round little man with Jerry Colonna eyes — and asked in excellent French if we were enjoying our "ragout de singe." A telltale pallor spread over Helga's face as she essayed a weak smile. As soon as the *maitre d'* was out of earshot, she said, "Let's go." We went. By that time we had all remembered that "singe" is French for "monkey."

Ultimately we recovered.

Out of desperation, I located a market where I bought Libby's corned beef, a large sauce pan, a can of Sterno, half a dozen potatoes, an onion and a pat of sweet, fresh buffalo butter.

I set my Sterno galley in the bathtub (fire protection) and in short order had concocted a fine corned beef hash that was gratefully devoured by five hungry people. Nothing has ever tasted better.

And so, on to Tuy Hoa by train from 5 A.M. until 7 P.M.

If American troops, stationed in Vietnam, spotted a sign reading, "Tay Garnett Slept Here," it was a lie. The five of us were domiciled in a "bungalow" in the midst of a desert, whipped by a gale that blew out our oil lamp and shredded our shutters.

The next morning, with eyes hanging on our cheekbones, we boarded a bus for Nah Trang. In those days it was an island summer resort. Our hotel, "Le Beau Rivage," overlooked the sea; we cracked out cameras and took a couple of plates and a pan shot from the top of an ancient Annamite temple, as I'm sure hundreds of American G.I.s have done.

Our next transportation was an incredible vehicle that was, for some obscure reason, expected to advance us to Saigon. Mechanically the contraption was by Studebaker, out of Maxwell, with an assist from Hupmobile. Its gas tank bulged between engine and dashboard, and its transmission sounded like New Year's Eve in Shanghai.

Its tonneau had been designed to seat fourteen small Indochinese, but twenty-five members of an informal United Nations were collapsed together, jouncing, bouncing and elbowing in steamy intimacy. And eating bananas.

As we started up the first of a series of hills, our motor sputtered and all but died. Instantly an apparition consisting of fragile bones encased in brown skin and an inadequate loincloth, hopped onto the hood of the bus. He had come from the roof, where, we decided, he had been installed as standard equipment.

He began to BLOW into our gas tank with all the lung power he could muster. The engine took heart as the boy continued this artificial respiration until we reached the top of the hill and headed into another little valley. Settling down, with his skinny back blocking the windshield, he ate a banana and waited for the next hill.

My chief complaint was that I couldn't figure how to photograph the stunt without being left on the jungleside as our Studemax topped a rise and stormed downhill.

I had other photographic complaints. As we forged on through the tropic night, our headlights illuminated jungle communities of four or five grass huts. In front of each was a huge teak table on which couples were so deeply involved in what they were doing that they didn't even stop doing it long enough to see what *we* were doing. With that footage nowadays, I could make a film that would be a cinch for an "X" rating, several million at the box office, and an Oscar.

Speaking of Oscar, nearly everyone in Hollywood has laid claim to the distinction of having nicknamed the Motion Picture Academy Awards statuette. On close scrutiny it will be noted that Golden Boy looks a lot like Everyman. Or Every Woman, for that matter.

The first time I saw the statue, I said, "My God, that's Oscar Miller, my former father-in-law, except that Cedric Gibbons (sculptor of the figure) has substituted a broadsword for Oscar's tennis racket."

End of my claim to baptismal fame.

At the end of seven indescribable days and unbearable nights, we reached Saigon. I had never seen a more beautiful sight than the *Athene,* standing white and stately at anchor midstream in the Saigon River.

We moved aboard, glorying in the cleanliness and sweet fragrance of our boat. However, there seemed to be a certain aroma from our trip that clung stubbornly to the very air. But coming from our galley?

Guess what we had for dinner that night.

Yeah.

Baked, with coconut syrup.

In a bitterly contested election, we voted 3 to 2 against drowning Israel Oliver, our Nubian cook.

On to Singapore.

When we docked, I was interviewed by a reporter from one of the Straits papers. I've always enjoyed interviews, because I've found that the average reporter can tell me more than I can tell him. Especially when I've been at sea for several weeks.

This particular reporter's news was that Charlie Chaplin and Paulette Goddard were arriving that afternoon aboard one of the Dollar Line ships. I had never known Charlie, but Paulette was a friend. I respected her quick mind; in addition, she was — from north to south — a landscape to refresh the eye.

"Where are they staying? The Raffles?" I asked.

The reporter grinned. "Nope. The word is that they'll check into a little dump on a side street to 'avoid crowds.' You know how 'Retiring Charlie' hates fans."

I was at the dock as the ship was tied up. My idea was to welcome the Chaplin party to Singapore, and to suggest they join us at the Raffles for a few laughs.

I was refused permission to go aboard, and the Chaplins remained in their cabin until all other passengers had disembarked. Finally a mountain of handsome luggage was brought down the gangplank and turned over to a hotel porter who loaded it into and all over a cab.

"Follow that taxi," I told my driver. "There's something odd about this."

The luggage was unloaded and stacked on the walk before a down-at-the-heels hotel with hot and cold running rats on the veranda. A skinny little Malay kid was lifted to the top of the trunks and cases, in spite of a persistent drizzle, and told to guard them against the expected crowds.

After waiting twenty minutes, I grew bored. Traffic swooshed along the street without pausing, and pedestrians circled the leather Everest without a backward glance.

Total indifference to the great man was not the result of his being incognito. Stenciled in large white block letters on either side of each piece of luggage was the legend:

CHARLES CHAPLIN

I went back to the hotel, grinning. The cabby said as he let me out, "Chaplin, big man? In Hollywood — MAYBE?"

The Chaplin party checked into the Raffles an hour later, depressed and dripping, but completely free of autograph-seekers.

Nearly everyone in the world yearns to move to Hollywood, with certain notable exceptions. One night, we (Paulette Goddard, the Friedlobs, and the Garnetts — Charlie had a headache) decided to check the scene at The New World, a huge open-air taxi dance spot in an amusement park. We were warned by the desk clerk at The Raffles that The New World might be *"lively."* Leave it to the English to underplay a description.

As we entered the place, we could make out — through smoke as thick and hot as clam chowder — a tide of British, American, Malaysian, German, Dutch, French, Portuguese, Brazilian, and Chinese sailors that surged and swirled against the bar, and eddied into the shadows in distant corners. Abruptly someone took exception to a chance remark, broke a bottle against a tabletop, and a few seconds later a blood-gushing gob was rushed out a rear exit, as the police arrived in force.

"I hate these slow starts," I said.

[197]

Helga was not amused. "I want to get out of here FAST," she gasped.

"Just a moment," suggested Paulette.

I followed her nod and beheld the most beautiful female I'd ever seen in that or any land. Obviously Eurasian, she was tall and willowy with huge cat's eyes set in a cat's wide-cheeked, small-chinned face.

My wife said on a held breath, "Sign that girl and we'll take her back to Hollywood with us. I've never seen anyone to equal her."

That sentence substantiates the rumor that there are women who can rise above jealousy when a million dollars is to be made.

I wanted to play it very British, to impress this taxi-dance tramp with the legitimacy of my offer, so I called for the manager to introduce us, which he did — leering with every syllable.

I explained to our scantily-draped Aphrodite that I thought she had a chance for motion picture fame, and detailed my qualifications for giving her a career. I wound up with the clincher, "Would you like to sign a contract, and go to Hollywood with my wife and me?"

Shoulders stiffening and eyes narrowed, she said, "Oh, NO. I *couldn't* do a thing like that!"

I was stopped cold.

"Why not?" Paulette wanted to know.

The girl straightened to her full height as she said, "I've HEARD about Hollywood. IT IS A VERY, VERY WICKED PLACE."

I had enjoyed Bert Friedlob on a now-and-then basis while our touring party had been fellow passengers on a series of *President* liners, or when domiciled in a city, or even when condemned to travel on the Devil's Dishpan across Southeast Asia.

Once aboard the *Athene,* however, I was forcibly reminded of a law of physics that had slipped my mind: salt air inflates the human body; as a passenger expands, the capacity of a boat shrinks.

During our intimate dinners, Bert outlined his plans for the future in generous detail; his plans to build a mansion in Bel Air — shrink; his plans to set up a film producing company — shrink; his intention to establish his own film distributing company — shrink; his blueprints for starting a nationwide theatre chain — shrink.

In ten days the *Athene* had become a kayak.

I was able to hold back tears when Bert announced that he had made a firm date to meet his brother in Bombay to go on a tiger hunt. The *Athene,* Captain Flob observed critically, was moving too slowly to conform to his schedule.

He and Jeanette (who seemed immune to sea air in that she took up practically no space at all) left the *Athene* at Columbo, Ceylon, to board another *President* liner. Tigers may come and tigers may go, but I remain convinced that the REAL reason for Bert's departure was a desperate need for a new audience, one that didn't take to counting sea gulls in the midst of his Executive Planning Sessions.

Our crew turned the suddenly spacious *Athene* toward Bombay.

While studying *The Pilot's Manual* I was seduced by a line reading, "The Laccadive Islands lie green and fertile off the Malabar Coast of India in the Arabian Sea, lat. 10° 20′ 20″ N. and long. 72° 74′ E. When last visited, in 1880, the natives were not unfriendly."

Androth (pop. 700), the major island of the Laccadives (and still, today, lacking a Hilton-Sheraton) was surrounded by a coral reef. We dropped anchor to leeward, well off the reef; by the time our hook was down, we were surrounded by dugouts. (Incidentally, such hardwood dugouts were carved out of solid logs on the mainland, and paddled over 200 miles of Indian Ocean to the Islands.)

The craft were manned by locals who had brought us hundreds of freshly cut coconuts. The lightly clad members of the welcoming committee swarmed aboard with gifts underarm and hands extended for fair exchange. Things were different from 1880, when beads and mirrors were legal tender; this gang wanted one currency, and one currency only: American cigarettes.

We were invited, through an effective sign language, to go ashore. The idea appealed to me, so I took the Eyemo along. I was still enthusiastic about the expedition, although the entrance to the lagoon — crystalline to a depth of thirty feet — was crowded with hungry sharks eighteen to twenty feet long.

We were greeted by the village mayor, a patriarch in a rumpled white kaftan and a shark's tooth necklace, who asked after the health of "Her Majesty, Queen Victoria."

I lacked the courage to explain the cavalcade of Edward VII,

[199]

George V, and Edward VIII, but mentioned that the coronation of George VI was imminent. The good chief beamed, said he hoped Her Majesty's "son" would reign as long and wisely as had the great queen, and the amenities were satisfied.

Luncheon was served at that point: a hard-boiled egg that had been peeled by grubby fingers. The FBI would have had a field day identifying those responsible.

The egg had been sliced paper thin in order to serve about twenty guests; the slices were passed around on small wooden plates. This hors d'oeuvre was accompanied by a grog that would have converted W. C. Fields to Alcoholics Anonymous.

Fortunately, I'm not one of those jealous cooks, keeping my best recipes secret. I'm happy to pass this one along:

Take one green coconut, top it and place aloft in convenient tree.

Allow to ferment for one week. (Fermentation is a natural process resulting from the drowning and disintegration of local ants and bugs.)

When coconut liquid begins to work AUDIBLY, cocktail is ready.

Do not strain or stir as scum is, to epicures, infallible evidence of vintage.

Protocol: Host takes first sip from bowl to check quality, passes bowl to guest on right and so on around the circle, bypassing the boys now well separated from the men.

Long before refreshments were served, my beautiful blonde wife had grown bored. Hoping to avoid sunstroke, she strolled through a coconut forest that bordered the lagoon, and — finding a secluded retreat turned twilit by interlacing branches — stretched out on a mossy mound and fell asleep.

She was awakened by girlish giggling. Cautiously, she opened her eyes a mere slit, expecting to find herself staked to the ground, ready for broiling over an open fire.

The heat felt by Helga came not from conflagration but from humiliation: two girls were holding up the hem of my wife's skirt while ten or twelve others were studying comparative anatomy. Their discovery of a blonde woman elicited no scientific awe — merely incredulous hilarity.

That incident may have had something to do with our eventual domestic discord. There are some women who are totally unable to adapt themselves to the social circles in which their husbands move.

We were peacefully en route to Bombay when our radio operator came down to the salon, wearing a pumpkin grin. "I was just talking to the Dollar Line radio operator," he said. "They're a day out of Bombay, bound for Cairo. He says they have a Hollywood big shot aboard, name of Friedlob, who owns the yacht *Athene.* Seems that Friedlob plans to rejoin his boat at Calais. He's just riding the Dollar Line because he grew tired of the limited social contacts on the *Athene.*"

Dear old Captain Flob.

We laughed all the way to Bombay. We stopped laughing when we learned that no one from the *Athene* would be permitted to set foot on Indian soil. The harbormaster was coolly courteous, saying, "If you need provision, we'll send a ship's chandler to you."

Our skipper, Captain Jack Harris, would have been an ornament to the U. S. Diplomatic Service; he suggested that I go below so he could have a chat with his old friend, the harbormaster.

The first misunderstanding that had to be cleared up was the identity of the legal owner of the *Athene.* Our log proved that Bert Friedlob had been a guest and nothing more from Saigon to Ceylon.

That settled, the harbormaster explained that the local animadversion was not directed against the *Athene,* per se, or her crew, but against Mr. Friedlob alone, "as a matter of national pride."

It seemed that when Mr. Friedlob reached Bombay, he had been interviewed by local reporters and had led them to believe that Captain Flob was a very large wheel indeed. He had been invited to speak to a meeting of local dignitaries and businessmen to discuss his plans for filming a major motion picture in Bombay!

Bert's first modest statement set U. S. public relations back fifty years. "I am here," he said with a sweeping gesture, "to put India on the map."

The Indian hometown boosters ushered Bert to the nearest exit and expressed their appreciation with a farewell gift: an atlas.

Anyone who has traveled as far as Disneyland knows that a trip always costs more than anticipated. Multiply that fact by the distance around the world and you have an idea of my financial situation when the *Athene* reached Port Said.

The crew had to be paid, and there were to be other pressing expenses when we reached England; my fiscal condition reminded me of a Biblical verse to the effect that "the sack needs grain." But first I had to get the sack.

Helga, Shack, and I left the *Athene* and set off by land from Port Said and Cairo, filming as we went. On to Alexandria, then by ship to Marseille and via train to Paris. Meanwhile, the *Athene* was to proceed through the Suez, across the Mediterranean, then sail up the Atlantic coast to Calais.

We reached Paris at 9 P.M. in a drenching rain, and registered at the Chambord Hotel.

On an off-chance, considering the hour, I called the Selznick office in London; the blessed, familiar tones of my agent, Noll Gurney, answered.

In a small voice I said, "Help — help — help."

"Where in hell are you?" he boomed.

"Broke in Paris," I confessed.

"At least you've never been broke *there* before," laughed Noll. "Okay, don't leave your hotel tomorrow until you hear from me."

The next morning he gave me the beautiful news that he had contracted for me to write and direct a script for Douglas Fairbanks, Jr., who — with Marcel Hellman — had established a producing company in London.

Gurney had also arranged a hefty advance for me.

"Before we go to London," Helga said tentatively, "aren't you going to see your cousin?"

For a moment I was stopped. What cousin?

"No doubt she'll want to thank you for the bracelet."

Never underestimate the memory of a woman.

Still, why not telephone Countess Joan? I placed the call while Helga, overplaying indifference, stood by. The maid said the Count and Countess were in Nice on holiday.

I refused to regard the slightly hollow feeling in my midsection as painful disappointment.

A few days later, right on schedule, the *Athene* arrived in Calais; we boarded her for the cross-Channel trip to the Yacht Club basin at Southwick, near Brighton.

First business in London was leasing living quarters, because we knew my shooting schedule would take six months with luck, longer with standard foul-ups.

We found a handsome flat in Tilney Street, half a block from the Dorchester Hotel, and put down the magnificent Oriental rugs we had bought during the *Athene*'s cruise. Helga ordered her family antiques out of storage, and we were London householders. I even contemplated carrying a brolly — "umbrella" to you colonials.

With zest I settled down to the most concentrated job of writing I'd ever done. In three weeks I had a rough draft of the script, a thud and blunder story of the Border Wars. Arrangements were made to shoot several Scottish castles, and feelers were put out to acquire five thousand British cavalrymen, equipped to bivouac themselves and their mounts.

Let the record show that the production man in charge of making location plans WAS BORN AND REARED in the Newcastle-upon-Tyne area, our initial location, and SHOULD have known something about district weather conditions.

Meanwhile, during London evenings, I covered every play in the West End, searching for our leading lady. At the Savoy Theatre, I spotted one of the most talented and beautiful redheads I had ever seen. She was feminine and alluring with incomparable legs, but she also gave out an aristocratic air that a French parfumeur could have bottled as "Essence of Great Lady."

I sent a note backstage, asking for an appointment and explaining that my interest was purely professional. She bought the disclaimer and responded that she would be happy to meet me and my associates in the lobby of the Dorchester for tea the next day.

Hellman and Fairbanks were as taken with the lady as I. We promptly arranged for a comprehensive screen test. It was a smash: The girl's image lit up the projection room like summer lightning.

We three rubbed our hands and turned to less fascinating details of production.

The Fairbanks charm worked a miracle in securing from His Majesty's Government (George VI) the services of 5,000 cavalrymen.

[203]

This coup assured a lavish production, but unavoidable delay was caused by our having to manufacture thousands of authentic period costumes, along with caparison for the horses.

Further delay resulted from our having to manufacture lances, crossbows, and long bows, as well as arrows, because the short-memoried British military no longer stocked them!

I decided to take advantage of the lull by arranging a pleasure cruise on the *Athene.* We loaded the boat with friends (among them Thornton Delahanty and Lord Donegal — New York and London columnists respectively) and sailed through the Canal to Kiel. We caught a few chukkers of the Olympic Yacht races, run Nazi-style, i.e., according to rules guaranteeing the success of the Super Race's entries.

After a couple of days in Copenhagen (aquavit and Tivoli) we proceeded to Kristiansand in Norway, cruising the fjords in our inboard-powered fishing boat.

The port authority at Kristiansand had just put up full gale warnings — the tourist steamers, freighters and airlines were secured — when a radiogram arrived saying that 5,000 men and horses were en route to Northumberland, and did Director Garnett plan to attend?

Said director collected his lower jaw and checked with Captain Harris who muttered, "That's a helluva blow kicking up in the North Sea."

"Can the *Athene* take it?"

His pride was piqued. "The Athene can take anything, *anywhere.* But it'll be rough. R-r-r-r-rough."

"Let's go," I said, trying to sound gung ho. Under my breath I added, "And may the luck of the Irish prevail."

I had heard of the fury of the North Sea, but nothing ever written could have prepared me for that ripping, battering, screeching, tearing gale. At one point a wave like an almighty fist crashed under our inboard-powered fishing boat — slung in davits that were bolted through two inches of teak and pine — ripping it free and depositing it on the skylight of the main salon.

Captain Harris piped all hands on deck so we could lash down the fishing boat, then stuff mattresses around it to hold it steady and to keep the ship from foundering.

My gallant *Athene,* bruised, battered and thoroughly seahandled, still sailed boldly into port as the sun set. Her valor can be appreciated in realization of the tragedy of two British trawlers that foundered and sank within a fifty-mile radius of our position.

Helga and I, exhausted beyond exhaustion, went to the Inn and fell into dreamless sleep. We were safe in Northumberland.

The next morning I awakened to a strange light in the room. It wasn't sunlight. It was more like — reflections from snow?

I jumped to the window and gaped. There were people passing along the street below, but they appeared as disembodied heads. Below chin-line there was an opaque blanket of ground fog, thicker than marshmallow syrup.

I dressed with shaking hands and took the steps two at a time, thumping against the front desk with a breathless inquiry, "What's outside?"

"Oh, THAT," laughed the desk clerk. "That's Scottish Mist. Surely you've heard of it?"

"Only on the rocks," I admitted. "How long before sunlight burns through?"

"About three months. Happens annually, y'know."

I staggered to the telephone and told Noll Gurney, in London, the story.

"You mean Hellman, Fairbanks, and five thousand horses and men are en route to zero visibility?. . ." Gurney cleared his throat. "Look, Tay, if you can board the *Athene* and shove off instantly, you may get out of there before the lynching."

"But I'm innocent," I protested. "It was the 'expert' location manager employed by . . ."

"Get!" yelled Gurney.

We managed to get out of the harbor and head south.

Hellman and Fairbanks lost a bundle, and all three of us lost our anticipated association with the glorious redhead.

A few years later, L. B. Mayer happened to be in London negotiating for some story properties and players; someone showed him my test of the redhead.

"Sign her," Mayer said, halfway through the test. "Sign her and send her to Hollywood as quickly as possible. What's her name, did you say?"

"Greer Garson."

"We'll have to change that to something more feminine, of course, but she'll be a valuable property under any name."

"Property" — that is the term used in the film business to describe contract actors and actresses as well as plays, novels and other script sources. In Greer's case, the "property" — when talked to — talked back! It did NOT change its name.

We sent the *Athene* across the Atlantic, through the Panama Canal, and up to her berth in Wilmington, California, at a leisurely pace. Helga and I dismantled our London flat (acquired and furnished when we believed we would be living in England for the better part of a year), and stored our silver, our Steinway, our Oriental rugs, our handsome French antiques, even our heavy coats, in Cook's warehouse. Then we boarded the *Queen Mary* for New York, never imagining that one day she would be living in Long Beach, California.

Never imagining, either, that all our treasures would be wiped out during the buzz-bombing of England.

Hangover House looked good to me. I strolled through the rooms, relishing our expanded space (quadrupled from the layout of my original blueprint) and generally feeling with Stevenson, "The hunter is home from the hill."

My poesy was not shared by Helga.

We tossed a homecoming party for a guest list including Tyrone Power, Loretta Young, Sally Blaine, Carter and Pollyanne Young Hermann, Clark Gable, Kay Francis, Bill and Dottie Wellman, Spencer Tracy, Bob Taylor, John and Josie Wayne, Frank Borzage, King Vidor, and what seemed like a cast of thousands.

I thought it was a Four Star affair, but the next morning Helga had a number of things to say. Boiled down to the nitty-gritty, it was my wife's opinion that not even Elsa Maxwell could give a decent party at Hangover House.

Two days later Helga greeted me with the news that she had closed a deal for a house on Stone Canyon Road in Bel Air. She concluded, "I know you're going to LOVE it."

I loved every inch of those two acres, including each of the eleven bathrooms. Of course, it needed a little dab of something here and there such as a swimming pool, a bathhouse with bar and grill, *His* and *Her* dressing rooms, and a trout stream.

I'm not being facetious when I say, "a trout stream." There was actually a stream that flowed across the sweeping front garden under giant sycamores.

Being a natural lily-gilder, I had the stream bed cemented, installed a waterfall with a circulating pump, and screened the stream's inlet and outlet. Regularly I bought a barrel of trout from Noah Beery's Trout Farm, and invited my sporting friends to a Fish Fry.

In hope of eventually owning more of the house than the bank did, I went back to 20th-Century Fox to direct a comedy written by one of our more brilliant scripters, Harry Tugend.

The story was called *Love Is News,* and starred Loretta Young, Tyrone Power, Don Ameche, and Slim Summerville.

A highly useful comedy device in those days was the *double entendre,* although we didn't know how to spell or pronounce it. Slim Summerville was particularly effective in erotic situations because no one could connect carnality with that woebegone pan.

Take, for instance, a sequence in *Love Is News.* The situation started with Slim, as a rural sheriff, arresting Tyrone and Loretta for hitchhiking.

Furious, they demanded to be taken before the local magistrate at once. The sheriff complied by driving them to the courthouse. There, Slim removed his sheriff's hat and badge, donned a black robe, and mounted the judge's bench to hear the case.

He found the hitchhikers guilty and sentenced them to ten days in jail unless they could pay a fine of $100. They admitted they were broke.

Slim, putting on the gun belt discarded while he worked as magistrate, picked up a jailer's key ring, and led the miscreants to the cell block where they were locked up in adjoining cells.

The arresting officer–judge–jailor then returned to the front office, whistling and jangling his keys.

Instantly the Loretta and Tyrone characters began to bicker, each blaming the other for their incarceration. The bickering became snarling and the snarling escalated into war. At the height of the battle, Tyrone tore off a shoe and hurled it at Loretta. Confounding all logic, it passed through the bars of his cell, through the bars of Loretta's cell, and fell at her feet.

The next morning, Summerville—shambling in to feed his prisoners—stopped short at sight of a male shoe in Loretta's cell. There it lay, damning evidence of conduct unbecoming the jugged.

Moral indignation blazing in his bloodhound's eyes, Slim said, "I cain't figger out how ya done it, BUT DON'T DO IT AGAIN."

On July 4th that year, Helga and I, Leslie Howard, and a beautiful blonde (I think it was Sheilah Graham), plus Lord Donegal spent several days on the *Athene,* anchored at Avalon, Catalina.

Leslie had a theory, on which he liked to expatiate, that water taken internally was lethal. He had tried Scotch and water, bourbon and water, brandy and water with resulting dizziness and violent nausea; in each case *water* was the common factor, so he regarded it as hostile to the human being and took his liquor neat.

I took a different tack to prove Leslie's theory of aquatic malevolence.

The public relations official for the Avalon Water Carnival, spotting me as an outstandingly patriotic citizen with a death wish, approached me with his problem. An aquaplane stunt, involving two speedboats, had been planned as part of the afternoon's entertainment, but one of the aquaplaners had turned up in jail.

Would I replace him?

I had done a few acrobatic didoes on skis, surfboards, and aquaplanes, so I felt adequate, not to say superior, to the job.

I was standing on my head on the board, skimming waves at forty miles an hour, when the other half of our aquaplane team introduced an unrehearsed thriller: The driver cut across our bow and I got caught in the wake.

I bounced, complete with board, about four feet into the air (there was wild applause from the spectators) and came down upon the concrete sea, still rigidly perpendicular.

As from a great distance my ears picked up the sound of male seals locked in tusk-crushing battle.

The *Athene* was moored about three hundred yards from my point of impact; once I had reassumed the horizontal, I set out for home via the sidestroke, because I couldn't raise my head.

I was hauled aboard by friends armed with wisecracks; I was unable to parry, because I had to hold my head on. I found that by directing my eyes straight ahead, and imbibing in a dignified, almost clerical stance, I was able to take on several cups of Irish coffee. That accomplished, I went below to rest on my laurels and a bunk apparently stuffed with rocks.

I endured several days of violent nausea and felt lousy for weeks, but I made light of my accident. I didn't want Helga, on the Bel Air dinner party circuit, reporting my athletic achievement as the greatest marine disaster since the *Titanic*.

About three years later, in the midst of a standard physical checkup, Dr. Marcus Rabwin asked, "When did you break your neck?"

"Never," I said.

"No? According to these x-rays, you're dead."

"Take my word for it, Doc, those x-rays lie."

"Look—one of the vertebrae in your neck has been cleanly fractured. A segment is still wandering around in the trapezius muscle. I think I'll write a paper on it."

I posed for several additional x-rays, so that Dr. Rabwin could astonish his colleagues, topping his presentation with word that the patient was alive, and in what is laughingly called his right mind.

I have told this story only to extol the wonders of the human body, and to warn people against the dangers of associating with water, internally or externally.

25

MY NEXT PIC AT FOX TOOK ME, ONCE AGAIN, TO SEA IN *Slave Ship*.

The script, produced by Nunnally Johnson, was devised to costar Clark Gable, Wallace Beery and Mickey Rooney. Playing Gable against Beery automatically implied a battle of titans.

I was high on *Slave Ship* and about to start shooting when—one noon—I met Darryl Zanuck and his entourage on the sidewalk outside the Cafe de Paris (studio commissary in English).

Zanuck always carried the short weighted handle of a polo mallet which he swung persistently in the conviction that it would strengthen his wrists. Between swings he told me offhandedly, "MGM has crossed us up. We don't get Gable." Swing. Swing.

"Good Lord! What'll we do?"

"We'll shoot the picture, of course."

"With whom?"

Swing. Swing. "With Warner Baxter."

"Against Beery? A duel between 'The Ceesco Keed' and King Kong? They'll laugh us out of McKeesport."

"You have a choice. Warner Baxter or Michael Whalen."

The great Academy-Award-winning director, Norman Taurog, plus several of his buddies, were sitting on the nearby curbing, kibitzing.

Zanuck loved an audience when he was going to pin back a director's ears. (Rhetorical question: Has time changed him?)

I said, "You're giving me a choice between leprosy and Oriental syphilis."

The cheering section, led by Normie, went into the belly laugh of the century.

Thereafter, I was never one of the favored few at Fox. Neither was Normie.

During the filming of *Slave Ship* Warner Baxter and I became good friends; he was a fine actor and a man who could talk about his hobby, chess, with so much excitement that it sounded like sex. Working with him was a gas.

Beery played a different game.

As I've explained, fight sequences need not be brutal as long as raspberry syrup doubles for blood. Yet there have always been realists who regarded raspberry syrup as a copout.

In our script Rooney—The Mick—was cast as the cabin boy. In one sequence, he slipped ashore, hoisted himself onto the first available barstool and ordered a drink.

At that point, Beery—the first mate—swaggered into the bar, slapped the kid around, then lifted him by his lapels and promised him a cracked head if he ever again went into a saloon. This action was intended to clue the audience to Beery's "heart of gold" under all those layers of flab.

Instead of faking the slaps, Beery whacked the kid hard.

I yelled, "Cut!" Mickey slipped off the set and ran to a darkened corner of the stage.

When I caught up with him, a thin trickle of blood was sliding down his chin, and he was trying manfully to suppress tears of rage.

I promised Mickey it wouldn't happen again.

It didn't. While the cameraman was lighting the next setup, I called Beery aside and said, "Look, Wally, every guy on this set and UP IN THOSE CATWALKS, loves that kid. You're awfully good in this part, and I'd hate to lose you because somebody had parted your hair with a sun arc."

Slave Ship proved to be highly successful, but Zanuck never came on his knees, begging me to sign another contract. I'm not downgrading Zanuck as a creative powerhouse, but magnanimity and a sense of the ridiculous were not among his outstanding characteristics when I knew him.

Even the brilliant Jim McGuinness was fired from Fox when Zanuck took over, presumably because Jim had been a friend of the previous Fox landlord, Winfield Sheehan.

As a result, McGuinness (erstwhile of *The New Yorker* magazine under Harold Ross, and originator of the magazine's definitive "Pro-files" department) was unemployed all of ten minutes. MGM snapped him up. Before long he was their script and picture doctor and recognized throughout the industry as the unchallenged master in his field.

Jim had been my closest pal since *China Seas* days. When he heard that I was through at Fox, he telephoned to say, "Congratula-tions on your escape," and told me *his* Zanuck story.

According to Jim, when Zanuck had finished *Young Abe Lincoln,* he began to suffer serious misgivings about the film. He telephoned L. B. Mayer and asked him to come to a sneak preview that evening, and to bring McGuinness.

After the showing, Mayer, Zanuck and McGuinness paused in the foyer. Mayer, vaguely uncomfortable, turned to McGuinness to ask, "Well, Jim, what do you think?"

Jim said forcefully, "Zanuck is a goddam genius."

Zanuck puffed up like a blowfish.

Mayer asked with a straight face, "Why d'ya say that, Jim?"

"Because no other guy on earth could make Lincoln a 'B' presi-dent."

Unlike McGuinness, who had gone from corn pone to caviar, I went to Columbia, which was from hunger to starvation.

No Hollywood saga would be complete without a yarn about the Caliph of Columbia, the autocratic, vindictive, venomous Harry Cohn.

Gregory La Cava and I happened to sign directing contracts at Columbia simultaneously. Together we reported to Cohn's office to meet our new boss.

We cooled our heels for nearly an hour before Cohn's secretary told us, "Mr. Cohn will see you now." No one had gone in or out of the private office while we had been kept waiting.

When we entered the Presence, he was tipped back in his chair, his feet on the desk, his hat on the back of his head, and one of his monstrous cigars aggressively uptilted from the corner of his mouth. A squawk box on the side of his desk was a hot line to Santa Anita, where the third race was about to be run.

Cohn glared at us as if we had trooped, uninvited, into the sanctum. Around his cigar he demanded, "Can't you see I'm busy?"

As we had been ORDERED to report, we recognized this as Ploy One in the Cohn roster of intimidations. Cohn gave his attention to the race. When it ended he invoked forty kinds of hellfire on horse and jockey, because they had cost him a bundle.

When Harry, the Whip, ran out of breath, La Cava suggested that we return another day when Mr. Cohn had time for us.

Cohn turned up his volume and started again. His dialogue went something like, "If you guys are gonna work for me, you gotta get one thing straight. I'm the boss around here, and the ONLY boss. What I say, goes. I own this studio, and I run it to suit myself. Nobody on earth tells ME what to do. I don't give a good goddam for anybody in this town. I don't kowtow to nobody; if there's any kowtowing done, it's gonna be to ME . . ."

The intercom buzzed and Cohn's secretary said, "Mr. L. B. Mayer calling Mr. Cohn."

Harry removed his hat from his head, his feet from the desk, and the cigar from his mouth. He smoothed his hair, adjusted his tie, buttoned his coat, then lifted the telephone from its cradle and crooned in honeyed tones, "HELLO, L. B."

My first Columbia picture was to be a B. P. Schulberg production entitled *She Couldn't Take It,* starring George Raft, Joan Bennett, and Walter Connolly.

It was planned as a "comeback" vehicle for the talented Schulberg, the deposed monarch of the Famous Players-Lasky outfit. (Mr. Schulberg was the father of the novelist, Budd Schulberg.)

My feet were still damp on the job (and the same condition prevailed behind my ears) when I discovered that I had landed in the middle of a feud between Schulberg and Cohn. I've never been able to figure out whether I was put in to knock off Schulberg or vice versa. It worked both ways, which also may have been the play.

Considering Mr. Cohn's fast footwork, it should be recorded that he was once a hoofer in fifth-rate vaudeville houses of the Gus Sonne Time.

In those days Harry had a roommate who, unlike flat-footed Cohn, worked with fair regularity, and who practiced the share-and-share-alike principle, so Cohn lost no weight when unemployed—which was frequently.

Unfortunately, the day came when the roommate found himself at liberty. He had no savings because of his generosity, but he did have confidence in Harry.

That gentleman, contemplating sudden famine, got a job. On pay-day Harry came home with SIX lemon pies. Total groceries. The roommate groaned, "Harry, you know damned well that the one thing in this world I can't eat is lemon pie."

Smacking his lips, Cohn mumbled, "If you're hungry enough, you'll eat lemon pie."

The picture I made for Columbia was not exactly lemon pie, but I emerged with two substantial goodies: warm friendships with Joan Bennett and George Raft.

Errol Flynn's public image remains that of Hollywood's most enduring and bountifully endowed Don Juan; however, while Flynn was collecting the reputation, George Raft was quietly getting the job done.

George's marital situation was equivocal; long separated from his wife, George was unable to get a divorce under New York laws, and his wife refused to institute proceedings because of religious convictions.

In spite of his unavailability as a husband, George seldom looked at a girl without getting a subliminal "Go!" A discreet man, he never alluded to his successes; *that* news was usually broadcast by the girls themselves, unable to forego praise for the best snake in Eden.

Men, sometimes suspicious of Raft's dark good looks, were disarmed and won over after a few minutes of easy conversation. He wasn't out to prove a thing. Also, George was both admired and envied for an additional asset sometimes described as "a baby's arm with an apple in its hand."

There was a certain amount of talk around Hollywood at one time that Raft had been involved in the rackets. However, as nearly as I could make out, the scuttlebutt got started because Raft was once Tex Guinan's bouncer.

There were some rough customers around in those days, and drinking bootleg likker seldom civilized them. Raft had a system: he made it his business to know which was the heavyweight in every

crowd. If it became necessary to bounce a covey of gun-toting customers, George approached their big man and suggested softly that
closing time had arrived, displaying—flat in his palm—a .32 automatic pistol.

Invariably the overlord would grin at the undersized weapon and
ask, "Whatcha gonna do with that, sonny?"

George's instant answer was to slam the gun, with all possible
force, against the side of the recalcitrant's head, a procedure much
like slamming the barn door on a rat. It discouraged further conversation. George was never obliged to aim or fire his minicannon.

Being Irish, I've always cherished great respect for a guy canny
enough to win a fight without turning the scenery into the local
trash dump.

This story has been told before, but it bears repeating. In the
Sixties, George—like many other picture people—ran afoul of the
Collector of Internal Revenue. Raft's situation was desperate.

On one of his darkest mornings, George received a note from
Frank Sinatra saying, in general, "Use whatever you need." It was
accompanied by a check on which only one line had been filled in:
the signature of Frank Sinatra.

Some guys, hearing from Santa Claus midyear, would have kept
it secret. Not George. With tears in his eyes, he showed the check to
almost everyone he met for a week. Possibly the widespread Word
caused Frank some embarrassment, but a rose spotlight is mighty
becoming to the Good Guys.

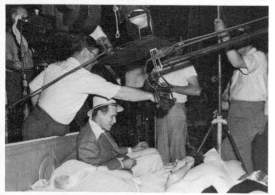

Left column, top to bottom:
Dear old C. Aubrey Smith had a birthday on the set of ETERNALLY YOURS, so I ordered a cake which he shared with Loretta Young and Broderick Crawford. If Brod saved his necktie, he could get good money for it on the Sunset Strip these days.

Advantage of being a director is that you tell *other people* what to do to achieve dramatic impact. Here I'm showing David Niven where I want him to land after a parachute jump executed for ETERNALLY YOURS. He made it okay.

Another proof of the unlikelihood of hanky-panky on a film set, no matter how great the temptation. Loretta Young, relaxing in preparation for a closeup during ETERNALLY YOURS, kids her director.

Billie and Aubrey and Brod and Loretta in ETERNALLY YOURS, during a tea break. Surnames: Burke, Smith, Crawford and Young.
Top right:
Here I'm teaching Pat O'Brien the underhand stroke in tatting, I think. If I'd known that our neat little whodunit was to be released as SLIGHTLY HONORABLE instead of under its original title, SEND ANOTHER COFFIN, I would have been teaching him to make Molotov cocktails. Others innocently involved were Edward Arnold, Eve Arden, and Brod Crawford.

Top left:
Here we are, on an ice boat, Loretta Young, David Niven, and I, for ETERNALLY YOURS. Note that I've forsaken my cane in favor of a hunting stick. Real swank, and handy besides.
Bottom left:
Aline MacMahon and Frank McHugh in a scene from ONE WAY PASSAGE.
Right column, top to bottom:
Kay Francis and William Powell emptying glasses before the ritual of breaking them in ONE WAY PASSAGE (Warner Brothers).

Lew Ayres and Maureen O'Sullivan in a bad moment from O. K. AMERICA (Universal).

Lew Ayres and Edward Arnold in O. K. AMER- ICA.

Pat O'Brien and a supporting player (whose name escapes me) in DESTINATION UN- KNOWN (Universal).

Top left:
Yours truly explaining scene to Alan Hale and cast in DESTINATION UNKNOWN.

Top right:
Clark Gable in a low moment, comforted by Jean Harlow in SLAVE SHIP (Fox).

Bottom right:
George Sanders, with monocle, failed to see eye-to-eye with Wallace Beery in SLAVE SHIP.

Middle:
Pat O'Brien, Eve Arden, and Phyllis Brooks in SLIGHTLY HONORABLE. How about that hat!

Bottom left:
Pat O'Brien fights Mother Bell; Eve Arden takes up hairdressing; and Broderick Crawford destroys music in SLIGHTLY HONORABLE (United Artists).

top left:
David Niven and Loretta Young in gentle clinch for ETERNALLY YOURS (United Artists).

top right:
The utterly lovely Martha Scott in CHEERS FOR MISS BISHOP (United Artists).

bottom left:
Greer Garson, as MRS. PARKINGTON, extols the virtues of her cane over mine (MGM).

middle:
Jean Pierre Aumont, Gene Kelly, Hume Cronyn, Wallace Ford, and Joseph Calleia decide who's going to do what in CROSS OF LORRAINE (MGM).

bottom right:
Greer Garson, Jessica Tandy, and Gregory Peck in a triangular moment from THE VALLEY OF DECISION (MGM).

26

AFTER WORKING EVERY WEEKEND FOR SEVERAL MONTHS—USUALLY aboard the *Athene* when we were at anchor in Catalina—I finished the script for *Trade Winds.*

With the script ready to go, all I needed was to find somebody interested in going with it.

For once in my life, I fell into a bed of shamrocks. Walter Wanger had set up a full staff and was ready to roll on a film at United Artists when the Breen office (formerly the Hays office, and now the Valenti office) had refused to okay it. Walter was stuck with heavy overhead.

Myron Selznick, whose business it was to know what was going on, sold Walter a complete package: me, the script, Fredric March for the starring role, Joan Bennett for leading lady, and Ralph Bellamy for a character-comedy role.

We still needed a character comedienne.

Freddie March said one day, "Florence has an idea for the comedienne's role. Now, don't laugh. I've learned, through the years, to take Florence's hunches seriously." (Florence was and is Mrs. Fredric March, Florence Eldridge, a star and a helluvan actress in her own right.)

After the big buildup, I waited dubiously.

Freddie went on, "Florence says she has seen this girl do comedy, and she's magnificent. Her name is Ann Sothern."

"The queen of the B's?" I said, but the more I thought about it, the better I liked it.

We sent the script to Ann, who brought it back personally, and said, "I like the role, but there's one thing that bothers me. I've never played a drunk. I'm not sure I could."

"That problem you can leave to me," I told her, a statement that should have given me something to think about right then, but my attention was on the picture.

Walter Wanger proved to be an excellent partner; he and I got along fine. He was a handsome man in a Marlboro way, a charmer born in San Francisco of a wealthy banking family. He had taken his degree at Dartmouth, an experience that had failed to ruin him.

When I first met Walter, he was newly a free man, having been divorced by Justine Johnston; although we didn't suspect it, he was not long fated to enjoy bachelor bliss, largely as a result of *Trade Winds.*

In addition to serving as a springboard for a celebrated romance, *Trade Winds* was unique in that it involved more process photography than any film before or since, with the possible exception of *Around the World in Eighty Days.*

The critics have always been kind to me, and in the instance of *Trade Winds,* they wrote as if they were doubling for my mother. The picture was a smash, and it delivered some fine fringe benefits.

The *Jeanie* character, a lightheaded, softhearted dizzy babe, was played to the hilt by Ann Sothern.

Several months after the film's release, I was working at my desk at U. A. when a blonde blur burst through the open door, body-surfed across my desk, and landed in my lap, wiping out the two of us onto the floor.

I had my arms full of glorious girl, but she was giggling, which unnerved me. "What the hell goes on?" I managed to say.

Kiss on the forehead. Kiss on the cheek. Kiss on the chin. "Oh, Tay! You'll never guess! You've done it this time—you've really done it. MGM has stolen your *Jeanie* character right out of *Trade Winds* and they're going to build a series around her for ME. They're going to call her *Maizie,*" chortled Miss Sothern.

And they did.

The next Wanger–Garnett opus was a Ben Ames Williams story improved completely out of its original shape by Towne and Baker. Granted, they *did* keep the original title: *Stand-In.*

We signed a fine cast: Joan Blondell, Leslie Howard, Humphrey Bogart, Gregory Ratoff, and Jack Carson.

As I've mentioned earlier, his role in *Stand-In* was Bogie's first sympathetic part and catapulted him straight into the arms of Ingrid Bergman, Katharine Hepburn, and Lauren Bacall (for real).

Leslie Howard, destined to reach his zenith as *Ashley Wilkes* in *Gone With the Wind,* and to meet his death through enemy action during World War II, was a delightful guy, a talented actor, and—at the time of *Stand-In*—a double-dedicated shutterbug.

We'd get set up for a shot and the assistant director would start yelling for Mr. Howard.

From the rafters seventy-five feet above the stage's concrete floor would come a cordial, although belated, "Yes, old boy?"

"We're ready to shoot," the A. D. would announce as if it were a big surprise.

"Half a mo', please," and Leslie's Leica would snap, snap, snap. He shot enough footage from precarious positions to have put together a second feature entitled, *Lloyds of London Blows Its Cool.* That foolhardy company was betting there would be no casualties among our troupe during the picture's production.

Joan Blondell, an important star then as now, was on loanout from Warner Brothers, as was Bogie. The result was that the roster of Warner stars frequently visited our set. In those days, picture making was fraternal, somewhat like college days with everyone plotting against the faculty, in this case *Les Freres Warner.*

One of our frequent callers was Jimmie Cagney, who always looked Joan over carefully. "For signs of a recurrence," he kidded. The background of the inside joke was this: About a year before Joan went to work with us in *Stand-In* she had been doing a film on the WB lot. Cagney, visiting almost every day, noted a new Blondell mannerism: She had been batting her naturally long eyelashes furiously.

"What's with the eyes? Some new character bit?" he asked.

"I just can't keep 'em open," Joan had confided. "Between the lights and the long hours, I can scarcely see. I've now been under contract to this studio for twenty-seven months, and I've made thirty-two pictures. I've been starred in all but the first film, which means I've been in almost every scene every day for over two years. Friend, I'm *beat!*"

Jimmie checked Joan's forehead and almost blistered his hand.

A peaceable man in his own concerns, Cagney can be a seven-foot tiger in behalf of a friend. He made so much noise that the studio doctor was called. After a quick examination, the doctor ordered an ambulance, and Joan was hauled to the hospital for emergency surgery: Her appendix had ruptured.

She was still groggy from anesthetic when her bedside telephone rang. A nurse answered, explaining to the studio representative that Miss Blondell would remain in the hospital for about two weeks, then would be obliged to recuperate at home for an additional two or three weeks. The sound on the other end of the wire was roughly that of a dock riot, unexpurgated.

Three days later, by some Warner magic, Joan was released from the hospital, ambulanced home and stretchered into her own bedroom, where she was to be attended by a private nurse.

Joan stared incredulously at surroundings which should have been familiar, yet were merely reminiscent in a vague sort of way. Giving up the puzzle, she went to sleep.

During Joan's three days in the hospital, studio workmen had repapered, repainted, redraped, and refurnished Joan's bedroom— even blocking out a large picture window—so as to duplicate the set on which she had been working when she became ill.

That transformation accomplished, director Mike Curtiz and a full crew barged in to film the final scenes of Joan's picture, while Joan recovered. Slowly.

When Cagney visited *Stand-In* one noon, about a year after Joan's hospitalization, Joan asked, "Well, Pally, what are you going to do with an entire afternoon all to yourself, seeing as how you finished a fillum this morning?"

"Start *another* picture at 2 P.M.," growled Jimmie. "Nowadays, whenever I have to go to the john, they pan me all the way to the W. C. and all the way back. Only because I'm prudish is the cameraman stopped at the door." ("Pan" is a picture term for a moving shot in which the camera swings with an actor in walking or traveling sequences. A pan shot is made possible by what is called a "free head," that is, it allows the camera to swing and photograph in any direction. Any questions?)

Another favorite Blondell story resulted from our making what are called "wardrobe tests," i.e. photographing a star's clothing in advance of actual filming to be sure the stripes don't jump off the screen or the earrings don't look like skillets hung out to dry.

One afternoon Joan was posing in a clinging satin gown that outlined her voluptuous curves like a wet-suit. She looked to be no more than a devastating seventeen.

The camera operator, ogling Joan through the lens to the extent that he was unaware of anyone else on earth, muttered softly, "Jeez, I wish she was pregnant and I was in the klink for it."

Out of sequence I want to tell another yarn about Joan. Several years after *Stand-In,* we worked together on an episode of *Bonanza.*

She came on the set one morning with her left cheek swollen halfway to Denver.

"I'm okay," she insisted, when I asked what door she had run into. "It's just this tooth—and all the aspirin I've taken."

I insisted on her seeing a dentist at once. She protested but finally agreed grudgingly.

She was back an hour later, short one tooth, but determined to finish the day's work. The crew, who always loved Joan, went around shaking their heads and murmuring the ultimate show biz compliment, "What a trouper!"

She deserved the accolade, because the last scene of the day required her to drive a team of horses at warp speed over a washboard road and across a stubble field right up to the camera, so the ride couldn't be "doubled." By that time most of the dentist's sedative had worn off, so every jolt was agony. Add to that the unchangeable fact that Joan loathes horses—very few broncs grazing near the theatrical trunk in which Joan was born.

As our gutty heroine left for the day, I tried to thank her. Out of the healthy side of her mouth she riposted with, "Forget it. I only did what ANY idiot of an actress would do for her career." Even her laugh was lopsided.

Back to *Stand-In.* Another visitor to our set was Akim Tamiroff (AhKEEM TAMiroff) who was a buddy of Gregory Ratoff's. After introducing us, Ratoff told me sincerely, "AhKEEM ees vun hail of en ektor; almoost es gude es I am, he ees. Eggseptink he's got thees gawd-avvul eggsent."

Somewhat later, when Ratoff was a director and producer at Fox, the word went around that Ratoff played gin rummy regularly with Zanuck, and usually took a terrific creaming.

When I ran into him one day at the Brown Derby, I asked, "What's the scoop on the rummy sessions?"

"So a leetle friendly cod game, wot's de difference? Ven I am owing a man money, vell de man is vanting, very personal, I should keep vorking," explained the crazy fox.

I knew *Stand-In* was a solid smash when I drove onto the lot one morning and the officer at the gate touched his cap and said, "Let me park your car, sir. Probably you've got a lot on your mind."

Still in partnership with Walter Wanger, I was enthusiastic about No. 3 on our schedule, *Eternally Yours,* also laughed onto paper by Towne and Baker. We had an impeccable cast: Loretta Young, David Niven, Broderick Crawford, Billie Burke, and C. Aubrey Smith.

Eternally Yours dealt, more or less hilariously, with the conjugal problems of a girl married to a vaudevillian, a traveling escape artist in the Houdini image. I remember that in one sequence, David was nailed in a weighted coffin and dropped into a bay. His responsibility was to continue breathing until he could develop gills or kick his way out. In another, he jumped out of a plane wearing a straitjacket which somewhat hampered his pulling the parachute's release toggle.

For his wife, Loretta, life was just one laugh after another.

During the shooting of *Eternally,* David was working Sundays on the Kraft Music Hall radio show. Sam Goldwyn (who had David under exclusive FILM contract) insisted upon collecting half of David's RADIO pay.

David considered Sam's demand unsporting; even so, David sent a check regularly to Goldwyn for half the weekly take. On one occasion, Kraft sent a huge basket of their (and allied) products to David. Meticulously, David cut each bar of cheese, each can of sardines, each box of crackers, and even the basket itself in HALF. He packed Goldwyn's share neatly, and dispatched the melange by special messenger to Sam.

When World War II was declared, David explained to Goldwyn

that an Englishman's place was with his old regiment. "I'm going home," he said.

Said Sam, "David, you're a noble boy. I'll never forget you, and for your patriotism you should be proud. BUT YOU'RE NOT LEAVING HOLLYWOOD."

David replied, hamming it up, "Visualize me, Sam, going over the top and yelling, 'Come on, Lads, for God, King, and Sam Goldwyn!' "

And he went.

During the filming of *Eternally Yours,* Broderick Crawford and Niven became buddies; when the picture was completed, they went to New York together for some excellent, if nebulous, reason.

Supported by the bar at "21," David was accosted by an undersized citizen who observed, "I BEG your pardon."

Niven, parting lip from glass, responded, "Yes, chum?"

"Aren't you David Niven?"

"I am, indeed."

The little man stepped back one pace, calculated distance, and delivered a roundhouse punch that knocked Niven flat on his wallet.

Crawford, having played the situation in many movies, knew his lines perfectly. "You can't do that to him. He's with ME," he roared.

Whereupon, Mr. Half Pint also flattened Crawford's wallet.

Brod tells that one on himself, and adds a yarn about his experience as an Army judo instructor during World War II. He had illustrated a number of techniques when he noticed one member of the class wearing an expression that read from left to right, "You gotta be kidding."

Said Brod, "Think you can do any better?"

"Yes, Sir," said the student.

"Okay, take ME," suggested Brod.

The recruit obeyed the order implicitly: He broke Brod's right collarbone.

With *Eternally Yours* on marquees and doing great business, Wanger and I bought the rights to a book entitled, *Send Another Coffin.* My pal, Ken England, sweated out a very funny script with a fresh, flippant, sophisticated approach to the standard murder mystery.

Actually, Ken's treatment was several years ahead of its time; so far ahead, in fact, that a few years later the approach was adopted at MGM and designated as *The Thin Man* pattern. Bill Powell and gorgeous Myrna Loy (now as then) made movie history as Nick and Nora Charles.

Our cast for *Coffin* was made to order for that sort of lighthearted homicide: Eve Arden, Pat O'Brien, Broderick Crawford (he was habit-forming) and Alan Dinehart.

Everything seemed to click; we finished well ahead of schedule and budget—which should have warned me.

With a feeling of "Well Done," I humored myself and went to bed with a ten-Kleenex case of flu. Wanger agreed to finish off the final odds and ends of the picture while I decided whether to live or go the easy way.

Possibly Walter made his promise to me in a daze, because he was getting ready to elope with Joan Bennett, a situation likely to upset any man's equilibrium.

By the time they were honeymooning, I had dried eyes and nose well enough to take Helga to the San Francisco premiere of *Send Another Coffin*. Pat O'Brien and Brod went along to make a personal appearance, a plan that always hypos the box office.

The film had been booked into a theatre whose owner I liked and respected as a perceptive showman. As we strolled across the lobby, he met me, his eyes blazing. He had prescreened the picture that afternoon.

"You dirty double-crossing s. o. b.," he said, touching all bases. "I bought this picture as *Send Another Coffin*. What in hell was the idea of changing the title to *Slightly Honorable?* That won't sell matinee ticket No. 1."

I stood there with my chin resting on my second shirt button. "I don't know what you're talking about," was all I could say, remembering that several years earlier there had been a Broadway play, followed by a successful film entitled *Strictly Dishonorable*. It had been a comedy-drama light years removed from our sophisticated whodunit.

The theatre owner showed us to the cheap seats, growling, "You'll know what I'm talking about after you've taken a look at your own private disaster."

[227]

What we saw was a badly mutilated, un-funny comedy. It had been cut with a jigsaw and reassembled with a Mixmaster. It was AWFUL.

One hundred and fifty prints had been made and were en route to theatres; one hundred and fifty catastrophes bearing *my* name as director.

My fever went to 103, and my temper burned a hole through the steel roof of Southern Pacific's crack "Daylight" as we rattled south the next morning. By the time we had taxied home, I had enough pneumonia to have started a national trend.

I was sick; I was furious. I should have ordered Helga to bind and gag me for two weeks, at which time I could have handled the situation sensibly. As it was, I telephoned Walter and outlined my feelings in detail, beginning, "Look here, you sneaky, double-crossing sonavabitch . . ." From there on, the conversation became personal.

I realized exactly how bad *Slightly Honorable* must be when the officer at the United Artists' gate (the man who had been parking my car) asked me for identification one morning.

It was many years before Wanger and I agreed to settle for a draw. Thank the Lord or Mack Sennett, or whomever was responsible for our reconciliation before Walter took the long count.

27

CENSORSHIP HAS ALWAYS BEEN A MAJOR HOLLYWOOD HANGUP. WHEN I first began to write, direct and produce, we even put pants on a Pekinese if there was any chance he might wander, naked, into camera range. That was in the days before the Swedes boiled over, filling the art houses with steam and paying audiences.

One of the worst examples of the horrors of censorship came to my notice while I was still writing for Ben Turpin, Stan Laurel, etc. Marshall (Mickey) Nielan was directing a drama in which the burly villain was supposed to lure the innocent heroine to a forest cabin, and—in the euphemism of the day—"have his way with her." Mickey was informed by the Hays office that he could show the villain chasing the girl around a table in the cabin—cut. End of scene.

Mickey accepted the challenge with a fiendish grin that should have warned the censor. Mickey had his cameraman dolly in on a dainty, daisy-picking girl of about eight, who was wandering through the trees; she spotted the cabin and tiptoed up to peer through the window. Her horrified reaction was held for a long, ghastly closeup, after which she went stumbling through the forest, screaming hysterically.

It was one of the most shocking connotive scenes ever made, but the audience didn't actually SEE anything, which made it kosher.

Years later, I—as a director—met up with censorship in one of its more virulent forms when I submitted Towne and Baker's delightful script, *Joy of Loving,* to the Hays office.

Those watchdogs in behalf of public morals explained icily that, to avoid corrupting the young, there must be no exploitation of the joy of loving. Loving was conjugal duty, involving a possible nod from the stork. All strictly business, and joy be damned.

Our title was mandatorily changed to *Joy of Living,* which is a gas if one accepts the Hays office premise that one may experience the joy of living, *only* if one avoids the joy of loving.

Philosophy aside, we had a tremendous cast: Irene Dunne, Douglas Fairbanks, Jr., Billie Burke, and Alan Mowbray. Music by Jerome Kern, and lyrics by Dorothy Field.

On the initial day of shooting I met Doug Fairbanks for the first time since the cavalry invasion of Scotland. He failed to mention it. So did I.

When *Joy of Living* was cut, scored, previewed and dispatched to a waiting world, Helga and I decided we were entitled to a vacation. Nothing platinum—just a breath of non-Hollywood air.

"I've always wanted to see the Cathedral in Mexico City," Helga ventured.

In those days before instant air transportation, the highway between the California border and Mexico's sky-hung capital had changed little since Father Junipero Serra had elected to walk. Thinking that a second man in the party might prove useful, I invited Schwegler to come along. Schweg, a Magellan at heart, cast all good sense aside and joyously jumped at the chance.

The trip was "uneventful," unless you count four flat tires, a ruptured fan belt, and no Spanish except *cerveza,* a beverage that anesthetized us between quandaries. (Quandaries are small Mexican towns consisting of one burro, seven chickens, half an acre of corn, and a garage in which no English is spoken.)

Mexico City, in our opinion, had a luminous evanescence implying that it might disappear at any moment. Even the Cathedral was slowly sinking into the swamp on which the city was built. My treasured silver cigarette case, encrusted with gemstones from our trip on the *Athene,* and engraved with the signatures of each of the stars with whom I had worked, simply vanished. One moment it was safe in the glove compartment, and the next—thin air. At that altitude, air is VERY thin; anything of value, short of a red-hot stove, is prone to dematerialize.

Helga had scarcely recovered from the *turista,* when someone at the Hotel told her that one hadn't *seen* Mexico until one had visited

Veracruz. Naturally, having come that far, Helga wanted to *see* Mexico, so we painted "Veracruz or Bust" on our luggage.

Schwegler, whose Magellan enthusiasm had been quenched by tequila hangovers, agreed to take our car home, and scattered sand northward at a speed that disregarded the Scotch-taped fan belt. We learned later that he made it to Los Angeles with only minor disasters en route, none of which concerned the fan belt.

Foolhardy in our optimism—traditional among world travelers— Helga and I boarded a TRAIN. It set out with a noisy braggadocio that lasted about twenty minutes before wheezing to a gasping stop.

Being one of the world's few Instant Locomotive Engineers, I felt obliged to lend assistance. The situation was worse than I had anticipated: there was hole in the steam line.

Standing clear, I ruminated on the probable distance to the nearest donkey market, and wondered how best to break the news to Helga, who sometimes lacked a certain sense of high adventure.

I was still working on an approach pattern when the fireman emerged from the jungle, pausing only to empty his bladder. In his unoccupied hand he held aloft a wooden plug carved out of an old log, and announced to the flabbergasted passengers, "Mira! Engine she ees fix!"

He and the engineer pounded the plug into the hole in the metal tube, assuring me with gestures that the steam would expand the plug to form an effective seal.

It worked.

Agog over the resourcefulness of the primitive, I hastened back to our dusty seat to share my wonder with Helga. She managed to restrain her enthusiasm.

When, at length, we looked upon the harbor of Veracruz, I told my strangely silent wife, "We should have made this trip on the *Athene*."

"Or on *The Spirit of St. Louis*," she responded in a monotone.

Subtle, but I knew what she meant: Veracruz, in the late thirties, was the resort that God, and all subordinate beings, had forgotten.

"What we should do," I ventured, still selling, "is go to Europe."

"How?"

It was a fair question. After an optimistic use of Helga's French, we learned that no cruise ships bound for Europe made regular calls at Veracruz. BUT, the clerk at our hotel admitted that a small steamship, bound for Havana, would put into port the next day. Si, he could sell us two first-class tickets.

Repeatedly, through that long Veracruz night, I assured Helga— each time she returned, whimpering, from the W. C.—that Havana would be positively swarming with ships freshly through the Panama Canal and bound for London. Inspired by tequila, I even decided that we wouldn't grab the *first* available boat, unless it delighted us completely. We might stay in Havana for several days until we could get exactly the accommodations we wanted.

Her whimper increased to gale force sobbing.

In Havana we had little trouble learning that there were NO ships from the Canal headed anywhere. We did break the language barrier enough to gather that, by taking a flying-boat to Port de France on Martinique, we could catch a French Line cruise ship bound for Marseille.

We took the flying-boat; occasionally it attained an altitude of maybe five hundred feet, coughing agonizingly every few seconds, but mostly the porpoises were leaping over us. In order to relax my crossed fingers, I gestured grandly and congratulated us upon our luck. Martinique was a name that had always intrigued me: steel bands; darkly romantic men and women in vivid costumes; moonlight on a coral lagoon—experiences valuable to a film director.

Forget it.

Also, forget the solemn assurances of the travel experts in Havana. The French Liner *Cuba* was not due for THREE days.

Lacking an alternative, we took "accommodations" in the eight-room hotel that was Port de France's version of the Waldorf. In order to be seated in the three-table dining room, we were obliged to shoo off a nesting hen. The resultant egg was greeted with cries of joy by the staff and hurried to the kitchen to provide Helga's omelet, which she couldn't eat, being averse to meeting her food socially before consuming it.

We discovered that there were three sources of entertainment in Port de France, in addition to chicken-shooing and egg-harvesting. The most popular was exploding the population. Second in appeal were the cock fights, which sent Helga and me back to the hotel on the verge of nausea. The third diversion was swimming, enjoyed exclusively by sharks.

When it eventually arrived, the French Line's *Cuba* looked like heaven with a Parisian accent. Helga instantly asked the room steward for a deck plan, so as to memorize the location of the *Cuba*'s emergency W. C.s.

After our first aperitif, Helga's complexion brightened from pale green to pale pink, and we began to exchange polite, if brief, courtesies; by nightfall, after a magnificent dinner polished off with a few beakers of Napoleon, we were acting like old friends.

Within two days the Napoleon had even subdued Helga's visceral irresponsibility along with a cherished secret plan to murder the motion picture director most conveniently at hand.

We docked in Marseille and caught the "Blue Train" for Paris.

Helga spent several days shopping—what else?—an activity that freed me to call Joan.

That marvelous voice lilted over the wire, "Oh, Tay-ee! Tell me how you happen to be in Paris. We *must* get together. You'll want to see Henri—he will insist upon it. You really made your mark in that area."

I hesitated. "You see—well, Helga thinks you're my cousin."

She chuckled. "Fine. That makes a kiss a family matter. How soon could you be here this evening?"

"Like six?"

"Like six. Be seeing you, Tay-ee."

After hanging up, I realized that the mere sound of her voice turned back my personal calendar. Ponce de Leon had been looking in the wrong places for the fountain of youth.

Helga was delighted by Joan's invitation. I suggested, "Wear that blue dress," and she batted her long eyelashes at me.

Joan met us at the door, extending her hand to Helga, then lifting her cheek to my kiss.

After that I performed the introductions—a little late in the program—and Helga, laughing gently—murmured, "So you're Tay's long-lost cousin. I must say you both come from a handsome family."

While Joan was trying to field that one, Helga added, "Don't let it bother you, Joan. I have a fascinating cousin or two whom Tay's never met."

[233]

At that the two women met one another's eyes squarely and both began to laugh.

I'll never understand women, but I was as thankful for the congenial atmosphere as I was bewildered by it.

Joan took us upstairs to see Henri. It was obvious that he was seriously ill yet was refusing to let it interfere with his grace or his cognac.

When Henri observed that Joan remained too much in the house, and needed fresh air, I persuaded her to join Helga and me at Fouquet's for dinner.

The girls had become friends by the time we had finished our aperitifs; they became bosom buddies over the onion soup, and by the time we had finished the sole meuniere, I had been relegated to the status of an acquaintance vaguely remembered.

While I was being largely ignored, I had time to discover that the years had not diluted the elation I felt at being with Joan.

As Helga and I were taxiing to our hotel, after having taken Joan home, I tossed out a question, "She's lovely, isn't she?"

"Absolutely charming," Helga said warmly.

"There'll never be anyone more beautiful."

Helga nodded. Tipping her head to one side, she considered a moment, then murmured sincerely, "She must have been *very* beautiful."

To me, Joan had not changed. True, her hair was showing a touch of gray. There were worry lines across her forehead, and smile marks radiated from her eyes. Still, she couldn't look over twenty-seven—thirtyish.

"Why so quiet?" Helga asked suddenly.

I hadn't realized that I *was* quiet. I had been thinking only that San Diego, my house in Laurel Canyon (which Helga hated), and the days with Joan during my first visit to Paris meant something to me that couldn't be explained or shared with anyone.

At that moment Helga's hand covered mine. "She IS beautiful. Very beautiful," Helga said.

On to Berlin. I wanted to find out what had happened to that lovely city since my *S. O. S. Iceberg* days.

I telephoned Major General Ernst Udet at the Air Ministry.

"Tay!" he shouted. "Where are you?"

"At the Eden Hotel."

"Don't move. I'll be there in seven minutes."

At the end of six minutes I heard sirens screeching to a halt in front of the hotel. In the midst of a twelve-motorcycle escort, a Bavarian hot rod discharged my resplendently uniformed pal, Ernst.

I was halfway across the lobby when he spotted me, grabbed me in a bear hug, and kissed me on both cheeks, a greeting inherited, no doubt, from his French father. Arms around each other, we rode the elevator to our floor, and—still entwined—were ushered by fawning hotel employees to our suite. I realized that the servitor who asked, "What may I have the honor of bringing you to drink?" was the hotel manager himself.

Upon meeting Helga for the first time, Ernst exclaimed, "Ma blonde superbe!" and covered her face with kisses. Leering over her shoulder at me, he announced, "She is much too much woman to waste on you."

I explained to Helga, "He's just getting even. That's exactly what I said to *his* wife the first time I met her."

On that cozy note, Ernst insisted that we three have dinner at Horcher's that evening. Frau Udet was visiting friends in Paris.

At that time Horcher's was the smartest and most ambient of Berlin's many superb restaurants. The wealth and beauty of Europe were often gathered in its dining rooms and gradually it became the favorite haunt of Nazi big shots. (Shortly before World War II ended, the Horcher's enterprise was moved to Madrid where it is again justly famed.)

After cognac that evening Helga asked to be excused. We dropped her at the Eden, and Ernst dismissed his car so that we could walk and talk in privacy.

As background material, I should mention that Udet was half-French, half-German, and had been eighteen years old when World War I broke out. He became one of the youngest members of Baron Manfried von Richthofen's Flying Circus, and was credited with shooting down sixty-two Allied planes.

In 1919, Udet went back to designing, manufacturing, and testing pleasure aircraft, which were intended only for private use (in strict accordance with the Versailles Treaty). Although Udet was totally uninterested in politics, he and Goering—who had been his Squadron Leader—remained close friends.

My own flying experience was undoubtedly one of the reasons for the instant rapport between Udet and me. Now and then during our association I paused to contemplate the mysteries of time and place. Here we were, Udet and I, buddies. Had I been a few years older so as to have been shipped overseas before the war ended, Udet might well have shot me out of the sky over France. Or vice versa, if I'd lived on a diet of four-leaf clovers.

As Hitler had gained power during the Thirties, prominent Germans were pressured to join the Nazi party, and "German War Heroes" (who were permitted to wear a distinctive armband on civilian jackets) were urged to return to uniform. Udet was the product of a cultured traditionalism; his contempt for Hitler was unbounded, as indicated by the story he told me to explain his wearing the uniform of a major general in the Luftwaffe.

Several months earlier, while still a civilian, he had made plans to seek asylum in France (where he had been educated). He souped up an experimental plane he had originally built for exhibition flying. He knew he would need all the money he could get, but neither he nor his money could be removed from Germany legally. So, whenever he thought it prudent, Udet would draw several thousand marks from his bank account and go out on the town.

In one night he'd hit half the bars on the Kurfurstendam, and in each he'd toss handfuls of fresh reichmarks to squealing barmaids, and watch them scramble for the loot. However, for every hundred marks he squandered, he managed to save twice that amount. He sewed the currency in the lining of civvies and wadded the clothing in the tail of his aircraft.

His shakedown flights consisted of circling while performing various exhibition stunts carefully calculated to attract so much attention that no one could suspect him of furtive intent. Each day the stunting circles widened. Finally Udet was ready.

Taking off early one morning, he had circled to within a few miles of the French border when he was buzzed by a squadron of Nazi fighters. He was forced to land in a fallow field.

He was informed that he had been under SS surveillance for

months; even the hiding place of his getaway stake had been discovered. He was placed under military arrest.

The arresting officer, a young flight lieutenant, was deeply embarrassed at having to take a national hero into custody. When, under his breath, he apologized and asked Udet if there was anything he could do, Ernst said, "Get to Goering." (Goering was in Munich at that moment, a fact unknown to Ernst.)

Udet was flown back to the Air Ministry where he was marched the length of the courtroom. Its vast longitude was terminated by a raised dais on which the judge's massive bench was placed. Behind it rose a gigantic slab of marble inlaid with an enormous onyx *Hakenkreuz.*

(Later, during our visit, Udet showed me that appalling room.)

The SS judge, awaiting Udet, muttered the charge, found Udet guilty, and added, "You are hereby sentenced to be executed at once."

Udet was goose-stepped into the building's open quadrangle and placed against a bullet-pocked wall. He was offered a blindfold, which he rejected, and a cigarette, which he accepted. He smoked slowly.

Impatiently the SS officer in charge of the firing squad growled, "Mach schnell." (Hurry up.)

At that moment Goering—having flown from Munich in a speed-setting roar—stormed in, yelling, "What goes on here?"

"The Führer's orders, Herr Reichmarshal."

Goering thundered, "*I* will decide what are the Führer's orders." Putting an arm around Udet's shoulders, Goering marched the prisoner to the Reichmarshal's office, cursing Ernst every step of the way as an idiot, a fool.

Sinking into the nearest chair, Ernst said to his erstwhile and future commanding officer, "So—I have again joined the Luftwaffe."

At that point in the story I came up with one of my penetrating comments: "I'll bet you were scared."

Udet grinned. "I had rubber knees for three days."

As we paused under the leafy canopy of trees lining Kurfurstendam, a complement of motorized black shirts went scorching down the street.

[237]

Looking after them, I asked, "Where's it all going to end? What do you really think of Hitler?"

Udet said under his breath, "Who's afraid of the big, bad wolf? Goering will kill him eventually, but Goering is too wise a soldier to try until he knows he can succeed. Meanwhile, I have work to do. I have friends who need help in escaping. Time is the problem. *Time* . . ."

Helga and I left Berlin the following day. I never saw Ernst Udet again.

Sometime after the U. S. entered World War II, a Reuters dispatch announced the death of Major General Udet at the controls of an experimental plane.

At least, I thought, he had escaped the SS and had died as he would have chosen.

Then, in late 1944, on a set at RKO, an electrician drew me aside, saying he had a message for me. It seemed that the electrician's sister had met Udet during the National Air Races in Los Angeles in the late Thirties. After Udet returned to Germany, he had corresponded with the girl in a hands-across-the-sea friendship.

In the latter days of the war, Udet's mother managed to smuggle a letter to friends in Switzerland, who had forwarded it to the girl in Los Angeles.

It read, in part, "You may have heard that Ernst died in a plane accident. That is a lie. Ernst was shot in the back by SS troopers, because he was engaged in underground activities of which his friends in the free world may be forever proud."

28

Lacking clairvoyance, I saw no aureola around the film business to which we returned from our ad lib safari. How was I to guess that the era from (roughly) 1937 through 1948, was to be labeled by cinematic historians—about three decades later—"Hollywood's Golden Years." At least one reason for the designation was that motion pictures, in those quaint times, were actually made *in* Hollywood.

MGM was a city in itself, employing around six thousand people; 20th-Century Fox's payroll was almost as great; Columbia, Paramount, United Artists, RKO, Republic, and Universal were humming. A glance at the roster of players billed during those years will awaken nostalgia in anyone over thirty. (See Appendix.)

I hasten to explain that "television," during that era, was a filthy word, unspoken in the executive suites. More about that later.

Martha Scott's performance in my next film, *Cheers For Miss Bishop,* was a notable contribution to the "Golden Years."

Fundamentally, *Cheers* was an American *Goodbye, MRS. Chips.* It told the story of a dedicated teacher in a midwestern university who devoted herself unstintingly to her students, a devotion that cost her the one love of her life.

Our cast, in addition to Martha Scott (who had achieved national fame for her performance on Broadway in Thornton Wilder's *Our Town*), included Mary Anderson (fresh from Alabama for her first film role), Rosemary de Camp (in her first picture after a brilliant career in radio), William Gargan, Sidney Blackmer, and Edmund Gwenn (each as eager as if it were his first instead of his umpteenth film).

I would like to take bows for transplanting Rosemary de Camp from radio to pictures, but it was Martha who sold me on the idea of using Rosemary for the sympathetic role of a Swedish immigrant student. Few indeed are the stars who insist on casting another rare talent for a great part in their own starring vehicles. Martha did, proof of both her star quality and her magnanimity as a woman.

Our second unit, sent to Lincoln to shoot background footage of the University of Nebraska's beautiful campus, was headed by Mickey Nielan. In regard to that bit of casting, I have only one thing to say: I'm awfully hard to convince. Mickey had been THE top director when I came into the film business, and his comedy touch was superb. I idolized him, refusing to believe the rumor that he had become a hopeless lush.

I was appalled by the first footage that came from Nebraska: It could only have been shot from the back of a galloping horse at midnight. The mystery of the murky images was explained by a final shot: Instead of using the standard finale—a camera assistant holding up a slate with the scene's number slugged in for the convenience of the film editor—Mickey had chosen to be photographed between two coeds (?), an arm around each. One of the liquified dolls was holding the slate no better than her liquor, and the other girl plus Mickey were far better lit than the campus backgrounds.

A fast telephone call exchanged Mickey's sober cameraman for the stoned director. I was bitterly disappointed in my fallen hero. It didn't occur to me, for many years, to think, "There, but for the grace of God, go I."

There's a postscript to the *Cheers* production story. I met the highly respected film critic for the *Los Angeles Times,* Kevin Thomas, at a French consulate party in the spring of 1970. After shaking hands, he told me, "You directed the only picture that ever made me cry."

He added that because of *Cheers* he had chosen to attend a small liberal arts college (Gettysburg, Pennsylvania), and that he had planned to become a college prof.

My reaction was that journalism's gain had been the teaching profession's loss.

Back to the era of *Cheers:* Arrangements had been made to premiere the film in Lincoln. In a preoccupied moment I forgot to duck, and agreed instead to "add to the festivities" by making a brief talk about Hollywood to the student body. Incidentally, Irvin S. Cobb, whom I had known since Sennett days, was booked to plug *Cheers* at the University the following day. Thank God, I didn't have to follow *him*.

Helga and I decided to spend a few weeks in New York, catching the shows, before returning to Nebraska, and talked Jim and Mrs. McGuinness into joining us. Jim, who knew everyone of consequence in New York because of his *New Yorker* connections, jumped at the chance to renew old ties.

John O'Hara's *Pal Joey*—which was to make stars of Eve Arden and Gene Kelly—was opening the night we reached the City. "I'd give my shirt to catch that first night—not much chance for tickets this late—still, why not give it a whirl . . ." McGuinness ruminated.

He made a series of fruitless telephone calls; even the Friars Club was without an angle.

In the *non sequitur* of the year, he announced, "Tay, you ought to belong to The Friars."

"In order to get tickets to Broadway shows?" I asked, grinning.

He chuckled. "Not exactly—but because you'd run into someone you knew whenever you came to town. You've directed half the membership."

I said thanks and how about our having luncheon at "21".

The first person we saw in "21" was John O'Hara, hanging onto the newel post in the foyer and fielding good wishes from friends. He released the post long enough to embrace McGuinness. After a mutual exchange of compliments, McGuinness introduced me and asked John in the same breath, "I suppose we're dead ducks as far as seats for the opening tonight goes? We'd need four."

"You've got 'em," asserted The O'Hara. "I'll leave 'em in your name at the box office."

McGuinness thanked him to the echo and added, "One more thing: I want to nominate Tay for membership in The Friars. Will you second the nomination? And will you send me a membership application?"

"Absolutely," O'Hara agreed. "I'll leave the application with Jack Kriendler at noon tomorrow. Right here at '21'."

O'Hara sat with us for about an hour, declining food, but accepting a few grogs that seemed to raise his center of gravity.

No matter. We were set for the opening. Man, would our wives be impressed!

The theatre was mobbed when we arrived, Jim and I resplendent in full dress, and our wives looking like models from Bonwit Teller's windows. McGuinness, the epitome of assurance, stepped up to the box office and said, "I believe John O'Hara left four tickets here in my name. I'm James McGuinness."

The clerk shuffled through a stack of small envelopes. He shuffled a second time. And a third. Nothing for Mr. McGuinness. Jim's face took on an instant Hawaiian sunburn.

"I'm *real* sorry," the clerk said.

On a delayed take, he added, "Are you THE James McGuinness of MGM?"

Jim nodded miserably, growling, "That dirty, double-crossing Irish sonavabitch."

By that time the girls were chanting a song whose lyrics went, "I've never been so humiliated in my life."

As it turned out, all of us—Jim included—had underestimated the wattage of the McGuinness name. The theatre manager produced four seats in a box. We learned afterward that he had reserved them for members of his family, who had generously relinquished them to the West Coast visitors.

Lap dissolve.

Two years later I made a singleton trip to New York on business. As usual I reported to "21" for my first Big Town luncheon. Hanging onto the same newel post was a familiar figure in a familiar attitude.

"Hi, Tay, old boy," shouted O'Hara.

I thought, "What gall! If he thinks he's going to laugh off that ticket runaround."

I said, "What was the big idea of pulling that dirty trick on us the last time we were in New York?

"I'm ashamed," John admitted contritely, "but I'm going to square it right now. I'll be back in five minutes with that *Friar's membership application.*"

I never saw John O'Hara again.

After the *Pal Joey* premiere, the McGuinnesses returned to Hollywood; eventually Helga and I entrained for Lincoln and checked into the Cornhuskers' Hotel. I felt lousy but ascribed my misery to a hangover assembled in Gruesome Gotham.

In addition to my personal troubles, we were all horrified by the Japanese bombing of Pearl Harbor. My country was at war, and there wasn't a damned thing I could do about it. I cussed my gimpy leg bitterly.

After my brief talk to the Nebraska student body—such a talk seemed fatuous under the circumstances—Helga and I were invited to have luncheon in the faculty dining room. As we were about to be seated, one of those odd, sudden silences fell upon the room. At that moment a youngish voice was observing loudly, "What do we care if the Japanese hit the Pacific Coast, and the Germans land in New York at the same time? It will still be two years before they can reach Nebraska."

My fever passed the boiling point. I said, "Gentlemen, I've made a terrible mistake. I'm American, but I've just discovered that my passport is not visa-ed for Nebraska." Turning to Helga I added, "Let's go back to the U. S. A."

We returned to the hotel and I fell into bed with a four-star case of pneumonia.

Incidentally, I want to emphasize that a glance at the roster of Nebraskans who laid it on the line for their country between December 7, 1941 and August 14, 1945, will indicate how out-of-touch with his nation and his own university a college professor can be.

Two pleasant things happened in the Cornhuskers' Hotel while I was meandering in and out of delirium: A superb doctor took care of me, and Irvin Cobb came to call one afternoon.

Being Cobb, he was impelled to tell me a story. Possibly it has appeared in a collection of his works, but I had a hunch it was one of those yarns he saved for ailing friends.

A small country boy, according to Cobb, concluded one morning that things weren't going right for him at the farm, so he collected his bow and arrow, a box of crackers, and a roll of toilet tissue, and set out for the West.

He was observed along the way by neighboring farm families who telephoned his parents with progress reports.

As afternoon oozed into twilight, the small pioneer became depressed. He hadn't seen a bear, a buffalo, or an Indian; his feet and legs were heavy, and he was out of crackers. As the wind began to sharpen, he decided that he should return home that night and Go West another day.

His backtracking was duly reported by neighbors.

The boy entered the kitchen expectantly, but the tea towels were drying over the oven, signifying that supper was over and the dishes done. Tiptoeing into the living room, he found his father—shoes off and pipe glowing—reading the weekly paper. His mother was humming softly as she darned socks beside the fireplace.

Only the cat arose from its cushion, wandered over and rubbed against the boy's legs.

Leaning over to stroke the kitty, the frontiersman asked, "Hey, Ma, is this the same cat you had when I went away?"

Back in Hollywood, the first friend I spotted in Romanoff's was Joe Pasternak, my erstwhile Budapest benefactor.

"Where in hell have you been?" he greeted me. "I've been trying to get you on the telephone for a week."

Who could ask for a heartier welcome?

Joe had a script lined up to star Marlene Dietrich, but there was a catch. He outlined his quandary, "The story's entitled *7 Sinners*—which is the name of a South Seas night club. The hero is a Naval officer who falls in love with Marlene, a singer in the night club. It's *Poor Butterfly* in reverse. The singer falls for the lieutenant, but in order to save his career from the contamination of being associated with her, she runs out on him. We need a big, rugged he-guy type with competent fists, plus sex appeal. T'aint gonna be easy."

I had an inspiration. "How about a guy under contract to Republic? He has a vacation coming up, so we wouldn't have to borrow him and pay Yates some fantastic sum. Our guy would get the total check; his name's John Wayne, and he fits your specification right down to his handmade boots."

"By me it's okay," Joe said, "but he's gotta be cleared by Marlene."

I set a lunch date with Marlene at the Universal commissary.

[244]

When we walked in, Wayne was where he'd promised to be—just inside the door, talking to a couple of friends.

Dietrich, with that wonderful floating walk, passed Wayne as if he were invisible, then paused, made a half-turn and cased him from cowlick to cowboots. As she moved on, she said in her characteristic basso whisper, "Daddy, buy me THAT."

I said, "Honey, you've gotta deal. That's our boy."

At a sign from me, Duke joined our table. I performed the introductions, and seconds later understood the full meaning of "superfluous."

Superfluous Garnett excused himself—an unnoticed gallantry.

7 *Sinners* was a fun picture in the filming, and when released it was a box office smash. The cast, in addition to Dietrich and Wayne, included Oscar Homolka, Albert Dekker, Brod Crawford, Billie Gilbert, and marvelously melancholy Mischa Auer.

What is Marlene Dietrich really like? She is all the things one couldn't guess from her sensuous appearance. She is one of the most compassionate women I've ever known. She always had time to listen to everyone's troubles; a girl with a sick mother was given Dietrich-brewed chicken soup to cheer the invalid; children were sent toys; a troubled husband was reassured about his wife's health by word from Dietrich's doctor. She was, to each individual, precisely what the situation called for.

In those Hollywood days it was customary for the director, sometimes the producer, sometimes the stars, to give a "close-of-picture" party. At such a time food and drink were brought onto the sound stage, and presents were exchanged. Big Duke wanted to cut himself in on the cost of the party, but Marlene and I ruled him out. He wasn't earning a huge salary in those days, but he always had an open pocket. He was as lavish with his friends as Santa Claus. I've often thought how wonderful it is that he's made millions—it's the only way he's been able to balance outgo with income over the years —or almost!

7 *Sinners* led directly to my first experience in radio. Through my good friend Norman Winston, I sold NBC a story line, based on a Ken Englund script, for a series to be entitled, *Three Sheets to the Wind.* It was an international spy thriller in which Helga was to play the love interest. The detective hero, John Wayne, was a lush.

So delicate were the sensibilities of that era's censors that a lush couldn't actually *be* a lush. Our hero's drinking had to be strictly a cover.

Nowadays, a lush on the screen is a "goddam drunkard," and "cover" is what an Eskimo wears outside his igloo. If you don't know what he doesn't wear inside, you haven't seen a movie for five years. It was about that long ago when imagination was outlawed; today you've gotta SHOW it where it's at.

While I was waiting for Wayne to finish a picture, I took a job directing a Harold Lloyd production starring Kay Kyser. The title was *My Favorite Spy,* and the script was prepared by Bill Bowers, one of the best comedy writers in the business. (Millions laughed themselves hoarse recently at his *Support Your Local Sheriff* starring James Garner.)

The best thing about *My Favorite Spy* was its title. Several years after our low-altitude bomber had been mothballed, Bob Hope made a film under the same title. *His* version was funny.

If I were forced to pick a "worst thing" about *MFS,* I'd say it was filming in downtown Los Angeles's Philharmonic Auditorium. With its doors wide open, that tabernacle was a California Cave of the Winds. It was battered by more breezes than Miami in hurricane season.

I had taken up residence in the Biltmore Hotel, catty-corner from the Philharmonic, where I could nurse my raging flu each night so as to be able to work the next day.

Between agonizing over our *Spy* disaster, and consuming enough quinine to make my head ring like Sunday in Salzburg, I put off calling Helga from day to day. When I did call, explanations were ineffectual, as they had been since our European trip, a situation many women will understand.

Once *Spy* was in the cans, I went out on the town with convivial pals, and got royally smashed. Thanks to a talkative friend, Helga heard a lurid and (I felt) exaggerated version of the episode before I had a chance to read her my prepared denial. I came home to a silence that thawed only slightly after Helga had read a few of the *Three Sheets* scripts, and noted how many juicy scenes she was to play with big Duke.

Troubles multiplied. Because of the war, two of our writers—Jerry

Lawrence and Bob Lee — were drafted. (As a team they were recently responsible for much of the fun in *Auntie Mame,* starring Rosalind Russell, and *Mame,* starring Angela Lansbury.) Their contribution to *Three Sheets* undoubtedly would have been considerable if only Goering had liquidated Hitler as prophesied by Udet.

At about the time our company wrapped up the final, or twenty-sixth, episode of *Sheets,* an eight-pound boy was born to Helga and christened William John Garnett, in honor of Helga's father and mine. He was a beauty: bright, handsome, good-natured—or I may have been prejudiced.

Unfortunately, the job of adjusting the difficulties between Helga and me was a chore to which neither of us was dedicated at the time. Constantly increasing pressures of the motion picture business, augmented by my heavy drinking, made it impossible for us to maintain a comfortable domestic situation.

Helga wanted to return to London, taking the boy with her, as soon as the war ended. In order to avoid excess baggage charges, she discarded our marriage in court.

When I saw William John a few years ago in London, he struck me as being the ideal young Englishman: handsome, socially poised, highly intelligent with a twinkle—altogether a lad of whom anyone could be proud.

Helga had wanted only cash out of our divorce settlement, so I emptied a couple of bank accounts in order to keep for myself the Stone Canyon house and the "Kentucky Ranch" at Paso Robles, California.

"Kentucky Ranch" had been established as a breeding farm by the fabled Lucky Baldwin who brought the first Kentucky thorobreds to California. Although legal title to the property has changed hands several times over the years, the romantic name of the spread has been maintained, along with the original big red barn.

At first I spent weekends at the ranch, and the week at the Stone Canyon house, fighting off a strait jacket. I lived in one cell just off condemned row. The nights were the worst. Helga never stopped talking in the other cell. She said all the things she should have said before leaving me, but hadn't. I said all the things, *again,* that I never should have said in the first place.

She won every argument.

Telling myself that everything happening to a writer is stock upon his shelf, I determined to get back to writing. It was tough, but I made it: I wrote to Joan Marshfield.

I copped out in the first paragraph, telling Joan that Helga and I were divorced through no fault of Helga's.

Henri had appeared to be so frail when we saw him in Paris that I was afraid to ask about him. Instead, I invited both of them to California, where—I warned—civilian suffering was great. No meat on Tuesdays, no eggs, sugar, shoes or toilet tissue. A guy had to wait nearly four months to get delivery on a new Cadillac. Hardships aside, it was still better than Paris, where, I'd heard, all cognac and champagne had been commandeered by the Occupation Forces.

Sick humor, but I knew Joan would understand—many things. As I addressed the envelope, I wondered abruptly if Joan and Henri were *in* Paris. They might have moved to the south of France. Or to England. Or—New York? Shrugging, I dropped my letter into the Beverly Hills post office with a mystical Irish trust that it would reach Joan somehow, somewhere.

When I heard that *Bataan* was to be made at MGM, I went after the directorial assignment with determination and forensic zeal. I even volunteered to take a hefty cut in my established salary—that turned the trick.

BUT, a week after I was set for the job, all salaries were frozen "for the duration." I've often wondered if Louis B. Mayer had checked out the future on an ouija board.

Bataan was worth whatever it cost me to get the directorial credit. Take a look at the cast: Robert Taylor, Robert Walker, Lloyd Nolan, Desi Arnaz, George Murphy, Tommy Mitchell, Barry Nelson, and Lee Bowman.

The entire *Bataan* schmeer was shot on Stage 16, where a real-as-hell jungle had been constructed. We had everything except sixteen-foot snakes, an omission unprotested by the crew's grievance committee. However, there was an occasional invasion of cannibals. They call themselves by their tribal name—agents.

In general, we worked on a happy set. Bob Taylor was one of the world's great gentlemen. He was serious-minded, hard-working,

Top left:
Robert Taylor and I, also on the BATAAN set. Bob knew at this time that his next role would be that of a lieutenant in the U. S. Navy, authentically and "for the duration."

Top right:
1945 winner of *Photoplay*'s Gold Medal Award (selected by theatre patrons throughout the world as the most popular picture) was VALLEY OF DECISION. Our table at the award banquet consisted of Macfadden's vice president, Greer Garson, and in the shadows, L. B. Mayer and the film's director, me.

Bottom left:
Robert Walker and I on the set of BATAAN. It was his first film. The injury was simulated to dramatize a plot sequence in the picture.

Bottom right:
BATAAN'S magnificent cast will never be duplicated: George Murphy, Thomas Mitchell, Lloyd Nolan, Lee Bowman, Robert Taylor, Robert Walker, and Desi Arnaz. We cried a lot during the filming, but we laughed a lot, too. What else is there?

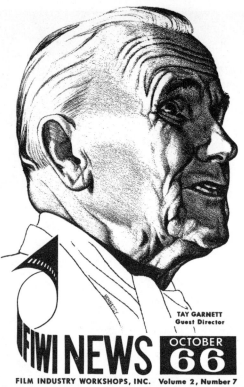

TAY GARNETT
Guest Director

FIWI NEWS OCTOBER 66

FILM INDUSTRY WORKSHOPS, INC. Volume 2, Number 7

A.P. GIANNINI

Top left:
I like this pen-and-ink sketch as well as if I'd done it myself. You must admit that's a face that has been lived in like a pair of CPO's fatigues.
Top right:
Dorothy Malone and I in a conference moment on the DEATH VALLEY DAYS set. What a trouper that gal is. (I am ignoring the handsome cowpoke in the background.)
Middle:
On the set for "The Little Cayuse" segment of DEATH VALLEY DAYS, Ken Murray and I, and a horse deciding whether to kick or bite.
Bottom right:
Tony Martin (on right) as A. P. Giannini (California banking tycoon), in a segment for DEATH VALLEY DAYS. Man at right was a v.p. of Bank of America, where all that money grows wild.
Bottom left:
On the set of DEATH VALLEY DAYS—Tim McIntire; the man about to become governor of California, Ronald Reagan; and Shari Marshall. I'm always in Ronnie's corner.

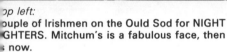

op left:
ouple of Irishmen on the Ould Sod for NIGHT
GHTERS. Mitchum's is a fabulous face, then
s now.

ight column, top to bottom:
n the set for CONNECTICUT YANKEE, starring
ng. I had just finished WILD HARVEST with
lan Ladd, so he stopped by to give us a few
ggestions. A pair of svelte stars make Old
ad seem a mite heavy. Purely a photographic
usion.

a break on DEATH VALLEY DAYS—Katy
rado and Ernest Borgnine (married at the
ne), as was Old Dad, a temporary condition all
ound.

sitors on the set of FIREBALL—1949. Mickey
ooney; my mother, Mrs. William Garnett; Mrs.
iedlob, mother of Bert; and "Captain Flob"
mself.

tertaining Cubby Broccoli's visitors on the
ndon set for THE BLACK KNIGHT. Alan Ladd
fourth from the left, a great gentleman and
y good friend. Note his bare arms in contrast
the wardrobe of all others. It was *cold* in
gland, but Alan's role was athletic enough to
ep him warm.

Top left:
1955—two of my friends who paid a call to our Madrid location for THE BLACK KNIGHT—Mr. and Mrs. Michael Wilding.

Top right:
Mari and I on the castle set for THE BLACK KNIGHT.

Middle:
A happy, happy man. Mari Aldon and I outside Caxton Hall, London, the day we were married, August 13, 1953.

Bottom right:
Tiela in the garden of our cold-water canyon house. Tiela selected the cap, personally, in the boys' section of a department store and wore it on a twenty-four-hour basis for several months.

Bottom left:
Cameron Mitchell and I on the set for the television series THE BEACHCOMBER. Cam went from that to THE HIGH CHAPPARAL which took him to affluence. Couldn't happen to a finer guy. *(Lane Lester.)*

op left:

bert Roland and his director on location for
ATH VALLEY DAYS (1967). Señor Roland is
own by his devoted friends as "Amigo."
ofessionally, he is tops. Personally, he is a
lished diamond.

op right:

chard Egan, Charles McGraw, and Robert
tchum in Colorado for ONE MINUTE TO
RO. ZERO had nothing to do with the temper-
re (RKO).

ottom left:

rtrude Berg, the team of Rodgers and Ham-
erstein, Faye Emerson, Rex Harrison, Lilli
lmer, Josh Logan, Leo Durocher, Thelma Rit-
r, Tallulah Bankhead, Cornell Wilde, Tommy
naco, Agnes Moorehead, Ethel Barrymore,
identified, Mary Martin, Louis Calhern, Helen
yes, and Lionel Barrymore, in MAIN STREET
BROADWAY (MGM).

ottom right:

bert Mitchum and Richard Harris in THE
GHTFIGHTERS! (United Artists).

Bottom left:
Joan Marshfield as painted by Dega Vierra.
Top right:
Tay Garnett, lighting his torches and pulling up
his tights.
Bottom:
May 1971—three old boys swapping lies at the
Vidor retrospective film festival presented by
the Los Angeles County Museum. To right: King
Vidor, his beautiful daughter and George Cu-
kor.

and keen. In spite of his astounding good looks, he was determined to be a fine actor, not merely a star. (The terms are not synonymous.) After having played a gross of "Tennis, anyone?" roles, Bob had turned down another dozen before he was given the part of the hard-nosed, regular Army sergeant in *Bataan.*

After winding up *Bataan,* Bob went into Naval Aviation. I had the satisfaction of signing a recommendation for him. Bob spent most of the war training cadets, while he burned to get into combat. He was a fine pilot and would have been an asset in the air war on either front, but the Navy had other plans. The funniest description of Bob's flight capability was once voiced to me by Barbara Stanwyck who said laconically, "Bob can do anything a bird can do, except balance himself on a barbed wire fence."

Robert Walker, whom I admired deeply, became a star through his *Bataan* role. We had found him in Chicago where he and his actress wife, Jennifer Jones, were doing what are called "open-end platters," i.e., entertainment for radio syndication, open front and back so that commercials could be cut in to suit local sponsors.

Bob was a talented, sensitive, fey guy who combined the comic abilities of Jack Lemmon and Bob Montgomery, plus a heart-grabbing, little-boy-lost appeal. Much of his quality appears to have been inherited by his son, Robert Walker, Jr.

An incident that took place between camera setups provides an insight into Bob's gentle naivete. When our huge sound-stage doors were opened briefly to air our jungle, music came drifting in. Astonished, Bob asked, "Where's it coming from?"

I said a Judy Garland picture was shooting on the next stage.

His eyes opened like blossoming parachutes as he asked softly, "D'ya suppose I could meet her?"

I said, "Let's go."

As I introduced them in Judy's dressing room, Bob's gaze was frankly idolatrous.

Judy, a prime sophisticate even at that age, caught the whole bit and was amused. She went into her act, saying in Mae West tones, "I've been hearing a lot about you, Honey. Drop around some evening and we'll have a few belts, and get REAL well acquainted."

Bob's jaw dropped as a crimson wave spread to his hairline. After a few seconds that I filled with small talk with Judy, Bob said, "I g-g-guess I'd b-b-better get b-b-back . . ." Backing out of the dressing room and tripping over the step, he added, "N-n-nice to m-m-meet you."

While we were walking back to our set, Bob said miserably, "Golly, I'm sorry I met her."

"Why?"

"I've adored her since the first time I saw *Wizard of Oz.*"

"And? . . ."

"Gosh, Mr. Garnett, you saw how she acted, and she's GOT to know that I'm married to Jennifer Jones."

To Bob, wholly unaware that he was, even then, being set up for a lethal kayo, any deviation from absolute fidelity was totally unthinkable.

A few weeks later it became apparent that something was seriously wrong with Bob. He seemed to be falling apart: his color was pasty, his eyes were bloodshot, and he couldn't remember his lines.

Taking him aside, I asked, "What's wrong, Bob?"

Fighting tears, he blurted, "Jennifer has left me."

The happy man on our set was Lee Bowman, a delightful gent who looked as if he were a young ambassador to the Court of St. James; had he gone into politics, I'm sure he would have made it.

According to Lee's report of his hungry young years around New York, he fended off starvation by bottling New York's excellent tap water and selling it under the esoteric title, "Branch Water." Lee had selected a simple bottle design, and a distinguished label, and shortly "Branch Water" was selling for $2.50 per split—as a mixer —in all the better restaurants. Lee's enterprise thrived until he was signed by MGM and brought west where the water was less appetizing, hence no temptation to entrepreneur Bowman.

The *Bataan* story dealt with the members of a rear-guard suicide mission, protecting the American retreat down the peninsula. Taylor, as the sergeant, was the last man alive. Having buried the other members of his detail, he dug his own grave, mounted a machine gun on the perimeter, and—half-mad with jungle fever—set himself to stall the enemy as long as ammunition lasted.

For dramatic impact, we decided to make use of the ground fog customary in jungle country. To create this, our special effects man dumped dry ice into tubs of water. Immediately, heavy white emanations formed on the surface of the water. By using an electric fan at low speed, our technicians were able to blow this vapor into the desired areas. Being heavier than air, it settled into prearranged hollows, giving the terrain the appearance of hummocks arising from a patchwork of partly melted snow.

The attacking Japanese were supposed to advance upon Taylor's position through this misty camouflage.

We warned our extra talent that the fumes were dangerous; when submerged, they must keep their eyes closed and hold their breath. They could only breathe when lifting their heads out of the goop. To be sure we had no mishaps, I established a lookout on a stepladder —one of my more logical moves; we had to rescue two of the boys who believed they had lung power superior to chemical assault.

Back to the illusion of war: As the enemy soldiers, slithering through the pools of vapor, reached a hummock and had to crawl over it—exposing themselves—Taylor mowed them down with machine-gun fire.

In a close angle shot we picked up Taylor firing and yelling wildly, "Come on, you bastards, I'm here. I'll ALWAYS be here."

The camera moved forward so that the spitting Browning filled the screen.

Abruptly, the firing ceased. Only a tiny wisp of smoke curled up from the silenced gun.

The End.

Well, not quite.

Mr. Mayer ruled that, from the lifeless machine gun, we must dissolve to a shot of the Stars and Stripes snapping in the breeze; the accompanying sound was the resonant voice of General MacArthur vowing, "I shall return."

So, all right! Our country was at war and morale was vital. However, I still deplore what I regarded as a betrayal of artistic integrity.

I continued to torch for Helga; Duke Wayne stood loyally by during those miserable months, keeping me company. However, I felt in my nerve ends that the Stone Canyon house expanded a few feet every night; stealthily, it grew and grew. I talked to a real estate agent about selling it.

"Forget it," he advised. "You can't GIVE a big place away these days. Keep it a little longer; it's a beautiful home and eventually you'll make a mint."

I didn't need a mint; I needed peace of mind, so I insisted on listing it. We finally sold for thirty-five thousand; not long ago the persom to whom I sold told me laughingly that she had been offered three hundred and fifty thousand, but she wouldn't think of giving it up. Her name is Greer Garson. Proves what I've often said: Beauty and brains are frequently found together.

After settling my obligations, I had enough scratch left to make a down payment on a two-bedroom house on Redford Avenue in the San Fernando Valley. It was situated about two blocks from Republic Studios, now Cinema Center.

It was a great little house with a fabulous bar-den that overlooked the patio. The living room was pleasant, the kitchen compact, and the bedrooms generous. I kept thinking, "Joan could give this place some excitement, some distinction. Okay, I'll just ride it out until I hear from her."

Meanwhile, I discovered that any room in my digs, walked through fast enough, and assuming you didn't trip over something, looked as tidy as if a maid had just left.

With *Bataan* cut, scored, and released to excellent notices, I was assigned by producer Edwin Knopf (my buddy from *S.O.S. Iceberg* days) to direct a script developed from Hans Habe's novel about the French Resistance Movement, *A Thousand Shall Fall*. The New York sales office, for reasons that escape me, changed the title to *The Cross of Lorraine*. There's a rumor that the film was awarded a citation by General De Gaulle, but—if memory serves—I've never been kissed by a French general.

Our cast consisted of the multitalented Gene Kelly, Jean Pierre Aumont, Hume Cronyn, Sir Cedric Hardwicke, and Peter Lorre.

We were in the depths of the war, so the set of *Lorraine* proved to be a Mecca for visiting V.I.P.s. Harry Truman, then a senator and busily investigating something important enough to justify the cost of a senatorial junket, called upon MGM. It was a delight to behold the Republican magenta of Louis B. Mayer's face as he, personally, provided top-drawer courtesies for the dapper little Democrat.

On another occasion our set was being honored by a galaxy of star-grade Army brass with Our Boss in full charge. We happened to be filming the grim simulation of a Nazi prisoner-of-war camp. Peter Lorre, as a black-clad SS sergeant, was doing his diabolical damnedest from the depths of his Jewish heart.

Between scenes, the Great White Father summoned Lorre, introduced him, patted his shoulder patronizingly, and observed, "Well, Peter, you look fit—almost as if being a storm trooper agreed with you."

Peter, accustomed to, but unappreciative of Mayer's ten-ton "little jokes," laid those enormous, guileless eyes on Louis B. and said in the tone of the top sergeant, "Oh yes, sir, it does. I eat a Jew every morning for breakfast."

The brass roared, but Metro's Golden Mayer left the set hurriedly.

Another *Lorraine* incident involved Sir Cedric Hardwicke, who played a provincial priest. Hardwicke was a wonderful human being whose title was carried with a touch of majesty and a ton of humor.

One noon, Cedric—still in his cassock and clerical hat—set out with me toward the commissary. En route, we passed the stage where Tommy Dorsey's band was rehearsing for the aforementioned Judy Garland musical. The jazz was what was called "hot" in those days, probably would be "funky" in 1973; a group of actors, directors, cameramen, and sound engineers from other sets had gathered before the huge open doors.

Cedric and I joined the ad lib audience. After a few minutes I reminded Cedric that we had only an hour for lunch, so we turned to go and Cedric bumped, full force, into Greer Garson, who was working in *Mrs. Miniver* at that time.

Greer, confused by the clerical robe, dropped her eyes without recognizing Cedric, and murmured in confusion, "I'm *so* sorry, Father."

Cedric, deadpan, blessed Miss Garson with the sign of the cross, then—in time with the music—executed a slow, sensuous grind ending in a violent bump. In his priestly costume, it was outrageous.

Greer caught her breath, glanced upward into the stern face of her fellow countryman, and almost popped her wig with laughter.

For a long time afterward, it was Cedric's practice upon meeting

Greer anywhere to say solemnly, "Bless you, my daughter." Neither ever bothered to explain the joke to the uninitiated.

From *Cross of Lorraine* I was assigned to another big one: *Mrs. Parkington,* to be produced by Leon Gordon (who will always be remembered in theatrical circles as the author of *White Cargo*).

The script was fashioned from the novel by Louis Bromfield. Greer Garson, having been awarded an Oscar for her work in *Mrs. Miniver,* was assigned to the title role. Additional stars were Walter Pidgeon, Agnes Moorehead, Edward Arnold, and Dan Duryea.

During the first scenes it became obvious that Greer had not yet caught onto the "Susie Parkington" character.

"Susie" was a bright, spirited, western mining town girl, bouncy and bubbling with vitality but without artifice. Greer was playing her too Great Lady, too British.

Wise Walter Pidgeon saw the problem, and—grinning wickedly—slapped Greer on the neatest derriere in Hollywood (a stunt he had used earlier in *Mrs. Miniver*), and said offhandedly, "Relax, Honey. It was LAST year that you won the Oscar."

Greer laughed and relaxed. End of problem.

We had another foulup on *Parkington.* We were doing a light comedy bit, planting a running characterization gag that I had dreamed up for "Susie." Whenever her volatile temper boiled over, she would thrust out her chin and exhale violently, bouncing the stray wispy curl on her forehead.

We tried the business several times, but it was no good. I knew it SHOULD work, and so did Greer. Then I caught on. I said, "It looks as though you were amusing *yourself,* as if you were doing it consciously to BE funny, but you know that amusing yourself—Red Skelton's technique notwithstanding—is one of the surest known ways NOT to amuse an audience."

I got no further. Twinkling those green eyes at me she inquired with a grin, "You mean I'm wearing a spangle on my nose?"

"Neon," I conceded.

"After this, when you see me getting a bit too Christmas-pantomime, just place your forefinger on the tip of your nose and I'll get the message," she said.

From that day on, whenever I felt she was pressing, I had only to tap my nose. She would smile and say, "One more take? I know I can do it better."

Such rapport is rare between director and star.

Usually Greer's humor was packaged by her intellectual turn of mind. I relished it, but sometimes it left others cold.

For *Mrs. Parkington,* the great couturier Adrian designed an elaborate period gown that dripped lace and furbelows and came to a climax with an enormous taffeta bow perched on the stomach.

Greer tried on the dress. Doubt arched her eyebrows. Turning a full-length profile toward the mirror she said solemnly, "But Adrian, it makes me look as if I had a marsupial pouch."

Rumor has it that Adrian was not amused.

In 1946, Greer and Clark Gable worked together in the disastrous *Adventure* with which I, thank God, had nothing to do at all.

The best brains in the MGM publicity department pooled wits and produced the promotional catch line, "Gable's back and Garson's got him."

A second choice was "Gable puts the arson in Garson."

Greer objected to both. "They're ungallant," was her complaint. "Why don't you say, 'Garson puts the able in Gable'?"

Arson or Able, there's never been a better actress or a more delightful human being than the redhead from England.

Incidentally, after Louis Bromfield had seen the film version of *Mrs. Parkington* he sent me an autographed copy of the novel. I was particularly gratified by the inscription which read:

"Malabar Farm—1944
My Dear Tay Garnett:
    This is just a line to thank you for the beautiful job of transferring "Susie" to the screen. She's one of my favorite people and I'm grateful to you for having captured her essence and for having embellished it. This is something for which an author must be deeply grateful. Thanks again.
    With the best of everything
                                        Louis Bromfield."

Usually an author is deeply offended by what a director has done to his resplendent masterpiece, so praise from Bromfield was the cherry in the Manhattan.

My next assignment at MGM was a job of resuscitation. Wesley Ruggles, a superb director, had been working on the hilarious wartime comedy, *See Here, Private Hargrove,* from the novel by Marion Hargrove.

The last third of the picture had gone to worms, an infestation predicted by Ruggles and Jim McGuinness from the start. The brass had insisted that the rough and tumble comedy of service life, totally outrageous and wonderfully funny, be given—at the end—"significance, importance, and relevance." (Incidentally, McGuinness referred to Louie B's collection of head-nodders as the College of Cardinals.)

Ruggles, deeply unhappy over the picture, which he knew had a tremendous potential, was obliged to leave Hollywood before *Hargrove* was previewed, because of a previous commitment with the Rank Organisation in England.

The preview audience's reaction to the latter portion of MGM's *Hargrove* was just short of tar and feathers. A quick call from Mayer to Ruggles across the Atlantic brought the response that Wes would like me to do the retakes.

I agreed, with the proviso that we would stick to the spirit of the original work. We weren't, dammit, going to go "noble."

Here's a fact of Hollywood: When a picture is in trouble, everyone on the lot knows it. The Small Pox sign, invisible but scentable, goes up, and no one will admit having been exposed to the original idea, the script, or the paper on which it was written.

On the contrary, when a picture begins to give off that unmistakable aroma of success, everyone in sight indicates obliquely that he, she, or it, created the fragrance.

I realized that the air had cleared for *Hargrove* when I began to hear stagehands referring to it as "my picture."

At the subsequent preview, I had the satisfaction of hearing an audience whoop and holler over the kind of comedy Wes and Jim would have achieved in the first place, if they had been allowed to use the talents for which they were being paid.

Hargrove established Bob Walker as a top star; his personal life was less than bright. He had begun to drink heavily. One noon he came into the small bar just outside the MGM auto gate, belted a few —quite a few—then walked carefully to the cashier, check in hand.

A tall, gaudy cigarette machine, decorated with a rococo mirror, stood next the cashier's counter. As Bob swung away, pocketing his change, he caught sight of his reflected face. In spontaneous savagery, he drove his clenched fist through the mirror, scattering shards of glass in every direction, breaking several knuckles and severing an artery.

He was carried to the studio hospital where the doctor patched him up and gave him some fatherly advice. Bob heeded it. Briefly.

I hate to sound like one of those "and then I wrote" types, but what *is* a man except what he has done, the people he has known, and the things he has learned from both?

So, next I was offered *The Seventh Cross,* to be produced by Arthur Freed. Set to star was that unexcelled actor and superb human being, Spencer Tracy. I had always wanted to work with Spence, but I had to pass up *The Seventh Cross,* because a week earlier I had agreed to direct the next Garson picture, *Valley of Decision,* scripted from the Marcia Davenport novel, and to be produced by Eddie Knopf.

I'm thankful that I couldn't foresee that I'd never have another opportunity to work with Spence, because I can't bear to hear a man sob—especially me.

We had a formidable cast for *Valley.* Opposite Greer was the brilliant newcomer from Broadway, Gregory Peck; other superlative talents were Lionel Barrymore, Jessica Tandy, Gladys Cooper, Donald Crisp, and Marshall Thompson (his first picture, which gave no clue to his eventual association with a cross-eyed lion named Clarence.)

We worked on a happy set. By that time Greer and I had become firm friends. Lionel Barrymore and I always hit it off beautifully— he got a kick out of knowing that his younger brother, John, Gene Fowler, and I occasionally applied a bright coat of paint to the local scene. Donald Crisp and I had been friends since the old Writers' Club days, and Gladys Cooper had always enjoyed Instant Popularity.

One of the stories Peck told on himself concerned the days when he was leading man for the incandescent Katherine Cornell. In one long, difficult scene, Greg was required only to lie silent on a deep, comfortable velvet sofa while Miss Cornell carried the anguish of the plot. The evening was warm, the sofa was lulling, and Greg fell asleep; he slept so soundly that he had to be shaken awake by a sympathetic—and magnanimous—star.

Through the years, Greg has worn his stardom with distinction, using his position to benefit many people through the Motion Picture Relief Fund, along with several other charitable interests.

Our cameraman, rounding out an able crew, was Joe Ruttenberg (a three-time Academy Award winner).

The combination of cast and crew won Photoplay-Gallup Poll Awards for Knopf, Garson and Garnett's version of *Valley of Decision*.

Not only were things going well professionally, but something great was added to my personal life. I came home one night to find a letter written in a familiar hand, and postmarked "New York."

Joan wrote that she and Henri had lived out the war in Estoril; they had come to New York so that Henri could be examined by a famed heart specialist. Helga, whom Joan had seen in London before sailing for the U.S., had supplied my address.

I thought, "God bless Helga. How does a man—lacking at least one loyal ex-wife—get along in this world?"

Joan's final paragraph was the haymaker: "I plan to be in California for several weeks. I'll call you from the Beverly Hills Hotel."

She did.

We spent several weekends on Coronado, checking chums of by-gone days. We spent a week at Avalon on Catalina Island, and a long weekend in San Francisco.

One day I asked, "Why go back to France? Why not live in Rancho Santa Fe or somewhere not too far from Hollywood?"

Taking my hand in both of hers and pressing it to her cheek, she said earnestly, "You know I can't leave Henri while he's so very ill, and if you and I were only a hundred miles apart, our lives would become hopelessly complicated."

She was right, of course, but, Lord, how I hate it when a woman is practical. Joan flew back to New York, and I did a lousy job of lighting my torches and pulling up my tights. For months.

One thing helped. I went to work on *The Postman Always Rings Twice,* from the smash novel by James M. Cain. We had a triple whammy cast: Lana Turner (at her best, which is *awfully* good), John Garfield, Cecil Kellaway, Hume Cronyn, lovely Audrey Totter, Leon Ames, and Allan Reed.

Lana, more than any other actress, including Marilyn Monroe, has been publicized as a sex symbol. Actually she is as soft as a baby rabbit, as sweet as cotton candy, and as frustrated as a maternal woman can be; she has always wanted a houseful of children, but since her daughter, Cheryl's, birth, motherhood has been denied Lana because of an RH Negative blood factor. Lana, the envy of a million women, envies a million women—those with a household full of youngsters.

John Garfield—awesome actor, lovable human being—had been warned by his doctor that he had a heart condition. When I saw him playing handball after lunch one day, I asked, "D'ya think that's wise, Julie?"

He called off the game and walked back to the set with me. Shrugging, he said, "So all right, I've got a tricky ticker. So what?"

Softening the words with a grin, I explained, "Don't get me wrong. I don't want to louse up your fun, but I've gotta finish this picture. That's Item One, naturally—you know how things are in this business! Item Two is I'm kinda fond of you, ya big lug. So how about no more handball—ever?"

He slapped my shoulder. "Don't worry, kid. Nobody's going to get me off this stage without a good exit speech."

It has always saddened me to know that the end came so abruptly for Julie that he was cheated of his tag line.

Hume Cronyn has always been one of the great talents of show business. He is gifted to the extent that he can play villainy as well as comedy or straight roles, so, since brilliant heavies are scarce, he has been entrusted with a collection of diabolical roles. The public has little idea of the man's personal charm and sense of humor. He tells this story on himself.

When he walked onto the set one day, an electrician high in the catwalks yelled down, "Hi, baby. How's tricks?"

Hume glanced up and responded uncertainly, "Oh, hi!"

A second electrician asked his mate, "What're you tryin' to prove? That guy's a star. You don't even know him."

"Whadaya mean I don't *know* 'im," sneered the greeter. "Me an' *Human Crone's* been pals f'years."

"Human" and his equally talented wife, Jessica Tandy, like to tell the story of their meeting, marriage, and attendant difficulties.

Jessica came to the U.S. from England to appear in a Broadway play; by the time the play's run ended, Germany had marched on Poland, Britain had declared war, and there was no way for Jessica to go home.

During the war years, Jessica and Hume met and fell in love. Jessica secured an American divorce with the aid and understanding of her first husband. That detail settled, Jessica and Hume were married and a few years later acquired a son.

When the war was over, Jessica and Hume wanted to accept certain British film offers, but a problem presented itself: She was divorced and remarried according to American law, but at that point in history, England recognized only divorces granted in English courts, if one of the parties to the action were a subject of the King.

After long negotiations, the British decree was about to be handed down on the only permissible grounds: adultery. Jessica had submitted photostats of her American divorce decree and marriage certificate, along with their child's birth certificate. However, it seemed that one more proof of cohabitation was needed: an affidavit from the Cronyn's housekeeper that she had seen the Cronyns together, emerging from their bedroom some morning, wearing robes and slippers.

Divorce granted.

Small wonder, considering the script and cast, that *Postman* realized its full potential. In fact, it has become a perennial realizer, although I note that in recent years it has acquired the distinction of being a late, late, late realizer, say from two to four A.M. on TV.

Postman brought me to the end of my MGM contract; I was subjected to the 5-star MGM sales pitch aimed at keeping me in the Mayer stable, but the truth is that I'd *had* the MGM all-kneeling routine at that time, and Gemini Garnett was restless.

I restlessed across town to Paramount. Actually, I was on Destiny's leash because, at Paramount, I rejoined Bob Fellows, a top producer on that lot. Another great guy was Henry Ginsberg, head of the studio.

My first assignment was a script developed from an original screen story entitled *The Big Haircut,* all about an itinerant harvesting crew in wheat country. The top star was that all-time A-1 right guy, Alan Ladd. To my intense dismay, and Alan's, that *Big Haircut* title was almost immediately changed by the front office to the (they hoped) sexually connotive *Wild Harvest.*

Much of our comedy–drama was shot on location near Bakersfield, California. Probably this is as good a spot as any in which to explain that a picture crew, on location, becomes happily close-knit and fraternal, or goes in the other direction to a condition of total loathing and the contemplation of murder.

We were lucky; the *Wild Harvest* gang, made up of Dorothy Lamour, Lloyd Nolan, Robert Preston, and Alan Jenkins, in addition to Ladd, worked together, played together, and spent our evenings exchanging yarns.

One of the best stories starred Alan Jenkins. A few days before a certain Christmas, Alan was on a stepladder, helping his wife trim the tree in their San Fernando Valley home.

At the top of the ladder, Alan found the altitude very dry, so he told his wife, "Honey, I'm fresh out of cigars; I'll just drop down to the corner bar and pick up a batch."

Mrs. Jenkins grimaced as she surveyed Alan's soiled, badly worn sneakers, and a pair of trousers that looked like a sewer-digger's Friday pants. She said, "Surely you can't let anyone see you looking like that. You haven't even shaved for days!"

Alan shrugged. "I won't bump into anybody I know, and besides, I'll be right back."

Lap Dissolve.

On New Year's Day, Pat and Eloise O'Brien were strolling down New York's Fifth Avenue when Eloise pointed ahead to an approaching apparition, a windblown, shaggy pedestrian inadequately clothed in a grimy, tattered sweat shirt, trousers that would have ended a washing machine's life, and sneakers ventilated by portholes.

"Why, ALAN!" Eloise gulped. "I didn't know you were in New York."

Pat added, "Where's MRS. Jenkins?"

Alan didn't miss a beat. "Home—trimming the Christmas tree," he said cheerfully.

Here are a couple on my longtime buddy, Lloyd Nolan. He came to California heavy with accolades and trailing a long list of theatrical credits. However, he quickly discovered that in Hollywood he was merely another face in the crowd. He went out to dinner with old buddies Pat O'Brien and Jim Cagney; they were besieged by autograph seekers. Nolan was ignored.

Nolie bided his time. Part by part, he began to duplicate his stage fame in filmdom. Mature citizens (inclined to assess the work of the stalwarts who carry a film, rather than that of the gorgeous youngsters who attract the popcorn trade) began to recognize him in public places, and smile. Nothing hysterical, you understand, simply calm appreciation.

Even so, no actor has arrived—in his own opinion—until the audience aged ten to twenty clamors for his signature. To have made it BIG, the actor must have climbed the rungs of the fan magazine polls.

One summer Nolie took his pretty wife, Melinda, to Catalina on a brief excursion. After dinner they walked to the Casino (misnamed because there is no gambling, only dancing) to find out what the young were doing with their feet.

Two pretty girls, dancing together—proper in Avalon on a bell-ringing basis—passed Nolie several times. Finally one asked in ringing tones, "Isn't that Lloyd Nolan?"

Nolie thought, "The darlings. The sweethearts. At last I've made it."

Caroled the second little sweetheart, "Yeah, that's Lloyd Nolan. He stinks."

A subsequent confrontation with fame was equally unnerving for Nolie.

He was asked by a friendly columnist one day, "Nolie, do you have a stepdaughter?"

"Nope. Why?"

"Oh, a guy in my business gets his ear bent by a lotta nuts. Forget it."

Nolie was unable to forget it. A query of that sort can invade a man's consciousness when he is trying to memorize lines, and pluck at his sleeve when he is walking the dog.

Furthermore, Nolie seemed to sense a sudden chill in his neighborhood shopping center. The druggist was less than his usual cordial self; the grocer had little to say; even the florist, with whom Nolie maintained a sizable account, appeared uneasy and formal. As for the cleaner. . . .

One afternoon Nolie remembered that he had, several weeks earlier, selected a "characterization suit" from his wardrobe to be cleaned in preparation for a role in his next film. He hadn't worn the suit since his appearance as Dr. Matthew Swain in the film version of *Peyton Place*.

Film buffs will remember that the dramatic climax of the picture was the trial of Allyson (played by Hope Lange) for the murder of her stepfather (played by Arthur Kennedy).

Allyson was saved when Dr. Swain produced from his coat pocket a signed confession from the stepfather which read, "I hereby admit that I raped my stepdaughter."

After using that climactic prop, Nolie had simply returned the alleged "confession" to his pocket; he had forgotten to remove it when the suit went to the cleaner. Said "confession" was enclosed in a cellophane envelope and pinned to the coat lapel when Nolie claimed his garment.

"I can explain," he said, and did—to general and greatly relieved merriment.

Nolie also telephoned the columnist to thank him for checking the story before destroying an innocent, although absentminded, actor.

I'm often asked what sort of guy Alan Ladd was.

He was generous, gentle, considerate, possessed of both a fantastic screen personality and a delightful spontaneous wit.

He wasn't the tallest man ever to face a camera, but he was superbly built—an Atlas in miniature. Like many a talented man who feels Nature has shortchanged him, Alan had a hangup about his height. When he did do a scene with a big guy, Bob Preston, for instance, we laid down planks three inches high for Alan to stand on. Those planks were the equalizer.

When *Harvest* was wound up, we tossed a big bash in one of our bar sets on the sound stage. Naturally, thanks to excellent free chow and limitless grog, we drew a full quota of crashers.

Most of them were studio people whom we knew, visiting from other sets; however, there was one—a giant of a man with a beat-up puss, who leaned on the bar and started to belt 'em. With each fresh drink he demanded more elbow room.

I told Alan, "That big mug is bad trouble, and nobody has a line on him."

Said Alan, "*I* know who he is. He's the big bastard who's leaving as of NOW."

Before anyone could stop him, Alan strode up to the surly monster, and reaching up, tapped him on the shoulder. The behemoth turned around and grinned down at Ladd, saying, "Hi, Shorty."

That didn't get him any votes.

Alan said, "You weren't invited to this party."

By that time Nolan, Preston, and I had moved in, close behind Alan, as Gargantua sneered, "And you intend to do something about it, huh?"

Alan nodded emphatically, then turned toward the crew and yelled, "GET MY PLANKS!"

It got a helluva laugh from all hands except Mac Colossal.

Before the bewildered crasher could recover, Bob Preston had locked the guy's arms from behind. Possibly the troublemaker had heard of Bob's exploits as a heavyweight in the service. In any case, he cooperated in his fast trip to the door.

From *Wild Harvest* I segued into a remake of *Connecticut Yankee in King Arthur's Court,* starring Bing Crosby, luscious Rhonda Fleming, Bill Bendix, and Sir Cedric Hardwicke. (Another reunion.)

A favorite Crosby story of mine has to do with the time when one of Bing's brothers was selling oil leases. He did pretty well, but, as in all sales ventures, he had lean weeks, a new mortgage, and a crop of kids who went through shoe leather as if it were whipped cream.

He needed tideover money: about forty grand. He approached Brother Bing.

When Bing asked if the leases were any good, his brother's candid answer was, "How can they be? I'm getting fifty percent commission."

Bing checked with his attorney who suggested that Bing invest to the tune of eighty grand. That would give his brother the necessary forty grand, "And you won't owe me a penny," said Bing. "I can wrote it off as a capital loss."

Inevitably, the drilling company struck oil on Bing's leases.

Rhonda Fleming was a beauty, and one of the spunkiest gals I've ever known. I invited the cast of *Connecticut Yankee* to spend a weekend at my ranch at Paso Robles. By that time there was a rugged ranch house and two guest houses on the tree-shaded portion of the 1,700 acres; also a sixty-foot swimming pool, and at a strategic distance a stable for my four saddle horses.

Several of us set out briskly along a winding bridle trail one morning; Rhonda's horse stubbed his toe, lurched forward, and tossed the lovely carrot-top over his head. By the time I reached her, Rhonda was brushing herself off while bringing the horse up to date on the basics of sportsmanship. Every time I looked at that horse for the next two days, he lowered his eyes sheepishly.

My old high school and Naval Air–M.I.T. pal, Bob Stephens, moved into "The Kentucky Ranch" to operate the spread for me. Bob and I did most of the cooking for our string of guests, while one of the invited tended bar; all things considered, we got a helluva play for many years.

Connecticut Yankee completed my chores at Paramount.

One day while I was making final cuts of the picture, Henry Ginsberg said, "Let's take a stroll." We wound up sitting on a pile of lumber on the back lot—the best business conference site in Hollywood.

"We don't have anything for you immediately," Henry said, "but I don't want you to get away from Paramount completely. I'd like to make a deal, guaranteeing you a picture a year for three years, at a hundred grand per picture."

Before I could reply, he went on, "We could make the deal nonexclusive, so you could work elsewhere as much as you liked, just so you would be available once a year for us."

I swallowed hard; it was the greatest of compliments. I thanked Henry fervently, explaining that I couldn't sign anything at that time, but whenever Paramount wanted me, I'd come a-running.

To be frank, on that March afternoon I could almost smell the Chestnut trees blooming along the Champs Élysées, and hear a smoky voice saying, "Dear Tay-ee! It's so good to be with you again."

I was packing—my airline ticket in my pocket—when my agent telephoned with word that Loretta Young had been signed by MGM for a suspense-thriller entitled *Cause for Alarm,* and wanted me to direct.

Tom Lewis, Loretta's husband at that time and a nice guy, was set to produce; a tall, dark-eyed, highly impressive Irisher from the New York stage named Barry Sullivan had been signed to play opposite Loretta.

I figured it to be a fast, pleasant eight weeks' chore—*then* Paris.

The script was a challenge; it played almost entirely in three rooms: the living room, entrance hall, and upstairs master bedroom in a small house. The problem of avoiding the show's becoming static was considerable. A single set is fine for the theatre, but movies must MOVE.

Loretta, adding a glamorous note to production conferences, suggested that we rehearse the entire story in the actual sets before we rolled a camera. It was a sage idea.

We rehearsed for a week; Joe Ruttenberg, our cameraman, sat in. During the last two days of rehearsal, Joe added his camera operator and gaffer. The result was that when we were ready to shoot, we not only knew the playing of every scene, but each camera setup for the entire show.

We wound up with a taut, exciting suspense picture, made in eleven no-overtime days—a schedule unheard of at MGM, or any other major studio.

I started to pack for Paris once again. Humming, I was closing my suitcase as the postman arrived.

A letter from Joan.

She said she was writing hurriedly from Lucerne, where she and Henri were to spend the summer. It had come about suddenly, doctors' orders—she was already homesick for Paris—and for me.

In Paris there would have been plenty of work for me; in Lucerne . . .? After all, I'd already learned to ski, disastrously, during *S.O.S. Iceberg.*

Silently, during the ensuing weeks, I thanked God that I had gone back to MGM; the faces were familiar, the studio routines comfortable.

I signed immediately to direct *Soldiers Three,* an adaptation of the Kipling novel. The stars were Stewart Granger, Walter Pidgeon, David Niven, Robert Newton, and Cyril Cusack.

Those ingredients should have made a good picture, but the miscasting of one principal, which I failed to recognize until it was too late, threw the show completely out of balance. Trying to restore equilibrium with jokes and gags was like trying to cure bubonic plague with warm beer.

(P.S. Recently I caught a television presentation of *Soldiers Three* after not having seen the film in decades. I was astonished at how well it had stood the changes in time, attitude, and vocabulary, and how effective were the performances of the celebrated principals. Perhaps I judged the picture too harshly.)

In any case, in the midst of my professional exasperation, my personal life improved unexpectedly.

I went to a cocktail party one night—one of those obligatory things. Because I didn't drink while I was in production, I found the function to be what Barbara Stanwyck once described as "a fete worse than death."

I had to get the hell outa there, so I eased into the kitchen and out through the service entrance which opened onto the corridor. As I closed the back door, I heard a second surreptitious click from the apartment's front door.

I swung around. A tall, handsome blonde girl swung around. We faced each other—a pair of party-poopers.

[273]

"My watch has stopped," I said, as though that explained everything. "Do you know what time it is?"

"Nine-fifteen, and I was bored too," my fellow fugitive admitted.

"How about a quick cup of coffee at Musso's?"

She said gently, "I don't believe we've met."

"Let's remedy that. I'm Tay Garnett."

"Oh yes—*The Postman Always Rings Twice.* I'm Mari Aldon."

"You're an actress?"

"Yes, I've just finished a tour with the National Company of *Streetcar Named Desire.* I played the younger sister."

We talked for two hours over coffee and flannel cakes. I asked her to have luncheon with me at the Brown Derby the next day, to go on with the conversation.

That luncheon lasted until the waiters began to hum, "Good Night, Ladies."

We had luncheon the following day in the Lanai Room at the Beverly Hills Hotel.

During the previous restless night I had decided that I must be absolutely honest with this young, beautiful, talented, and fascinating girl. I said, "I like you very much, and I want to see you as often as possible, but in all fairness I don't want our association to rule out some guy who might offer you a future. I'm a two-time loser, and I don't intend to marry again."

She smiled and shrugged. "I'm sure we can be good friends, because I'm not interested in marriage either." She added lightly, "I am *intensely* interested in a career, and I KNOW something wonderful is about to break for me."

She was right; she signed a term contract with Warner Brothers the following week, and her first assignment was the lead opposite Gary Cooper in *Distant Drums,* directed by Raoul Walsh. Not bad.

As for me, Quixote Garnett was about to embark on another windmill tilting.

Bert Friedlob (of *Athene* fame) came back into my life, a condition guaranteeing my need for millions in insurance and a task force of guardian angels.

Bert's first question was whether I could write an exciting, romantic, pathetic, funny, action story against a Roller Bowl background.

The gimmick was that Bert owned the International Roller Speedway (a Roller Derby type of operation), that had made, he said, a terrific hit in Europe.

Bert's big price for my services was right (and so, at the moment, was his bankbook), so I telephoned Horace McCoy—with whom I was collaborating at the time — and we went to work on an exciting, romantic, pathetic, funny, action story. (The film from Horace's novel, *They Shoot Horses, Don't They?* won a full set of Oscars in 1970.)

Our completed script, entitled *Fireball,* dealt with an orphan boy who was skating-mad, and whose every dream was of becoming a pro roller bowl racer. Just as he was getting a professional start, he contracted polio; however, after a dramatic interlude of suffering and heroic determination, he put on his skates again and eventually achieved his ambition.

The ideal casting for the boy was Mickey Rooney; he read the script, liked it, and agreed to do it. We signed two additional big names: Pat O'Brien and Milburn Stone (the beloved "Doc" of today's *Gunsmoke*).

Seeking a picture backer, Bert and I talked to Joe Schenck about, maybe, thirty grand. Joe chewed his cigar, then said, "The odds are long, but it's still a good bet. I'll finance the picture and release it."

I couldn't believe our good luck. To put it simply, I was a profusion of apprehensive incredulity.

I was right.

An accountant's reestimate of the picture's cost was around fifty grand front money. Bert and I scurried to see Joe again.

"I said I was with you, and I am," Joe reiterated. "When do you need the fifty thousand?"

We said, No particular hurry—but the following morning would be nice.

The following morning Joe was found unconscious on the bathroom floor. Rethinking our project had nothing to do with it; apparently he had slipped and struck his head. We were heartsick over Joe's condition, and despondent over our own consequent problems.

We underestimated Joe. When he regained consciousness in the hospital, his first act was to telephone his bank and say, "Lend Bert Friedlob and Tay Garnett fifty thou. I'll endorse it." Then he passed out again.

[275]

Bert and I took a solemn vow that Joe would never regret his endorsement. He never did, proving that miracles are still available.

At that happy point, Bert had another of his recurrent brainstorms: why not take his Roller Speedway to GUAM, and film the picture's backgrounds during the Speedway's island appearance.

GUAM! WHY GUAM?

Bert explained that in order to entice laborers to work on government projects on Guam, Congress had passed a law exempting all Americans from income tax liability on Guam earnings.

I'm as greedy as the next man, in a nice kind of way, but I began to shake my head. Bert insisted on checking with a tax attorney who had been in the Air Force during WW II; he said we'd be doing the U. S. a favor by supplying amusement for The Rock, which was without excitement once the poodle-sized pack rats had retired for the night. He predicted that we'd make a mint.

I protested, "But, Bert, Joe's backing does NOT include a trip to Guam."

"Don't worry," advised Bert with a sweeping gesture. "I've got a coupla pals—David May and Bud Nast—who are born pigeons; I've already talked to them about Guam, and they want a piece of the action. Naturally, they're not included in the picture deal."

There is no easy way for a man to get off the summit of a roller coaster. I was stuck for the rest of the ride.

Once financing was set, we began to line up equipment. First step was to have seating built. This consisted of "circus blues" (2 x 12s painted blue) made to stretch horizontally between vertical stepped racks set at intervals of about four feet.

Next, the same carpenters built the heavy plywood Speedway track in portable sections.

It does my soul good to remember that this extensive feat of carpentry took place in Bert's patio on Crescent Drive in industry-free Beverly Hills. Only a Friedlob could have pulled it off without having the entire City Council, the Mayor, Wally Berry, and Lewis Stone screaming on his doorstep.

Our equipment ready, our next worry was acquiring acreage on Guam, which was, and is, U. S. Navy. Fortunately, I had a high brass friend who—in TWO short months, by using diplomatic muscle—made it possible for us to be assigned a twenty-acre parade ground.

"Absolutely beautiful site, jutting into the tropic sea," our benefactor rhapsodized.

Upon that lovely spot we made plans to install our prize piece of housing, a portable hangar, designed originally to accommodate two B-29s. Bert had bought it from a surplus outlet.

"Natch, I beat the regular price," he said.

"What was the regular price?" I asked innocently.

"How the hell should I know?" was Bert's exasperated answer.

So much for the Friedlob sense of humor.

We shipped our "physical environment," including a man known as a "canvas master" borrowed from Ringling Brothers, aboard a wallowing tramp steamer; later we bought round-trip airline tickets for our skaters and picture crew.

According to our time plan, the tent should have been up for a week or ten days in advance of our arrival. As our plane neared the island, we were jubilant with anticipation.

We looked, and looked, and looked; we couldn't spot that huge blob of khaki canvas.

I attributed this failing to the fact that I, personally, had never seen a portable B-29 hangar in my life. That condition prevailed even after we had reached the tent site.

We listened, aghast, to our canvas master's fantastic report. Separated from his profanity, the key words were, "No progress."

Because the hangar was constructed without center poles, it had to be supported by outside poles held in place by cables attached to sunken six-foot sections of steel rail, or "dead men."

Here and there an oldtimer had cautioned against trying to drive post holes through coral, but our drill-operator had announced pridefully that he had a bit that would cut coral as if it were birthday cake.

Twelve bits later, at around twelve hundred dollars per bit, reinforcements had to be ordered from the mainland. Pretty tough birthday cake—like the meringue on a restaurant pie.

"What in all HELL is under this parade ground?" the infuriated operator asked rhetorically of the wind, the sea, and a group of laughing natives who, for three weeks, had been watching our operation with gleeful incredulity.

"Steel," said one of the gabbier ones, explaining in gestures and pidgin that when the U. S. forces had returned to Guam after WWII, they had bulldozed all Japanese heavy armament into the sea, then compacted it with a few feet of topsoil to complete the parade ground.

Bert turned to me at the end of this report and yelled, "YOU'RE the *director*. Why don't you look into these things before you go off half-cocked? Now we'll have to find another location for the tent."

"You just do that," I suggested wearily. "Meanwhile I'll go home for the two or three months it will take to get Navy permission to use another area."

"Oh, YOU and your goddam Navy," growled Bert.

"Hey, wait a minute." I turned to the canvas man and asked, "Isn't there some way we could hook our cables onto that mass of metal down there instead of using the 'dead men'?"

His eyes widened. "Why not? We can cut in with torches and weld them."

Shouted Bert, "Well, don't just stand there talking about it. Let's get going."

By the time our hangar had been put up and our show was ready to roll, we were three hundred grand in the red. I was worried half out of my skull. Bert snapped his fingers and said pityingly, "Stop chewing your liver; everything I touch turns to gold."

At first I believed him. Our Roller Speedway was an instant success. Night after night we played to packed, screaming audiences. Everyone on The Rock seemed to select a favorite skater and root for him as if they'd been born of the same mother.

We paid off the three-grand local debt, as well as David May and Bud Nast, and began to hope for the jingle of coins in our own jeans.

Yet we had failed, for the second time, to consider a contingency: Professional skaters are expert stunt men who know how to take spills without suffering serious injury. When our thrill-hungry audiences realized that the apparent mayhem on the track was carefully timed and choreographed, and unlikely to end in murder, they lost interest.

Some wisenheimer, noting our dwindling attendance, suggested that we take our show to Manila, saying there was even less to do in the Philippines than on Guam; we were assured that we could return Stateside as millionaires. Bert decided that was what he had always wanted to be.

On we went to "entertainment-starved" Manila. Almost at once, we discovered that Manila had opera, ballet, a fine symphony orchestra, excellent theatre, movies from everywhere in the world, not to mention baseball, jai-alai, horse racing, boat racing, and dance contests featuring an ankle-breaking little number called the *Singkil.*

Manila was not hungering for a Roller Speedway.

Well, okay. Bert and I still had *Fireball,* an exciting film calculated to bail us out and bolster our bank accounts with maybe a measly million or two.

As things turned out, *Fireball* earned a few thousand for each of us, but the Big Money was forestalled by scandal.

I have to laugh, these days, when I see what appears on motion picture screens, and hear about what actors and actresses do without creating a ripple on the sea of public opinion, then contrast that with what happened twenty-odd years ago to our clean, upbeat little picture about roller skating.

A member of our cast fell for the badger game, except that—in place of an irate "husband"—the scene was crashed by police who had been trying for months to bag the hustler.

News of the actor's folly would have been buried in the want-ads if it hadn't been for a miserable coincidence: On the night of the actor's arrest, his wife gave birth to their first child.

Outraged women's clubs had *Fireball* boycotted in *thirty-two* states!

Fireball itself was as pure as Himalayan air, but it was tainted, according to the guardians of public morals, by the presence of one luckless actor.

And you mean to sit there and tell me you still want to go into the motion picture business? On GUAM?

A man is always glad to get home, loaded or broke. He's glad-plus when he hopes a gorgeous blonde is waiting for him.

I telephoned Mari Aldon and, ignoring my three months' absence during which I hadn't written a line, asked, "How about dinner at Chasen's tonight?"

She answered enthusiastically, "Mmmmmm—okay. I haven't anything else to do."

At Chasen's every man I recognized and several I'd never seen before, hurried over to our table to say "Hello" and be introduced to Mari. Obviously they were overwhelmed. Mari appeared to be underwhelmed.

Here is another truth about the picture business: The demands are such that it is almost impossible to maintain any semblance of social or domestic life. By the time I was combining business with pleasure by taking Mari to a play or a film several times a week, the interlude was terminated by my agent. He had made a deal for me to direct *One Minute to Zero*.

Edmund Grainger was producing; extensive exteriors were to be filmed at Camp Carson, Colorado Springs. Too far away to get back to Hollywood over weekends. (A situation to be remedied by the jet engine a few years later.)

The story of *One Minute to Zero* dealt with the development of air–ground support during the Korean War, a system that employed low-flying fighter aircraft as heavy artillery. It had an exciting potential, and we had the cast to handle it: Robert Mitchum, Richard Egan, William Tallman (destined for fame as Hamilton Burger on the *Perry Mason* show), and delightful Claudette Colbert in a role calculated to build the boys' wartime morale.

Mention of Egan reminds me of one of his World War II experiences. Having attained the rank of major in the Marine Corps, attached to G-2 (Intelligence), he was assigned to a real cutie.

Burdened with two hundred pounds of equipment, Rich was parachuted by night into the jungles of a Japanese-held island in the Pacific. Assuming that he landed intact, he had to get his bearings, bury his parachute, and find a cobra-free cave in which to hole up during the day.

Having established a base of sorts, he was obliged to crawl around through a Stygian tangle of hostile animal and vegetable life, acquiring as much detailed information as possible about the occupation forces, their armament, equipment, supplies, etc.

That accomplished, his orders were to go to his place of concealment, and—at a prearranged hour—crank up his ship-to-shore radio and report his findings to a distant Navy plane standing by. It had to be assumed that the Japanese would monitor Egan, triangulate his position, and with all possible haste start shooting down his throat.

Cutting it very fine, he had perhaps sixty seconds in which to give his report, pack up his radio and survival equipment, and melt into a new forest hideout.

For months, Rich repeated this hairy routine at regular intervals while he subsisted on coconuts, tropical fruits, and occasional goodies liberated from a careless Japanese quartermaster.

At length the island was taken by American forces and Rich was sent home on leave: THIRTY beautiful, carefree days with plenty of stored-up pay.

He landed in San Francisco aglow with expectancy. Rich was born and reared in sight of the Golden Gate, so he had a massive case of the Home Town Hurrahs. First, he planned to surprise his brother, a priest. Mounting the steps of the rectory two at a time, he gave the bell a mighty jab. The housekeeper broke the news that Father Egan had been transferred to Rome.

Bitterly disappointed, Rich walked to the corner drug store and settled in a telephone booth with his little black book. After all, this was his home town; he knew every guy and gal in it.

He dialed a number—no answer. Another—a stranger answered, knew nothing of the previous subscriber. Another—another.

Everyone seemed to have disappeared into war's confusion.

At ten o'clock on the morning of the fourth day of the major's leave—having made contact with not one friend or acquaintance—Egan took up a spot at the end of a posh bar. He ordered a double bourbon.

A few moments later an Army colonel stepped up to the bar and ordered Scotch.

"Arrogant bastard," thought Rich, glaring insolently.

The A. B. glared back.

Rich ordered another double bourbon and, his upper lip curled, slid along the bar two seats nearer the infantryman.

The colonel motioned for another double Scotch and closed the gap from *his* original position by two spaces.

[281]

Seven double belts later the two branches of the Armed Forces were within striking distance of one another.

Egan asked, "You looking for something?"

"Trouble," said the colonel.

"You came to the right shop. I'm loaded with it."

"Fine. Shall we step out back?"

Rich, holding the bar steady to keep it from collapsing, said, "Be my guest."

"In all fairness," the colonel demurred, "I should show you this." He passed over a card.

Rich focused on it with difficulty.

It identified the colonel as light-heavyweight champion of the Pacific Forces.

"You've been more than fair," said Rich. "I can do no less." He tossed out three cards from his own wallet. The first certified him as a holder of the Karate Black Belt; the second recorded his pistol championship in the Marine Corps, and the third registered his qualifications as a knife fighter.

The colonel studied the cards. "Sir," he said, "may I buy you a drink?"

It turned out to be a nice day after all.

Back to Colorado Springs and *One Minute to Zero.*

Zero was the last picture Howard Hughes financed at RKO before selling the studio. One of the delights of working for Mr. Hughes was that his film companies went platinum-plated First Class. Our cast and crew (about 200 people) were housed in Anderson Company weatherproofed tents having plywood floors covered with heavy linoleum. Each tent had its own heating unit, private shower, and bathroom facilities.

As for the food—Henry VIII would have lopped off heads to get our chef.

Although my tent was ideal, I spent most of my time at the Garden of the Gods Club. I needed isolation, because I worked on the script every night, which wouldn't mix with conviviality.

As things worked out, we had the longest shooting schedule of any picture in recent years with the possible exception of *Cleopatra.*

Fortunately, nobody fell in love on the *Zero* set, or we'd be shooting yet.

When we arrived in Colorado, the trees had just come into full leaf. When we finally locked up the last can of film, we had wired alien branches to the denuded aspens so as to match the stuff we'd shot in the spring.

Our initial difficulty was that, three-fourths through the location shooting, Claudette Colbert came down with a four-star case of pneumonia. She was game, but 104 degrees of fever hospitalized her.

Eddie Grainger telephoned Howard Hughes, outlining our difficulty: Claudette's doctor had advised against her working for at least three months.

Not to be outdone, I also developed a short sequence of pneumonia. I was fresh out of the hospital when Mr. Hughes returned Grainger's call. H. H. suggested that I fly to Hollywood, because he wanted me, personally, to discuss the Colbert role with Joan Crawford.

Joan was represented by Lew Wasserman (then head of the MCA talent agency, and now president of Universal Studios). I've always felt that, because the male roles were dominant in *Zero,* Lew advised Joan against taking the lone female part. I was disappointed; I had known Joan for years and had always wanted to direct her. She brings a brilliant talent onto the set, and I'm convinced she would have been great in the *Zero* role.

In Hollywood I reported the situation to Mr. Hughes (by telephone) and was told to return to Colorado Springs the next morning, because Ann Blyth had been signed for the part.

ANN BLYTH?

Somewhat earlier, Ann had played (superbly) Joan Crawford's daughter in *Mildred Pierce;* obviously our entire script had to be rewritten to accommodate the younger casting. Time, as usual, was of the essence, so Grainger flew Bundy Solt into Colorado Springs to do that rewrite.

We could cope with cast and script problems; the location difficulty that gave us nightmares slithered under bushes, and rattled like gravel in a tin pan.

I asked the commanding officer, "What do you guys do about rattlesnakes?"

"Kill 'em!" he said firmly. "We shoot or hack up from twenty to thirty each day. Just don't step where you haven't looked."

Our still cameraman went batty over Colorado scenery. He often used an old-fashioned glass plate camera, and focused by covering his head with a thick black cloth. One morning he was lining up a scenic shot when our property man told him in a carefully normal tone, "Don't move. Whatever you do, don't step back. All right, slide your right foot to the right. Fine! Now slide your left foot up beside your right. Okay—JUMP RIGHT!"

The rattlesnake had been no more than two feet away when our cameraman executed his maneuver; lonely and frustrated, the snake chickened out and disappeared into some dried weeds where he could pout undisturbed. Another built-in headache was the erratic Colorado weather. New England could take lessons.

We were entertaining the S.A.C. brass at the Garden of the Gods Club one beautiful moonlit evening, when the power failed; instantly the room was illuminated by forked white lightning, and a second later it reverberated with thunder. Rafters were still ringing when the roof was hit by a cannonade of hailstones the size of golf balls.

So it shouldn't be a total loss, we used the hail to chill our Air Force libations.

There were days when the temperature would plunge from seventy at midmorning to the low thirties at twilight. An assistant director told me one such night, "Boss, we gotta get outa here—or finish this fillum on snowshoes."

The final scene was to show the American forces forging northward to regain territory lost before the institution of air–ground support. For that scene we had been granted a one-time-ONLY use of all the personnel and rolling equipment at Camp Carson, plus a squadron of tanks from the military depot at Pueblo.

Strung out on a winding, muddy mountain road, the cavalcade stretched from foreground to infinity.

My fingers ached with cold inside fur-lined gloves. Keeping an eye on a sky as purple as the devil's belly, I yelled "Roll 'em."

The camera began to grind.

The cavalcade moved forward. One hundred and eighty feet of film later I yelled, "Cut and print it!"

Clenching my fist at the sky I exulted, "I got it, you bastard! I GOT it."

The sky had the last word. It spat a snowflake right in my eye.

And you mean to sit there and tell me you still want to go into the motion picture business? In Colorado?

The next period in Hollywood history—a report the reader may skip if he is easily frightened—is essentially a horror story.

Television was abroad in the land.

It was dull beyond enduring, but the human animal is fascinated by the unlikely. The idea that images, blurry and bloodless in a haunting blue light, walking and talking and selling soap, could be brought into one's *own* living room on a tiny screen, held millions breathless AT HOME, night after night.

The neighborhood theatre was deserted even by termites.

Hollywood's finest minds wrestled with the problem. The theory that there might be something lacking in motion pictures was discarded in favor of the premise that "The damned idiot box is what's lousing us up. We gotta give the customers a BIGGER SCREEN."

So we had 3-D with blue/red glasses, Wide Screen, Wider Screen, and Let's Shoot It on the Sahara.

Another theory, of which I became the victim, held that we hadn't been giving audiences enough star power.

Lester Cowan, a producer who had taken offices at Goldwyn Studios, brought me a script written by Sampson Raphaelson. It was so good that, naturally, Cowan had it rewritten five or six times.

What was left of the story was "higher than Kansas in August." It dealt with an aspiring young playwright who fell in love with an ambitious young actress.

Playwright's play flops; actress scores brilliant success; playwright tries suicide; police stop him; wise longtime theatrical greats give him fight talk; tearful reunion with successful actress; fadeout on wedding-bound kiss.

On the abovementioned "more and more will do the trick" theory, we were given the following cast, listed alphabetically because I never know when I'll be working with them again, here or hereafter:

[285]

Tallulah Bankhead, Ethel Barrymore, Lionel Barrymore, Gertrude Berg (Molly Goldberg), Louis Calhern, Rex Harrison, Josh Logan, Mary Martin, Tommy Monaco, Mary Murphy, Lilli Palmer, Rodgers and Hammerstein, Herb Shriner, and Cornel Wilde.

What a waste.

I spent an entire summer on David May's boat—trying to recuperate.

For lack of a project I was beginning to throw kisses to seagulls when I had a call from Irving Allen and Cubby Broccoli in London. They had Alan Ladd under contract for several pictures, and were kicking around a story idea. All they had to go on was a title, *The Black Knight.*

I want to make it perfectly clear that our *Black Knight* had nothing to do with the Saracen in Sir Walter Scott's *Ivanhoe.* Or with Sugar Ray Robinson.

Alec Coppel had been signed to write the script, aided by snide comments from me. As planned by Alec, the story line had Alan Ladd in medieval armor and a midwestern accent, horsing around old castles in search of his Lady Love. You can't blame him: The gal was Patricia Medina.

Fundamentally, the plot was one of those bootblack-to-President things. Alan, as a kid, worked in a blacksmith's shop, hammering out armor. With diligence, courage, and lots of help from Coppel's script, he worked his way up to a fiery sword.

Alec was living in his villa ON THE RIVIERA, and asked me to be his guest. Inevitably, the work went slowly.

First, because of the climate.

Second, because of the supreme complication named Mari Aldon. I couldn't get her out of my mind.

I telephoned her in Hollywood and announced, "I want to get married."

She was ecstatic. She asked, "Why don't you?"

"I mean to you," I clarified.

"Call me back when you're sober," she said, hanging up gently.

I called the following morning—having calculated the time in California more carefully—and repeated my proposal.

It was then that I realized how long I had been *un*married. I had forgotten that no woman worth her bobby pins can go anywhere without a stitch to wear. Translation: without an entirely new wardrobe.

Okay, I said. How long would it take to round up a reasonable set of new threads?

Mari thought she could manage it in—oh, a couple of weeks—so we met in London SIX weeks later and were married in Caxton Hall, a ceremonial edifice comparable, I believe, to our Chambers of Commerce. (I was a divorced man, hence, under British law, denied a church wedding.)

Mari forgave me the unglamorous setting, but found it a little more difficult to work up enthusiasm over production plans that had advanced the starting date of *The Black Knight* one week. We had to leave for Spain the morning after our wedding; I pointed out that ours might be the only honeymoon in history that included 150 house guests. She was not amused.

Incidentally, Mari's trunk, packed with her beautiful trousseau, was crushed like marshmallows under a hippo's foot during shipment from Los Angeles to London. Although the trunk and its contents were insured, Mari never realized a penny, because of a tricky little clause having to do with "Acts of God."

I'd never believe *He* was that sort of Guy.

Although our story was laid amid the castles of Scotland, my recollection of the Fairbanks–Hellman Scottish mist recommended a more southerly climate for the sake of thrift.

Spain was a left jab to the heart for us. The Castellana Hilton had been opened only a few months; we had a suite on the fifth floor from which we could see an arc of the city against the magnificent backdrop of the Sierra de Guadarrama—roughly, very roughly, comparable to Palm Springs' Chocolate Mountains.

Spain offered a large variety of spectacular castles. We photographed several: Toledo, Segovia, Seville, Granada, but chose, for our major battle action, the plains before the walled city of Avila.

The Spanish government lent us a crack company of cavalry, which we costumed in medieval armor made in England of PLASTIC!

Our particular company of cavalry had just won the World's International Equestrian title, beating the Italians for the first time in twenty years. I doubt that anyone has ever seen greater precision and flexibility, or closer coordination between animal and rider.

As the battle raged, "The Black Knight" was supposed to leap from a castle wall and land ninety-eight feet below in the moat. The moat was dry, a matter of satisfaction to our stunt man, Paul Baxley.

He stacked cardboard boxes about ten feet deep in the moat beneath the crenelation from which he was to jump. While I turned purple, holding my breath, Paul made a spectacular leap and terminated it in a safe three-point landing. A little rough on the boxes, of course.

Things were going well for the picture; so well that when a cable arrived one morning, I refused to read it. Handing it to my assistant, I said, "*You* have a strong heart. After you've read it, let me know what's wrong—in a day or so."

He broke the news promptly and gently: He yelled, "MY GOD, ALAN LADD IS IN A HOSPITAL IN CANADA. HE'S BROKEN HIS ANKLE."

This explains why directors, operating under tight schedule and budget, become alcoholics and/or go mad, and/or drop dead.

When I regained consciousness, we laid out all our action stuff in medium and long shots with Paul Baxley—a perfect double for Ladd at a distance—and made scenic plates so we could process Alan in later.

As soon as we had finished our location stuff, we flew to London to await Alan's arrival.

Meanwhile, Mari was busier than a chaperone at a Miss America contest being judged by Warren Beatty. She appeared in *Barefoot Contessa,* starring Ava Gardner and presided over by Joe Mankiewicz; she starred in a live BBC production of *Once in a Lifetime;* David Lean, impressed by her performance, cast her in the newly-wed role in *Summertime* starring Kate Hepburn, Rosanno Brazzi and Darrin McGavin.

During this period Mari and I were living in a "maisonette" in Eton Square. We had been there for months before we were informed that we were ensconced in the Bel Air of London, and "How did you EVER find so delightful a place?" Oh, we just looked under our checkbook and there it was.

While Mari was occupied with a thriving career, I did two things. Bad news first.

Robert Ruark, newly returned from Kenya, told me many of the anecdotes later included in his brilliant novel, *Uhuru.* Since Kenya was still under British rule, I figured making a film there wouldn't be much more hazardous than making films on Guam or in Colorado.

I wrote a synopsis of a Mau Mau story, and asked Bob Mitchum (back in Hollywood) to read it. He liked it, and said he'd do it.

Next, I went to the film Finance Office in London and was assured of Edy Plan Participation, and what was called "split-hemisphere" financing.

Mari and I flew to Hollywood to firm up Western Hemisphere financing. Also to secure a letter of agreement between Mitch and me. Mitch was represented by my own agent, Bert Allenberg, so the negotiations were simple except for one problem: I had been unable to get a definite fix on the "no-rain" season in Nairobi.

East Africa House in London had given me two widely divergent dates. Opinion seemed to be split down the middle as to exactly WHEN we would risk getting our generator trucks bogged down in mud.

Bearing that in mind, we specified in our agreement that *one of two possible dates* would be mutually agreed upon as starting date as soon as I could get definite rainfall information.

Agreement in hand, we flew back to England. I was supplied with past rainy season statistics, so I telephoned Allenberg to stipulate our starting date.

Bert said lightly that he was sorry, but Mitch wouldn't be available. Bert had just signed him to star in *Blood Alley,* a Batjac Production to be directed by my old friend, Bill Wellman. It was set to roll on *my* starting date.

"But what about our agreement?" I gasped.

"Oh, THAT!" Bert said offhandedly. "It stated specifically that the choice of date must be *mutually agreed upon.* Mitch doesn't agree, so there is no mutuality."

I had been had. Looking back on it, I believe I used a lot of lurid invective. It didn't change anything, but it relieved some of the pressure.

[289]

The final irony was that Bob Mitchum—on the first day of shooting *Blood Alley* in San Francisco—shoved a longshoreman off the dock and was promptly fired from the picture by Bob Fellows.

This ill wind blew me no good; my London arrangements had been cancelled by a disenchanted Film Finance Office, so there was no way to reactivate *Mau Mau.*

In such emergencies, one turns to one's friends for consolation. There was a substantial Stateside contingent of homesick actors working in London, all yearning for U. S. chow—not necessarily better than London's, merely different.

Mari and I assembled an honest-to-Alabama fried chicken dinner, complete with corn-on-the-cob (canned), hot biscuits, mashed potatoes, cornbread, crisp chicken of course, and as a topper, apple pie made from an old Garnett family recipe.

The last guest to arrive was Ava Gardner. When Mari answered the door, there stood what could have passed as a Royal Duchess, about to attend a coronation ball. Spreading her arms and whirling about, Ava announced, "I don't care what anyone else is wearing; I bought this gown today, and I HAD to spring it."

She made a highly successful entrance to the applause of her show biz buddies.

Mari and I were all set to sing out, "Come and get it," when Mari realized that we'd forgotten to make the gravy, without which fried chicken just ain't.

Ava Gardner to the rescue. "Stand aside," she said. "Give me room according to my talent. I just happen to be the best country gravy maker on earth." She waved a large wooden spoon with authority,

I stared at her. At that time she was probably the most beautiful woman since Helen of Troy, and the best-dressed since Elizabeth I. The gown emphasized Nature's close attention to art on the day Ava went down the assembly line.

"You should be wearing an apron," Mari suggested.

"Don't give it a thought; I'm not one of your sloppy cooks. Here, taste!"

I took the spoon. The gravy was fantastic. Sheer Cordon Bleu.

Her hair was unmussed, her forehead dry, her gown without evidence of accident. I regarded my shirt and trousers ruefully. I looked like the testing ground for a leopard factory. Mari, of course, was wearing an apron.

Other guests that evening were Bob Taylor, John Huston, Lana Turner, Susie and Alan Ladd, Peter Cushing, Patricia Medina (who brought us greetings from Johnny Farrow), and Clark Gable who sat on the floor throughout most of the evening, crooning to a fifth of cognac. It should be recorded that he arose after a hearty dinner, leaving an empty Courvoisier bottle, and walked to his car as if he'd been drinking Uncola.

On another occasion, we decided to assemble a Mexican dinner. It took two weeks to collect the ingredients. We located "polenta" (corn meal) in an Italian grocery. A full day's search turned up chili powder in an Indian grocery in Soho. We found suitable cheese in a Dutch delicatessen, onions and tomatoes in a Spanish grocery. The alligator pears for guacamole came from North Africa, and at Simpson's we discovered U. S. canned hominy that I ground to make tortillas.

That dinner, served to the same group mentioned earlier, was an outstanding success. Sometimes I think I should have gone into the restaurant business; oysters on the half-shell might have paid better than turkeys on celluloid.

Incidentally, a terrible storm had blown in from the North Sea on the afternoon of the Mexican dinner. With all aircraft grounded, all shipping held in harbor by a full gale warning, and all England—to a man—sloshing knee-deep in ankle-high rubbers, we were flattered to have our entire guest list show up.

It was Robert Taylor who brought us a newspaper bearing, in scare headlines, Britain's commentary on the weather:

CONTINENT ISOLATED

29

With Mari's European commitments satisfied, and mine lying in state, we decided to hurry home.

We took an apartment on Wilshire Boulevard, and I signed with a new agent, Bob Coryell.

In Hollywood, business and pleasure walk hand in hand to the advantage of both. During our first week in California, Mari and Vera Peterson set up a dinner date. Mari and Vera had become friends on *Barefoot Contessa* in Rome, where Vera had been Bogart's hairdresser. And no comments about Bogie's NEED for a hairdresser. Vera was married to Walter Thompson, a film editor for Cinerama and a delightful guy.

Over dinner at Chasen's, Walter asked, "Are you totally committed for the next few months? If you aren't, I'd like to recommend you to Merian Cooper. He needs several directors for *Seven Wonders of the World.* Tey Tetzlaff is now shooting the Italian stuff, and Cooper is looking for additional guys like you who have filmed in unusual places and can combine diplomacy with picture business."

Two days later Merian Cooper (of *King Kong* fame) sent for me. Bob Coryell and I hotfooted over, and signed after a brief conversation about the wonders of INDIA. The deal included Mari as my secretary.

In preparation for my segment of *Seven Wonders of the World,* I spent a week in Warner Brothers' Hollywood Theatre (which had been newly converted to Cinerama), studying *This Is Cinerama,* the first production filmed in supercolossal Wide Screen, and directed by Mr. Cooper.

I sat in practically every seat in the house. I tried the front row, the back, each side in several locations, and the balcony; I needed to know how various angles fared when projected on that huge screen. For the information of the technical-minded, the Cinerama camera contains three heads, each with a 25 millimeter lens, slightly overlapping, giving the camera a close approximation of the scope of the human eye.

Few men have suffered more for their art than I; sitting in any position was pure agony, because we had started our course of immunizations the previous Monday—everything from yellow fever through typhoid, paratyphoid, typhus, tetanus, cholera and the standard smallpox vaccination. The latter in the arm, thank God. My posterior was the anguished color of a sacred baboon's after backing into a porcupine.

Those who saw *This Is Cinerama* will recall that the most hair-raising portion of the film was that in which the camera was taken for a roller-coaster ride. It was a four-scream experience that brought audiences back again and again: the wrap-around screen gave viewers a thrill far beyond that provided by an actual scenic railway ride.

Cooper asked me to keep my eyes open for anything that might provide a comparable hair-crimper, toe-curler, and spine-vibrator.

We flew Pan-American via London, Rome, and Beirut to Delhi; the Cinerama company chartered a DC-6 to carry the First Camera and crew; the Second Camera and crew were carried on a DC-3, piloted by Paul Mantz.

After flying all over India in search of things of broad, general interest, we decided to spend a few days in Delhi and New Delhi, the latter simply a modern extension of the old city. "New" in India is always comparative and repairable.

Naturally, we had to photograph a cobra vs. mongoose fight, as obligatory a tourist sight as the sidewalk comfort stations in Paris.

The average tourist never knows that what he is shown is almost as staged as a film fight. Whenever a cobra is to be used in a performance, he is first milked by his trainer, so that his poison sacs are empty. Any self-respecting snake must find total disarmament highly discouraging.

Add the fact that the cobra has probably made the scene thirty to forty times before, with the same mongoose. It is inevitable that the snake, a seasoned contestant, should do his best to escape the mongoose who has all the aces.

When we started to film our fight, the fakir set up his performers in the center of a large ring of seated natives, who wouldn't let the cobra escape. Turned back by the native perimeter, the snake zipped into his basket where he was safe. As for the mongoose, he seemed less than upset; he just sat back and breathed on his manicure.

When the cobra was again dumped into the ring, he shrugged helplessly and made a feeble pass at his enemy, at which point the mongoose closed his jaws on a point just behind the cobra's head. Before the mongoose could finish the job, the Fakir pried the mongoose's jaws open and stuffed the limp reptile back into his basket.

I refused to photograph a fixed fight; I insisted that a fresh snake and a mongoose without dramatic training be used. The result was some extremely exciting film. Women, descended from Eve, didn't much care for the sequence.

Incidentally, show biz cobras are the original Anna Helds of India. They are bathed daily in water-buffalo milk to heal the wounds of mongoose combat.

Next, the Taj Mahal. To avoid picture postal elevations, my cameraman and I crossed the river to the opposite mudflats at dawn. We lined up an ancient rowboat in the foreground against a REAR view of the Taj. I still gloat over filming Taj and boat reflected in the still pink waters of the river.

On we mushed to Benares, the religious capital of India, where we shot forbidden footage showing the burning ghats—funeral pyres—along the Ganges.

However, I still hadn't found my roller coaster.

A continued search finally landed us high in the Himalayas, near the Tibetan border at Darjeeling, home of the Ghurkha. These tough, bearded men were a photographer's delight in their cold-weather costumes, in contrast to the sleazy white nightgowns worn in the rest of India.

Each male Ghurkha carried a knife unique to this area. Near the hilt, on the back of the blade, there was a notch through which a man could sight his prey, then—relying on a sort of eye-to-arm computer system—hurl the knife. The Ghurkha were masters of the art.

They could kill game or what-have-you instantly and at remarkable distances.

In addition to Ghurkha, Darjeeling boasted another charm: a spunky, puffing little train on a mini–narrow gauge rail line that carried daily provisions from the valley, 6,800 feet below, up to Darjeeling. The moment I saw it, I knew I'd found my roller coaster.

That train wasn't really a train at all but a mountain goat with wheels. It clung to a narrow ledge circling a mountain; it had to gain altitude rapidly, and there were areas where there was no room for switchbacks, so it made occasional loops—tight loops not more than 150 feet in diameter—the track crossing above itself. One side of the train brushed the greenery clinging to the rocky mountain walls, and the outer side of the curve looked straight down to the bottom of the chasm between three and six thousand feet below. I'm being a bit careless in stating the depth of the canyons, because after you fall a thousand feet, the next several are only repetition without changing the ultimate result.

My train burned hard coal, but instead of the standard tender and fireman, this engine was equipped with a coal bin on top of the engine's boiler. A fireman, powered with a sledge, sat on top of the coal pile, cracking up huge chunks of fuel, and pouring the debris down a chute to the engineer in the cab.

On the front of the locomotive, in the position normally occupied by a cowcatcher, there was a flat plank about three inches thick and eighteen inches wide. Two men, one above each rail, stood on this informal platform with a box of damp sand between them. The grade was so steep that the men had to sprinkle the wet sand on the track to give the locomotive enough traction to drag the train up its mountain incline. At Darjeeling, the engine was run onto a turntable in preparation for the precipitous return trip, brakes courtesy of wet sand.

A train is a train is a train. To involve the audience with it emotionally, to personalize that one train in that one situation, the train had to become the principal character in a breathtaking drama.

I dug back into my Sennett experience for chase-sequence techniques. I decided to introduce a standard camera-bearing tourist, glazed of eye and unsteady of foot, thanks to his 100-proof cargo. He

—along with a dozen or so natives—boarded the train at the foot of the mountain for the trip up to Darjeeling. Inevitably, seeking solitude, our tourist sprawled alone on the very last seat in the open observation car.

Away went the train, chugging conscientiously upward toward Darjeeling.

On one of the relatively flat places in the track, a mother elephant and her baby—weary from traipsing through an upland forest—decided to take a siesta on the right-of-way. The exasperated engine screeched to a stop; its crew left the train, intending to shoo Mama Pachyderm away, and were joined by all the curious passengers with one exception. Our lush, involved with some pink elephants of his own, remained aboard.

Left unattended, our train began to slide backward, gradually at first, then on a wildly careening descent.

The engineer, noting a catastrophe in the making, leaped down the mountain, taking hazardous shortcuts through dense jungle growth in an attempt to intercept the runaway on a switchback. The passengers, yelling and perspiring, raced after him.

We intercut shots of the canting train with flashes of our peacefully slumbering drunk; then a quick cut to our engineer and passengers rushing out of the undergrowth in time to see the train zoom by; then viewpoint shots (what the drunk would have seen had he been awake) as the train pitched around loops suspended over the chasm's depths.

When this sequence was shown in theatres, every member of the audience was convinced that *he* was being hurtled around those dizzy curves. The yelling cracked glassware in a bar three blocks away.

Our train, abruptly regaining its dignity, slid to a stop in the station. It was a photo finish with the gasping, mud-caked engineer.

The drunk awakened, brushed his clothing, and with great aplomb descended from the car, telling the engineer grandly, "Thank you so very much for a lovely trip!"

Now for the technical problems.

Our little train couldn't be kept on the track if it descended faster than it ascended—a maximum speed of ten miles per hour.

Again, Sennett to the rescue. I told our cameraman to underspeed

[296]

the camera, so as to make ten mph look and feel like 100 mph when shown on the Cinerama screen. It worked.

There was an additional problem. As already mentioned, the train was the only means of transporting supplies to Darjeeling from the valley. To have tied it up for a film over a long period would have worked great hardship upon Darjeeling residents.

The government gave us wonderful cooperation, considering the difficulties involved. We were permitted to use the train for three or four hours per day, depending upon delivery problems, *over a five-day period.*

It took us an hour to get down from Darjeeling to the loop location, and an hour to return, permitting us—at the outside—120 minutes of actual shooting time per day. Subtract from that the minutes required to set up the Monster (the 500-pound Cinerama camera), and you have some idea how ingeniously and desperately hard we had to work to accomplish anything in the allotted time.

As *Seven Wonders of the World* worked out, my sequence was wonderfully received, but for my money the best sequence in the show was conceived and shot in Rome by Teddy Tetzlaff.

Teddy concocted a drama about an earnest, fat little guy who was determined to deliver his wife and five kids to St. Peter's Square in time to be blessed by the Pope on Easter Sunday.

The earnest, fat little guy's transportation was a motorcycle with sidecar. He was late in starting, so he was aflutter as he loaded the family on the frail and gasping vehicle.

A couple of "run-bys" later, the bike whimpered and conked out.

At that point, Teddy went to the old Sennett time-pressure pattern. He cut to a long-shot of a million people standing in St. Peter's Square, the Pope standing on his balcony addressing the multitude.

Cut to the fat guy getting his stalled motorcycle started again.

Cut to the multitude and the Pope.

Cut to the family—stalled again!

Cut to the Piazza as the Pope utters the final benediction and leaves the balcony.

Cut to the fat little guy and his load winding through the final narrow street and swinging into the Piazza in time to see a few stragglers taking pictures of an empty balcony.

In order to get a good close shot of His Holiness as he emerged onto the balcony, Tetzlaff (with the permission of His Holiness, of course) had his technicians build a "camera parallel"—high platform—facing the balcony.

The Pontiff was both charming and deeply interested in the camera techniques making possible his appearance to millions of theatregoers in addition to those gathered in St. Peter's Square.

Consequently he was completely cooperative, and even consented to stage the ceremony and benediction for the camera the day before the actual appearance was to take place.

The Pope was inclined to move about on the balcony while speaking.

Teddy Tetzlaff faced a quandary. How does one tell the Pope, in his own bailiwick, how he *must* approach the camera and why he must hold steady in one spot.

An English-speaking member of the Vatican Court came to Tetzlaff's aid by explaining the difficulty to His Holiness, who twinkled and understood.

It was decided that one of Tetzlaff's camera assistants, an Irish Catholic, would be admitted to the Pope's private quarters to chalk guidance marks on the balcony floor.

Il Papa was warned not to look down at his chalk marks as he approached them, because that would destroy the illusion of spontaneity.

After a try or two, His Holiness discovered that there was a knack to "feeling" the marks as seasoned actors do; it was a trick that took time to acquire, so it was agreed that the camera assistant would lie on the balcony floor and *manually* direct the Pontiff's feet into the proper position.

The Pope found all this preparation highly amusing. By that time the entire crew had fallen in love with that gentle, humorous, and most gracious man.

After Tetzlaff was satisfied with his tower closeup, he told his cameraman, "Cut and print it."

His Holiness called out to Teddy, "If you don't mind, could we do it over again? I'm sure I can do it better."

Shades of Greer Garson.

To be absolutely candid, I didn't know then, and I don't know now, why I was drinking so heavily during that period of my life. No man becomes an alcoholic overnight; the state is a creeper-upper, and one has to work at it.

I had always enjoyed a drink—par for the Navy course—but gradually I had gone beyond the social stage and had begun to "need" a couple of belts to get myself "even" because of widely varying provocations. I saw to it that a generous supply of the necessary provocations was always available.

Mari was patient. "You'll realize, one of these days, that alcohol isn't a human necessity," she said quietly.

"God, I *hope* not," was the way I countered that one.

One morning, as we were leaving the Imperial Hotel in New Delhi, a turbaned fakir sidled up to Mari and said, "I can predict your future, Memsahib."

"No, thank you," said Mari.

"There is MUCH I can tell you, Memsahib."

With an "I'll-bet" smile, Mari repeated courteously, "No, thank you."

"You are going to have a ginger-haired baby girl, Memsahib."

I tipped the fortune-teller rather more than necessary and asked Mari, "Are you?"

"Check with me next October," she answered, grinning.

On the crisp, sunny morning of October 25, 1955, in Stone Canyon, Bel Air, Mari awakened me with the news that, "I think we should go to the hospital. Call the doctor and tell him the pains are coming five minutes apart."

Mari didn't realize what I had been through: months of trepidation, consternation, panic, terror and alcohol. Women never know about these things.

In brief—I couldn't find the telephone with which to call the doctor. It was on a long, long cord, so naturally . . .

Mari placed the call while I packed for her. I was thorough. I included her opera glasses and a gold mesh purse but somehow overlooked her toothbrush, comb, and nightgown.

Without untoward incident, I managed to back the car out of the garage and drive to St. John's Hospital in Santa Monica. I felt like a fool; after all my *sang froid* during filming this sort of thing many times, I had lost my cool in the midst of reality.

As I was helping Mari out of the car, a nurse—just coming on duty —sized up the situation and ordered, "Don't walk one step. Not even ONE."

She hurried into the hospital and sent an orderly with a wheelchair to transport Mari. They didn't do a damn thing for me!

While Mari was being rushed upstairs, I reported to the Admissions Office to answer a lot of fool questions to which I couldn't seem to remember the answers—like Mari's maiden name.

"Steady, Mr. Garnett," someone said. "We've never lost a father."

If that cornball line ever shows up in a script I'm to direct, I'll make the writer eat the page without mayonnaise.

One of the nurses advised me to read a magazine and relax, because "everything" was going beautifully. I have always known that it is possible for the uninvolved to be philosophical about the troubles of others, but that hospital cheer was ridiculous.

Six hours and one hundred years later, Mari's doctor came into the waiting room to say, "Congratulations, Tay. You may see your wife and daughter now. They're fine."

Mari was still groggy, but she grinned and said, "The Indian fortune teller was right. We have a ginger-haired baby girl. Let's name her Tiela."

I looked the baby over critically; she *was* ginger-haired. She was also remarkably beautiful. I've heard new fathers say that before, but Tiela really *was* beautiful—in spite of Mari's observation that her daughter looked like a pink prune.

I telephoned Normie Millen with the news that Mari was fine, the baby remarkable, and the father parched.

Normie bought it. I had eaten nothing for twenty hours, so the liquor relaxed my stomach muscles and sent comforting messages along my veins. The ordeal was over. I didn't know whether to laugh or cry, so I had another drink to rationalize my emotional processes.

When Normie had to go back to his office, he turned me over to Corny and Gail Patrick Jackson. They bought me a few congratulatory drinks, then passed me on to someone else.

I awakened the next morning with a monumental hangover. Even

[300]

after a long, cold shower my hair was still several sizes too small for my head.

I had to see Mari and my daughter. I had to make certain they had survived my bad night.

Obviously a certain amount of medication was indicated; a full set of old-fashioneds enabled me to reach Mari's room.

Mother and daughter were in glowing health. Neither seemed to be bothered by the blinding sunlight or the deafening clatter of leaves on a tree just outside the window.

My concern allayed, I decided to avoid the elevator's swift descent —I hate discovering I've left my stomach on the third floor when I'm on the first—and take the stairs. I managed the trip from third to second without incident, but as I started down the marble staircase that leads from second to Main, my Navy knee gave way.

I awakened in a hospital bed, bound, taped, and splinted. I had a Colle's fracture of my right wrist, a compressive fracture of my left cheekbone, a deep laceration through my right eyebrow, one missing tooth, and four others undecided.

I was discharged from the hospital only a few days AFTER Mari and Tiela had gone home.

As soon as my face had returned to its normal color, my wrist had healed, and my dentist was taking bows for saving me from a latticed smile, I discovered that an epidemic called Television had swept the U. S. The country was hip-deep in soap suds.

The majors were pointedly snubbing the new medium, or as Wally Beery used to say, "They were playing the big ignore."

Otto Kruger, a genuinely nice guy and an adroit diplomat, was appointed by the Screen Actors' Guild to feel out the attitude of the majors about an idea perfected by players who could sense that the motion picture industry, as they had known it, was going down the drain.

The idea consisted of putting together, in a half-hour television show, an interview with a star, a visit to the set on which a feature film was in production, then a trailer of that picture. Today, a studio would pay a fabulous price for promotion of that kind; as originally proposed, the cost to studios would have been only cooperation.

Kruger and the Board of Directors of the Guild agreed that MGM

[301]

should be the first nut to crack. If Metro went for the idea, every studio in town would fall in line.

Kruger made an appointment with Metro executive Al Lichtman, who listened through Otto's forty-five-minute pitch, then tossed aside the pencil with which he had been doodling and asked, "How do you spell 'television'!"

Yes. Things were that bad.

A certain star had come to Hollywood from Broadway when Hollywood was considered Lower Slobbovia. He had done well in pictures, so he was open-minded about the possibilities of any fresh dramatic medium. He wanted to be informed about this new show biz baby, TV, but he also wanted to be safe from charges of sedition, should a studio executive drop in for a drink.

The dilemma was solved by installing a twelve-inch set in the MAID'S ROOM, where the entire family could huddle before the jiggling, twilight-blue figures.

Another star, born in New England, lived in a lavish "Country Barn," topped by a handsome weathervane designed to serve a dual purpose. Not only did the vane tell the direction of the wind, it served admirably as a television aerial—who could guess!

I was, emotionally, motion picture business all the way, but arrogance was a luxury I couldn't afford. Also, it has always been my practice to embrace every show biz novelty as quickly as possible, so I turned out three half-hour shows for the excellently conceived *Screen Directors' Playhouse,* working with such disparate talents as Yvonne de Carlo, Casey Tibbs, Rory Calhoun, and Michael Wilding.

At that point Bob Fellows went to Four Star Productions as executive producer, and assigned me to direct half a dozen thirty-minute segments starring Jane Powell (a sweet, malleable, sensitive girl) in some segments, and Jack Lemmon in others.

Like most comics, Jack—a magnificent actor—has an inborn sense of timing, an intrinsically amusing facial "mask," and a voice that goes over your funnybone like a feather. Yet the man himself is serious-minded, analytical, and "involved," which is today's package word for a sense of human and civic responsibility.

Next, on the *Loretta Young Show,* I directed segments that included able troupers Eddie Albert, Steve Cochran, Regis Toomey, Ralph Meeker, Royal Dano, George Tobias, and Jackie Coogan.

[302]

Jackie has a sneaky sense of humor; he's forever coming up with a deadpan crack that rocks the set for minutes. One of my favorite Coogan yarns has to do with his World War II experiences.

He started his military career by planning to end it abruptly: He applied for glider pilot training. Having survived basic, he and his outfit wound up in India for some reason lucid only within the Pentagon.

One day the outfit was ordered into dress uniform to stand inspection by a visiting Chief of State, Generalissimo Chiang Kai-shek.

The generalissimo's plane landed at the airfield where the U. S. military complement was drawn up in parade formation. Chiang shook hands with the American brass, then strode the length of the ranks at attention in the sweltering noonday sun.

Jackie was wearing an enormous black fusilier's mustache that effectively concealed the movement of his lips; he could ad lib at random and escape detection/discipline.

After what seemed an interminable visit to the troops, the Chinese generalissimo concluded his inspection, saluted everyone entitled to the courtesy, and with entourage sauntered toward the boarding ramp.

An admonition rang out anonymously from the eyes-ahead, motionless Americans, "NO STARCH IN COLLAR, PLEASE."

Between television assignments, I was frantically writing feature scripts, and selling none of them. I would have realized that a profound idea is never found at the bottom of a bottle had I not been chronically bottled in bond myself.

One soggy morning toward dawn, I checked into the Garden of Allah Hotel, afraid to go home to face Mari.

Fortunately, I was known at the Garden as a man who paid his bills regardless of how contracted. The bellman who showed me to my room steadied me over the doorsill and said kindly, "You're in bad shape. Do you know anything about Alcoholics Anonymous?"

"I sure do, and believe me, I'll join if I ever have a problem," I reassured him.

I was still trying to figure out how to unbutton my laced shoes when the bellman came back with a pint of vodka. "This will help for a few hours. Why don't you let me call one of your A.A. friends?"

Somewhat sobered by the vodka, I suggested that he telephone good old Kent Taylor, a guy I'd known and liked for a long, long time.

The bellman returned in a few minutes, saying that Kent would see me in the morning, which he did—at around 10 A.M. A ghastly hour.

"I'd like to take you to a drying-out spot in the valley. That's their business, and they do a good job of it—medical care and all that," said Kent as if he were talking about a brisk game of tennis.

En route, Kent stopped at a liquor store and picked up a half-pint of vodka which eased my going into retirement.

Three days later I went home. To my surprise, Mari let me into the house. However, she issued an ultimatum: I was to stay sober or she was through. She had HAD it.

I haven't had a drink of hard liquor since. Now and then I'll sip a glass of champagne at weddings or similar festive occasions, but that awakens no craving. Like a religious convert, a man who has "seen the light" abhors the possibility of a blackout.

Hollywood is essentially a small town, thank God. Word got around that I had jettisoned the booze bit, and Bob Mitchum asked me to direct *The Night Fighters*. Bob had bought the film rights to the novel, *A Terrible Beauty,* and was going to star in it for his own United Artists' company.

From the moment I read the first twenty pages of script, I was worried. It embraced every cliché ever written about the Irish troubles, harping on the ghastly poverty of the south of Ireland. (According to my friend, Dan O'Herlihy, that poverty is now a thing of the past. The wise heads of the Irish Republic encouraged heavy industry to move into the area by passing favorable tax laws, and by controlling unions rigidly. As a result, the once threadbare and hungry land is flourishing.)

In spite of my original uneasiness, I felt that I could hypo the script enough so that with a solid characterization from Mitchum, we might make a fairly entertaining picture from our cornball story. We were well aware that it could never stand up against an audience's magnified memories of *The Informer.*

We signed an impressive supporting cast: Richard Harris, Dan O'Herlihy, Anne Heywood, Cyril Cusack, Noel Purcell, and Nial MacGinnis.

Exteriors for the picture were filmed in and around County Dublin, and the interiors were shot at the Ardmore Studio in Bray.

It's a shame that some of the offstage action couldn't have been included in the film; it was livelier than the things called for by the script.

One night several of us were dining in a basement restaurant in

Dublin. The place was fascinating, dark with ancient smokes and echoing with voices long dead. For uncounted years it had been frequented by the Abbey Players and theatrical folk in general.

Dorothy Mitchum had flown in from the States that morning, so Bob was on his best behavior. As Bob opened the restaurant door for his wife, the owner himself greeted them, saying, "We're a bit crowded tonight, but I have a small table for two at the end of the room. There's only one chair—the other has been borrowed—but Mrs. Mitchum could be seated and each of you could study the menu while I look around for another chair."

"You've got a deal," Bob said cordially. "Take your time."

He was leaning down, menu in hand to learn his lady's pleasure, when he was poked vigorously in the ribs by a roughneck who thrust a piece of paper at Bob and growled, "Gimme your autygraph."

Mitchum regarded his fan coolly and said, "Excuse me, but I was talking to the lady," and turned his back.

The pest grabbed Mitchum's elbow and spun him around, snarling, "And *I* was talkin' to you."

Bob sighed and accepted the paper and pen. He wrote, "Screw you," and signed it, "Kirk Douglas."

That's how it started.

Bob's tormentor glanced at the inscription and slugged Bob hard.

Mitch pinned the man's arms to his sides and said softly, "You want to get yourself killed?"

At the far end of the room, Richard Harris's attention was attracted. "That's my buddy, Mitchum—in trouble! COME ON," he yelled to his Abbey Theatre brethren.

In ten seconds we had a beautiful donnybrook going.

Obviously Mitch had cast himself in an out-of-character role: For the first time in his life he was the only man present who did NOT toss a punch.

The following morning the local newspaper reported the incident with the snide headline, "MITCHUM REFUSES FIGHT WITH MUCH SMALLER MAN."

Mitch's reaction was characteristic: "I'm waiting for a midget. Him, I'll murder."

At the end of the picture we decided to give a party.

An entire stage at Ardmore Studios was converted into a nightclub. A bar and buffet table seventy-five feet long were set up, the band from the Great Northern Hotel was "laid on," and a dozen bartenders were hired.

Everything was going pleasantly when one of the dancers screamed. A bottle went through the bass drum. Frenzied women rushed to neutral corners. A mass of male humanity writhed and roared in the middle of the dance floor.

Eventually the conglomeration separated into countable individuals. Six men were carrying a seventh to the wide stage door. With a one, a two, a three, the horizontal one was tossed in a high arc into the foggy night.

The band crawled out from under the piano and the music continued. Once more the party oozed goodwill.

A dance later, another scream, another bottle, another rocketless launch for the same bandy-legged, red-headed little guy who had been thrown out originally.

I asked one of the crew, "What's with him?"

"It's the O'Casey. He's a slow man to convince," I was told.

I believed it when I saw him ejected for the third time.

Next day I made a cleanup trip to the studio to pick up the last of my papers. A janitor was sorting the debris left by the party.

As he came hobbling toward me, I recognized the defeated belligerent of the night before. His puffed lips parted in a painful grin to expose the dark vacancy left by a departed front tooth. One eye, the color of decaying eggplant, was swollen shut, and there was a mouse under the other.

Expelling the sigh of a man whose ruminations are deeply satisfying, the janitor said, "Good mornin', Guvnor, and wasn't it a *lahvley* parrty!"

It reminded me of Bogart, flat on his back on the carpet at "21," growling up at his huge assailant, "D'ya give up NOW?"

31

IN THE LIFE OF ALMOST EVERY GUY THERE ARE PERIODS WHEN HE COULD fall out of an airplane and land in a ton of goose down.

There are also periods when a man, crossing his own driveway, will trip over a local cat, fall in the path of a concrete truck, and get to his knees in time to be struck by forked lightning.

It took about ten years to heal my lightning burns.

I was not the only victim of calamity's vendetta. Everyone in Hollywood was in some sort of bind. A story told of the times has it that a New York actor desperately in need of a job, ANY job, started to drive to California. A Hollywood actor, equally desperate, decided to try Broadway. Midway through the loneliness of Texas, they met. Simultaneously arising from behind the steering wheel, each waved frantically and yelled at the other, "GO BACK."

At a party one night, John Barrymore—dying, but still the handsomest man ever to cross the American stage with the possible exception of Fredric March—wobbled up to me. Shaking his head sorrowfully, he rested a hand on my shoulder and recited in his finest *Hamlet* tones, "If you run, they bite you in the ass, Charlie, and if you stand still, they hose you."

I didn't think he had recognized me until he called me "Charlie."

When my pal, Joe Youngerman, secretary of the Directors' Guild, telephoned to say that an advertising agency had asked for a list of available directors, I said, "Put down the name Garnett, under Gee, I'd love the job."

It turned out that the sponsor was a cigarette company, and I went to work as if I'd been a Kentucky planter. I had quit smoking several years earlier, but in all fairness to tobacco I must admit *that* particular brand of cigarettes did no harm to my family. Actually, as between cancer and starvation, starvation is faster.

During those days, no matter how rough the going got, I'd say, "Forget it. We'll go up to THE RANCH." That's how we thought of it—in upper case.

Those 1,700 acres were our snug harbor from which we could look upon our storms in proper perspective. Above all other satisfactions was Tiela's delight in the place with its giant oaks trailing Spanish moss, its cheerful brook, its spring lupin and autumn holly.

Then, in one dreadful week my Jaguar was smashed by a truck, Mari's station wagon splashed its differential all over the street, and I was nepotized out of a top directing job by the producer's cousin.

We had to have money and RIGHT NOW. I harassed my agent to get me a job; poor devil, he was being harassed by every client on his list, because Hollywood had racked up a 75 percent unemployment statistic.

Mari and I agreed that we had more furniture than we needed; some of it consisted of signed antiques brought from our London flat. We checked with a used furniture dealer who tugged at his chin and finally offered us the approximate price we had spent on furniture polish over the years.

Eventually I faced up to what had to be done. Of our precious 1,700 acres, we kept only twenty-seven; we also retained the main house, two small guest houses, a two-car garage, and the stable.

I felt as the Dodgers would feel after losing four straight to Wellesley.

One afternoon Mari, Tiela, and I were exercising our poodle in Holmby Park when we met a longtime friend, Alan Miller, organizer and head of Revue Productions which had twenty-two series shows on the air at that time.

He said something like, "Wednesday is my half-day off, but what's your excuse?"

"At liberty," I answered, giving as jaunty a reading as possible.

"How about coming out to the studio tomorrow morning? I've been needing you," he said.

It was all I could do to keep from kissing the man. But in a public park? Although I refrained from embarrassing him, I believe Alan realized how grateful I was.

My first assignment was a segment of *Wagon Train,* starring Ward Bond, Robert Horton, Frank McGrath and Terry Wilson. I had known Bond casually for some time, but I had never directed him.

I was warned that he was rough to handle, that a few weeks earlier he had given a young director a very bad time. The y. d. had shot a dramatic "go-round" in a Western, then was shooting "reaction closeups" of each member of the cast. Somehow Ward managed to insert himself as background in each of the "one-shots." (One person's reactions only.)

Horseplay? Or sabotage?

Finally the exasperated director said, "We'll do all of the reaction closeups again—WITHOUT ANY OF THE BOND BROTHERS."

Forewarned is—for falling on your face—a great system.

Midway through production I explained a scene to Bond with elaborate care, then said, "Roll 'em."

Somehow the action and dialogue came off pure Hormel and Company.

We did it over; the second take had been left far too long in the smokehouse.

I said, "Okay, what's bugging you, Ward? Maybe you'd like to direct this scene."

"I would," admitted Bond.

"Be my guest." I was charmingly patronizing.

Ward made a couple of changes in the lines, altered the pitch of the dialogue, and shaded the characterizations. It came off like Gangbusters.

Even a director with a burr under his blanket senses the solid impact of a valid scene. After Bond had completed the scene HIS way I said, "Cut and print it. You were right, Ward."

Grinning, he said, "Aw, everybody's gotta guess right once in awhile."

After that, when I was told that Bond was hard to handle, I gave forth a piece of advice: "If that guy disagrees with you, better listen. He'll wind up making you look awfully good."

Next job: *The Deputy* starring Henry Fonda and Alan Case, plus great guest stars. *The Deputy* set was a happy one. Item one: We had Curly Linden, the fastest cameraman on the lot; Item two: If the shooting call was for 8:30 A.M., I was always there at 8:00. Invariably, Hank Fonda was ahead of me, lounging loosely in a canvas chair as if he were strictly a passenger. However, he managed to be near the stage door as other members of the cast arrived. To each he'd say a few words, and they would sit down together.

My curiosity prompted me to check up. Each person to whom I talked said, "Well, this is confidential, but Hank admitted he hadn't had time to study his script, so he wanted me to work with him over our scene."

(That'll be the day, when Hank hasn't learned his lines!)

The result was that when I was ready to shoot, Hank had rehearsed the entire cast. We always finished our segments well ahead of schedule.

After *The Deputy*, I worked on *The Tall Man*, starring my long-time friend, Barry Sullivan, as well as Clu Gulager; next *Riverboat*, starring Darrin McGavin; then *87th Precinct* with Robert Lansing and Norman Fell; on to *Overland Trail* with William Bendix and Doug McClure; followed by *Frontier Circus* starring Richard Jaeckel, John Derek, and Chill Wills.

Working on *The Untouchables*, starring Robert Stack, was particularly enjoyable because Bob's uncle and lookalike, Perry Wood, and I had been at M.I.T. together, and subsequently survived the H-boat at Pensacola. Bob and I have always found a good deal to laugh about; he's a Navy gentleman, and no greater praise can be heaped on any guy.

Naked City, starring Paul Burke and Horace McMahon with guest star Lois Nettleton (a tremendous little actress, just now being given proper recognition), was followed in my diary by direction of half-a-dozen ecclesiastical films made for the Southern Baptist Church Conference. One of the films starred James Drury, who subsequently became TV's "Virginian."

The job wasn't as far out of my line as it would seem at first glance, because, a few months earlier, I had completed—with Mari—a five-year course of study at the L.A Church of Religious Science. We were qualified for ordination, but we were so completely show biz that we felt our philosophy could best be practiced on a moonlighting basis.

[311]

And so to work on *Rawhide*—a director's delight. Its stars were Eric Fleming, tragically drowned in South America; Clint Eastwood, a real pro who rates his top success; and Paul Brinegar who is so adept that he makes everyone in his scenes come off handsomely.

Several segments of the perennial *Gunsmoke* were a great experience with Jim Arness, Ken Curtis, my good friend Milburn Stone, Amanda Blake, and such guest stars as Bill Windom, Lois Nettleton, and Barbara Luna.

I also directed a lot of the *Beachcomber* series, starring Cameron Mitchell, who is a frustrated baseball player. He pitches surprisingly well in the annual game between the flatfooted Press and the flabby Thespians. A partial guest list for *Beachcomber* included Cesar Romero, John Vivyan, Ann Helm, and my friend Glynis Johns.

Death Valley Days, patriarch of all TV Westerns, was a gas with Ronald Reagan, Keenan Wynn, George Gobel, Rory Calhoun, Gilbert Roland, Ken Curtis, Denver Pyle, and Ken Murray as guests. I did a jillion of them, never dreaming that one day I'd vote for Ronnie for Governor of California.

Bonanza with Lorne Greene, Mike Landon, and Dan Blocker was a ball. Patricia Blair, Marlyn Mason, Michael Rennie, Anjanette Comer, and my very special friend Joan Blondell were among the guest stars.

After that came a couple of short-termers: *The Loner,* starring Lloyd Bridges; *The Legend of Jesse James,* with Christopher Jones (who hit the Big Time in *Ryan's Daughter*) and Alan Case; plus *Please Don't Eat the Daisies,* starring Patricia Crowley.

All of which reminds me of Spring Byington's comment about television. A friend asked, after Spring had completed the last of the *December Bride* series, how she felt.

"Breathless," she gasped. "Television is summer stock in an iron lung."

Asked what caused the hectic pace, she explained, "It's simple: they don't want it good; they want it Thursday."

Just as I was beginning to turn hungry eyes at the lizards sunning themselves on our patio, I had a call from my agent who said that Nat Holt, once a successful independent Hollywood producer, was making a comeback (a situation so familiar during that era as to be trite. Make that "any era.")

My agent suggested that I get in touch with Nat's friend, Paul Donnelly, head of the Production Office at Universal. Donnelly was eager to see that Nat got rolling on his projected picture, *Cattle King*. When Donnelly told me that Bob Taylor had signed to star, and that the script had been written by Thomas Thompson, I took a deep breath of clean, clear hope.

Then Donnelly put it to me: "You've always brought your pictures in under budget and under schedule, and that's what we've GOT to have in this situation. Now, I know it's been a long time since you've drawn anything short of important money . . ."

"Look—Nat's a friend of mine," I said magnanimously.

Paul went on, ". . . enough of a friend for you to do it for a fifth of your bottom price. That's his limit!"

Hollywood is a place in which your professional worth is judged by the price you were paid for your previous job. That's why stars aspire to million-dollar salaries, even if there will be only $8.72 left after taxes.

I swallowed hard and said, "You've got a deal."

The lizards were safe.

When I telephoned my agent to say I had signed and was glad of the job in spite of the price—he blew up before I had finished the sentence.

"Are you CRAZY?" he yelled. "Why take that kind of money without consulting me?"

I said acidly, "YOU sent me to Donnelly in the first place—remember?"

The picture was shot in eleven and one-half days in Kernville, California, with a no-nonsense, beautifully professional cast starting with Bob Taylor, and including Joan Caulfield, Bill Windom, Bob Loggia, Bob Middleton, and Virginia Christine, who has since become famous as the Swedish lady in the Folger Coffee commercials.

Virginia's husband, Fritz Feld, was a longtime friend; Virginia and I became friends during the location. That was the first bonus of the picture. The second was a lasting friendship with the writer, Thomas Thompson.

Probably the motion picture industry is the only *business* on earth in which one man can control another man's professional life TOTALLY. The relationship between an agent and his client is more binding than a wedding ring; it is a combination of father–dictator and jailor–hangman.

At the time of my life presently under inspection, my agent took two of my original scripts to Paramount. A few days later said agent reported to me in glowing terms. He said Marty Rackin (head of Paramount at that time) had agreed to give me absolute autonomy in my own unit. Furthermore, Mr. Rackin was enthusiastic about the properties. The deal was looking great—all but locked in.

I was jubilant; my luck had changed.

Two weeks went by without final word. I called my agent. "Settle down," he advised. "Rackin's been busy, but this thing is all set except for details."

I waited another two weeks and called again. The master of my fate, more jovial than a clown on laughing gas, said that nothing was lacking to complete the deal but a signature—a matter of a few days.

Six nervous weeks later I had lunch with a friend on the Paramount lot and, by sheer chance, met Marty Rackin's assistant whom I had known for many years. After a few minutes of small talk, I asked, "How's my deal coming along?"

"What deal was that?" asked the executive.

I explained. My friend, aghast, said, "I look over everything submitted for Marty's consideration—that's my job. He often makes decisions without talking to me until later, but NOTHING goes to his desk that I haven't seen first. Why don't you talk to Marty?"

Marty Rackin, a gentleman personified, was cordial. He was also flabbergasted to hear of my "locked-in" deal. He had never seen the scripts, and my agent had never mentioned *them or me* to Marty.

How does a man who has been talking about a new house and car for his wife, a new wardrobe for his daughter, a car for himself and a dependable eating schedule, go home and admit that his "in-business-for-himself, sure-fire setup" has just been flushed down the Hyperion Disposal Plant?

[314]

I'm pleased to report that the legendary consolation of the desperate—the double old-fashioned—never crossed my mind. What I did think, with a small gasp of comfort, was, "I have a gasoline credit card that'll take us up to the ranch for a few days. Up there, I'll think of something."

I tried to be jaunty about saying, "Get your things together, girls, we're going to have a weekend in the country."

Tiela studied me, then went to her bedroom to pack.

Mari asked levelly, "What's wrong?"

Before I could answer, the telephone rang. The caller was the wife of the good neighbor who managed King Vidor's ranch adjoining our property. She was having difficulty controlling her voice, but she said, "I have terrible news for you—your ranch house has burned— it was gone, gone completely, before we could do anything—at three o'clock this morning—the guest houses were saved and so were the stables . . ."

She was crying too bitterly to go on.

I thanked her and said we had been packing to drive up; we'd stay in the guest houses.

No one can have any concept of the utter devastation of fire until he has sifted the ashes of a cherished home in search for some remnant of the mementos collected over many years and flavored by many emotions.

Mari and Tiela cried themselves to sleep in one guest house that night; I stayed awake in the other. Toward dawn, I remembered that I had been paying insurance premiums for years. Not enough coverage, not nearly enough, but *something.* The insurance money would have to be used for groceries until I could get set in another job.

Somewhat later I learned, to my impotent fury, that I was obliged to pay income tax on the insurance loot. If I had been financially able to rebuild or buy another home with the money, it would have been tax-free; because I had to have the cash to keep three people going to the table regularly, the I.R.S. had to gobble its bite, too.

So, you light your torches and you pull up your tights.

A few weeks later I moved into my office, which was furnished with a comfortable couch in addition to the usual office equipment, so that Mari and Tiela could have the apartment to themselves. We continued to gather for dinner as a family.

One evening, after Tiela had gone to bed, I said to Mari, "Honey, for a long time I've known there was something bugging you. Something you haven't even hinted to me, aside from the rough going you've handled like a thorobred. Why not get it off your chest? Maybe I can help."

She began to cry.

She is by nature a purposeful, forthright woman, so she quickly dried her eyes and gave it to me straight. She said Tiela was thirteen, and older in many ways than her years. Tiela would understand that people and conditions change, but she would love me always. Mari added that she, herself, would never stop loving me, but she didn't want to be married any longer.

It shouldn't have been a knockout blow, because—from the time I'd stopped drinking, and had developed a certain amount of awareness of my surroundings—I'd known that our relationship was not what it had promised to be.

So I didn't burst into tears at the news.

Later I didn't drive aimlessly for hours.

I didn't start drinking.

Also, I didn't sleep for weeks. I worked on a new script, wondering idly if adversity might not be a writer's creative yeast.

And I composed—laboriously as if a submarine were being raised from the bottom of the sea—a letter to Joan Marshfield. I apologized for my long silence, reminding her wryly that I had never been a G. B. Shaw letter writer; I told her something of the ghastly state of Hollywood production and said I was thinking seriously of moving to England, Italy, or Spain where hundreds of cameras were turning daily. And I added a phrase that I thought was a masterful throwaway: "I hope to make many plans, now that I'm a FREE agent, professionally and domestically."

I boasted to her that I had been sober for twelve years and didn't miss likker at all—rather gloried in my independence.

I asked after Henri's health, and closed with the bad joke that I hoped to hear from her more promptly than she had heard from some of her devoted, but unreliable friends.

Nearly everyone complains about the telephone and telegraph

service, and the cold-molasses movement of the mails. After rueful study, I've wondered if the deliberate pace of communications isn't a design of the goddess Hope.

I came back to my apartment late one afternoon, about a week later—after a carefully casual tour of studios (echoing with emptiness)—to find a Paris-postmarked letter.

NOT in Joan's handwriting.

It started:

"My Dear Tay:
   It was with the first sense of comfort I have felt in some time that I read your letter. It would have pleased Joan greatly to know she was in your thoughts.
   I have always known that you and Joan were truly in love, but I am a selfish man and could not bring myself to set her free. I held her with my long illness.
   You, I know, will grieve with me as I tell you that Joan slept away peacefully, on the Tenth of September last year. She had complained a day or so earlier of a pain in her arm, but dismissed it as of such triviality that she refused to let me call a doctor.
   Because you knew and loved Joan so dearly, you will agree with me that a merciful death was her due after a lifetime of unselfish kindness to others, and most unstintingly to me.
   If your European production plans mature, be warned that I shall expect you to come directly from the plane to my home. Together, we shall salute our treasured memory.
   Sincerely your friend,
                    Henri"

First there was shock.

Then remorse. Why hadn't I written, if only to say hello occasionally? She had been in my thoughts almost daily over the years. I loved her; I'd always loved her, but mistily, as in midwinter one remembers Hawaii in May. In my mind she had lived as a heartening loveliness, unchanging and indestructible.

Eventually there comes a horrible morning to be endured only with the thought, " 'Today is the first day of the rest of my life.' I must make something of it."

You light your torches and you pull up your tights once more.

32

ONE WONDERFUL MORNING, EARLY IN 1969, BOB FELLOWS CALLED TO TELL me that he had made a deal with some financiers in Tennessee to establish a picture-producing company using the trade style "Spillane–Fellows." He wanted me to write the scripts and produce–direct the films. The company's principal assets, in addition to Bob's forty years of film making, were to be the literary properties of Mickey Spillane.

First on the schedule was to be *The Delta Factor.* The story called for shooting in Nashville and the nearest possible approximation to Morro Castle in Havana.

Mickey Spillane and I worked together at his home in South Carolina, turning out a shooting script in about eight weeks; we believed we had concocted a taut, exciting cops-and-robbers screenplay. Its climax was a high-speed chase over serpentine mountain roads. I knew it could be made into a more galvanic pursuit than the *Bullitt* classic.

I was elated because I felt that we were launching an exhilarating and long overdue era of adventure pix.

We took preparatory offices at the Goldwyn Studios, then John Monks (my associate) and I flew to Nashville to arrange for studio space, and to cast local talent in the character roles. That done, we scouted the continental U. S. for a satisfactory fortress. No luck until we fell in love with Puerto Rico's Morro Castle; also, San Juan's rain forest offered magnificent backgrounds for our chase.

Back we went to California to report our progress and plans to Bob Fellows. My first sense of setback was sight of Bob; it was obvious that he wasn't at all well; to relieve him of some responsibilities we all pitched in, doing whatever needed doing.

We completed casting of the principals: Yvette Mimieux and Christopher George—things began to add up. We had a workable script, truly superb locations, a pair of handsome young players.

Donna Fellows telephoned one morning to say that Bob was in the hospital again. She added, "Tay, I think this is terribly serious."

I rushed over to see Bob for a few minutes, mainly to reassure him that the production plans were going well—pep-talk stuff. "But we need you back at your desk as soon as you can quit kidding around," I warned him.

"I'll do 'er," he said, and winked.

He suffered a final heart attack two days later.

I had lost my oldest friend in the picture business; he and I had been through a thousand experiences: the De Mille days, the Chicago kidnaping, the ski slopes of Switzerland, the belly laughs and belly aches of life in Hollywood.

I have never stopped missing him.

I have said many, many times that *The Delta Factor* should have been buried with Bob. Dirty trick on Bob, though.

I have more than sufficient reason for that statement, but as a kindness to many people, including Mickey Spillane, I shall forgo a recital of most of the tragedies of that misbegotten film.

Instead, we'll skip to the final chase location in the rain forest. Because we needed "point-of-view vertigo" shots, we set the cameraman with his camera in the back seat of the stunt car, and I rode in front with Roger Creed, our stuntman and driver. Our Volkswagen had been reinforced with a roll bar; its engine had been beefed up to equal a Porsche's performance.

We took the first three hairpin curves with only momentary whirring of tires and slewing of wheels; as we approached the fourth curve, which overlooked a 450-foot drop to dense foliage in the depths of the canyon, the spongy road seemed to ooze away. Roger did everything in the book to break the skid, but the VW had flight ambitions.

I said, "We're going over."

Roger yelled, "Not a goddam thing I can do."

[319]

We seemed to be suspended motionless in space, static, interminably; I learned later that the car made several end-over-end loops, then hit an outcropping of rock, which flipped us into a new series of revolutions, and on to the next outcropping, again into space . . .

Fadeout.

I was told afterward that passengers in a car coming from the opposite direction had seen us go over. They stopped and a samaritan demanded, "How do we get them out of there?"

The highway patrol officer who had just arrived, squinted downward, rubbed his chin and observed, "No hurry. There's nothing anybody can do for those poor devils." He repeated his opinion for the benefit of those who had missed the first reading: "Son muertes."

Dissolve.

The cameraman had been thrown clear and landed in a briar patch that did his clothes and complexion very little good. Roger had also fallen clear, but he picked up a T-shaped scalp wound that required forty stitches. Both of them were able to climb out of our informal landing field.

As for me, if it hadn't been for our grip, George Hill, our prop man, Bob Visiglia, our second assistant director, Stuart Fleming, and our transportation manager, Ray Tostada, I would have been in that forest yet. All four members of our crew happened to have taken a course in mountain rescue.

I knew what was going on, although I went in and out of focus intermittently. I was strapped onto a stretcher and snaked up the cliff by a truck pulling a pair of ropes. The rescue team clung to the four corners of the stretcher to prevent its slamming against rock ledges. In spite of being lashed onto the stretcher, I had to hang on with my left hand, because there was no foot rest.

I vaguely recall being shoved into a station wagon, and hearing a nurse say angrily, "This is outrageous; I have no sedatives."

Blackout.

I sensed, in the next episode, that I was in some sort of hospital. I heard a man say, "This poor guy just doesn't have a prayer."

I opened my good eye, saw a medic leaning over me and said, "Doc, don't you bet a goddam dime on it." That accomplished, I passed out again.

Four hours later I was in the Presbyterian Hospital where a genius named Dr. Salazar went to work. He asked, "Can you move your fingers?"

My right arm was lying outside its shoulder socket, alongside my face, but—all cooperation—I asked, "Like this?" and flexed my right hand.

"Well, I'll be damned," said the good doctor.

I considered that a fine exit line.

It was sunny when I was awakened by a nurse's traditional, "How are *we* this morning?"

"You're lovely, but what's wrong with *my* face?" I demanded.

"Oh, your eye and ear will be okay," she said, "but you fractured your cheekbone—it's an easy bone to break. You even fractured bones NOT easy to break."

All things considered, that was a pretty good review of my performance. X-rays indicated that I had broken all ribs on my right side; I had broken AND dislocated my right shoulder, tearing loose all pertinent tendons. I had a compressive fracture of my left cheekbone, and I had lost some conspicuous teeth.

Funny thing: During my entire hospital stay of three days I maintained a normal pulse, blood pressure, and temperature. Even my electrocardiogram was flawless.

Four days after escaping the hospital I was in Nashville, shooting the last of *The Delta Factor* from a wheelchair, my right arm in a sling.

Naturally, once I was back in California, I became the physical therapist's dream boy. I *worked,* and I mean diligently, at regaining the normal functions of my arm.

Physically I was in no shape to direct, but I was a helluva hunt-and-punch typist. My pal, Tommy Thompson, and I turned out a pretty good action Western, boasting a few new brands, and named it *Ride a Wild Mare.*

Once it was started on studio reading rounds, I dusted my hands and went up to the ranch to concentrate on two other stories. The first was the book for a legit musical play called *Have You a Little Problem in Your Home?* (sure to strike a nerve), and the second was a treatment for a film action–comedy called *Miss Felicia Oglethorpe.*

I had just typed "The End" on the musical script when King Vidor jeeped down from his house on the neighboring hill to say he had received a call from Hollywood to the effect that *Ride a Wild Mare* was under consideration by a major studio; I was wanted in town for powwows.

Instantly I was in physical shape to direct.

By the time I had moved back to my apartment, TWO majors wanted powwows.

My lights were blazing and my tights as taut as Raquel Welch's bikini when I received a THIRD call. A guy named Chuck Keen, president of Alaska Pictures, was planning to make a documentary about the longest midwinter manhunt in northern history. He called it *The Mad Trapper.*

Originally he had thought of George Marshall as possible director, but George had other commitments, so George and his agent recommended me.

After hearing Mr. Keen's pitch, I asked, "Do you have gluwein in Alaska? Oh, never mind." So I signed on with Alaska Pictures.

This Chuck Keen is a remarkable gent. He had already shot many documentaries about Alaska. He had also made nineteen trips to Vietnam to shoot actual combat footage—nineteen trips and nineteen documentary shorts—for Grumman Aircraft. It is said that he has logged more combat hours than any pilot who has flown in Nam.

A powerful man, although not as tall as Mike Mazurki (who had been signed for the title role), Keen gets it altogether like a bulldozer with a crew haircut.

One of my favorite stories about him has to do with financing one of his early Alaskan documentaries. Financing is where it's at, in today's motion picture business. The statement makes up in authenticity what it lacks in grammar.

Chuck had hocked everything he owned, right down to his longjohns, but still needed editing and eating money.

He outlined his problem to a local banker and closed his impassioned plea on a note of desperation: "I'm not just talking about a business venture, sir. I'm talking about putting food on the table for my wife and son. What d'ya say?"

The banker said, "No."

Chuck started for the door.

"Just a minute," called the moneyman. "Sure, you've had it rough.

So does everybody. I'll bet you've never noticed that I have a glass eye."

"I've noticed," said Chuck.

"Yeah? I'll bet you can't tell which one it is," challenged the banker.

"Easy," said Chuck. "It's the one with a little sympathy in it."

Chuck has never played a return date at that bank.

In California there is longitude and latitude in great abundance, but I've always been engrossed in other measurements.

Casually, I glanced at a map and discovered that Nome was roughly on the same LONGITUDE as the Hawaiian Islands. I was encouraged. I even said aloud, "I'll get a good tan."

Keen grinned, accepting me as a humorist. He said, "Aw, don't worry about clothes. We'll supply all you'll need up there."

I was still thinking in terms of crazy floral shirts with maybe a pair of hot pants and sand-resistant sandals when I lent the script to Mari for her opinion. (Mari and I are the best of friends, despite our divorce. Perhaps the divorce made all this possible, because a man can't be *friends* with a married woman.)

A day or two later she handed back the yarn, saying, "Great action story. You'll really get your teeth into this one. Incidentally, how about bringing back some mink and a couple dozen white foxes for Tiela and me?"

I agreed, regarding Mari as a humorist in her own right. However, I had fast recourse to an atlas, being nervous about that mink observation, and discovered that Nome is roughly on the same LATITUDE as Reykjavik, Iceland.

What one wears when shooting a winter Alaskan film is as follows: first, two suits of woolen longjohns, then two pairs of heavy wool socks. Add a snowmobile suit (a sort of jump suit quilted with glass wool), and an Air Force Arctic "parkie." (You cheechakos—tenderfeet—call them "parkas." We sourdoughs prefer the term "parkie.")

Next, one pulls on "inner shoes" made of quarter-inch felt; over them are added a pair of rubber and plastic mukluks. On the hands one wears two pairs of woolen mittens inside a pair of gauntlet mittens made of moose skin; the backs are either a very thick nylon velvet or wolverine fur. Wolverine is vital in the temperatures we were about to endure, because it is the only known fur (I am told) that resists moisture, hence won't freeze.

We made our headquarters at Cortino's Lodge, in Yukon Territory, an establishment you wouldn't believe without seeing it. Cortino's is a summer resort, about a hundred miles from anything except wolves, moose, and caribou. The exterior of the lodge is genteel rustic, built of milled logs, but the interior includes every known comfort such as a Swiss chef, a superb heating system, magnificent beds, and bathrooms awash with *hot* water.

Incidentally, when a sourdough speaks of "warm" weather in the winter, he means it is only 20 degrees below zero; when he regards the day as "cold," the thermometer is flirting with 50 degrees below. Add to that statistic a good brisk Arctic wind, and you have a cold factor that would freeze the rest of that brass monkey.

Chuck had written a story treatment before we got together; while we were still in Hollywood, he and I had rapped out a shooting script.

Essentially, the story deals with the final chapter in the life of a man who appears in the north country without known origin or background, a loner who talks to animals in the forest—each in his own tongue.

His troubles begin when he becomes outraged over the brutal carelessness of a drunken fellow trapper whose lines run parallel to his. When the traps are left unattended for days, the frenzied animals gnaw off a leg in an attempt to escape. The result is an agonizing, lingering death.

Our trapper comes across a magnificent animal, half-malumute and half-wolf, caught in the drunk's trap. He frees the animal, carries him back to the cabin and nurses the wolf-dog back to health.

The drunken trapper complains to the Alaskan Troopers, saying that his lines are being "robbed" by the loner. From that point on, the story concerns a lopsided chase over the white desolation of a northwest winter. The posse is equipped with eight dog teams and eight sleds loaded with food, shelter, and medical supplies. These are serviced from headquarters twice a week.

The pursued is merely a big, lone, bewildered man on snowshoes, his total equipment a back pack, a rifle, an ax, the wolf-dog he saved, and almost limitless strength and courage.

The enemy of both pursuers and pursued is the hostile ice and snow underfoot, and the glowering sky overhead.

One sequence has the trapper mushing along the bank of a river; he slips and falls into the icy water.

Men have fallen into Alaskan rivers before, but there is no record of anyone surviving longer than three minutes after emerging into subzero air.

The day we were to shoot the river accident, the temperature was around 42 degrees below zero, the chill factor in the subseventies.

Our stuntman had come down with a heavy cold, so Chuck Keen himself, president of Alaska Pictures (and at times he must regret it) said quietly, "I'll double."

We parked our camper, warmed to around 70 degrees, as close as possible to the point where Chuck was to emerge from the river. Even the blankets in which he was to be wrapped were heated.

Chuck, wearing snowshoes and carrying a rifle, made the fall into the river, losing one snowshoe in the process. He swam to a prearranged slope that he had decided could be negotiated and laboriously climbed out. However, beyond the lip of the bank, the powder snow was hip-deep; that lost snowshoe imposed a perilous handicap that we had not anticipated.

While the rest of us, *feeling* time tick away, tried to think of something helpful to do, Chuck simply kicked off the other snowshoe, and plowed doggedly through the bottomless drift in a swimming, loping gait.

Afterward, a doctor said that only Chuck's stubbornly supreme effort to make his way through that white muck had pumped enough adrenalin into his system to keep him alive.

With Chuck still in one piece and our picture in the can, we flew back to Hollywood to cut the film. My first suspicion, as I stared down on California from the air, was that the ecology fans had been out painting everything green.

Once *The Mad Trapper* was put to bed, Chuck said to me, "Well, now—we're going to have some concentrated summer in Alaska during the next few months. How about going back with me to direct *Timber Tramp?*"

"If you'll give me your word you won't even pick up an ax during the entire shooting schedule," was my way of signing the contract.

We signed a cast that made theatre exhibitors wash their hands in dreams of gold: Claude Aikin, Joseph Cotten, Tab Hunter, Leon Ames, Rosie Grier, Bob Easton, Stash Clemens, Cesar Romero, and two beauties: Patricia Medina and Eve Brent.

So what do you do when you go broke, your house burns, your wife gives up on you, and you fall off a cliff? YOU LIGHT YOUR TORCHES AND PULL UP YOUR TIGHTS.

Then, the other day, I met this blonde. . . .

Screen Credits

In the beginning, stories, scripts, gags, and incidental dialogue above and beyond the call of literature for:

Mack Sennett
Hal Roach
F.B.O. (Film Booking Office)
Cecil B. De Mille
Universal
Fox
Larry Seamon

TITLE		STARS
1922 BROKEN CHAINS	Screenplay with Carey Wilson	Colleen Moore Ernest Torrence
1923 THE HOTTENTOT	Screenplay with Frank R. Adams	Douglas MacLean
1925 DON'T PARK THERE	Coscript with Fred Guiol & Rob Wagner	Will Rogers
1926 THERE YOU ARE	Coscreenplay from F. Hugh Herbert novel	Conrad Nagel
1926 CRUISE OF THE JASPER B	Screenplay from Don Marquis Novel	Rod La Rocque
1926 THE STRONG MAN	Screenplay with Frank Capra, Hal Conklin, & Arthur Ripley	Harry Langdon Gertrude Astor
1926 UP IN MABEL'S ROOM	Coscript with F. McGrew Willis	Phillis Haver Harrison Ford
1926 THAT'S MY BABY	Screenplay with Frank Capra, Hal Conklin, & Arthur Ripley	Douglas MacLean
1927 LONG PANTS	Screenplay with Frank Capra, Hal Conklin, & Arthur Ripley	Harry Langdon Gertrude Astor
1927 WHITE GOLD	Original screenplay with Garrett Forte	Jetta Goudal George Bancroft

1927	RUBBER TIRES	Coscreenplay with Capra, Conklin, & Ripley	Phyllis Haver Harrison Ford
1927	GETTING GERTIE'S GARTER	Coscript with F. McGrew Willis	Phyllis Haver Harrison Ford
1927	NO CONTROL	Coscript with F. McGrew Willis	Phyllis Haver Harrison Ford
1928	POWER	Original screenplay	William Boyd Alan Hale Sue Carol
1928	CELEBRITY	Screenplay (from Willard Keefe's play) Direction	Robert Armstrong Clyde Cook Lina Basquette
1928	SKYSCRAPER	Screenplay with Eliot Clauson (from an original by Dudley Murphy)	William (Bill) Boyd Alan Hale Sue Carol Alberta Vaughn
1929	THE FLYING FOOL	Original screenplay Direction	Bill Boyd Marie Prevost Russell Gleason
1929	OH, YEAH?	Screenplay with James Gleason Direction	Zasu Pitts James Gleason Robert Armstrong
1929	THE SPIELER	Original screenplay Direction	Alan Hale Renee Adoree Clyde Cook
1930	HER MAN	Original screenplay Direction & production	Helen Twelvetrees Phillips Holmes Ricardo Cortez Thelma Todd Marjorie Rambeau James Gleason Slim Summerville Harry Sweet
1930	OFFICER O'BRIEN	Screenplay with Tom Buckingham Direction	Bill Boyd
1931	BAD COMPANY	Coscript with Tom Buckingham Direction	Helen Twelvetrees Ricardo Cortez
1932	PRESTIGE	Original screenplay Direction & production	Ann Harding Melvyn Douglas Adolphe Menjou

[328]

1932	ONE WAY PASSAGE	Screenplay with Wilson Mizner & Joe Jackson	William Powell Kay Francis Warren Hymer Aline MacMahon Frank McHugh
1932	OKAY, AMERICA	Direction	Lew Ayres Maureen O'Sullivan Edward Arnold Louis Calhern
1933	DESTINATION UNKNOWN	Direction (from a Tom Buckingham original	Pat O'Brien Ralph Bellamy Betty Compson Alan Hale Tom Brown
1933	S. O. S. ICEBERG	Direction	Rod La Rocque Ernst Udet Leni Riefenstahl
1935	CHINA SEAS	Direction	Jean Harlow Clark Gable Wallace Beery Rosalind Russell C. Aubrey Smith Akim Tamiroff Lewis Stone Robert Benchley
1935	SHE COULDN'T TAKE IT	Direction	George Raft Joan Bennett Walter Connolly
1936	PROFESSIONAL SOLDIER	Direction (script by Gene Fowler from a Damon Runyon short story)	Victor McLaglen Freddie Bartholomew
1937	SLAVE SHIP	Direction	Warner Baxter Wallace Beery Mickey Rooney Elizabeth Allen
1937	LOVE IS NEWS	Direction	Loretta Young Tyrone Power Don Ameche Slim Summerville Walter Catlett

1937	STAND-IN	Direction	Joan Blondell Leslie Howard Humphrey Bogart Gregory Ratoff Jack Carson
1938	THE JOY OF LIVING	Direction	Irene Dunne Douglas Fairbanks, Jr. Warren Hymer Alice Brady
1939	TRADE WINDS	Original screenplay with Frank R. Adams Dirction	Fredric March Joan Bennett Ann Sothern Ralph Bellamy
1939	ETERNALLY YOURS	Direction	Loretta Young David Niven Billie Burke Hugh Herbert C. Aubrey Smith
1940	SLIGHTLY HONORABLE	Direction	Pat O'Brien Edward Arnold Broderick Crawford Eve Arden Phyllis Brooks
1940	SEVEN SINNERS	Direction	Marlene Dietrich John Wayne Oscar Homolka Albert Dekker Billy Gilbert Samuel Hinds Reginald Denny Mischa Auer Anna Lee
1941	CHEERS FOR MISS BISHOP	Direction	Martha Scott Rosemary de Camp Mary Anderson William Gargan Edmund Gwenn
1941	WEEKEND FOR THREE	Production	Jane Wyatt Dennis O'Keefe
1941	UNEXPECTED UNCLE	Production	Charles Coburn James Craig
1942	MY FAVORITE SPY	Direction	Kay Kyser Jane Wyman

1943 BATAAN	Direction	Robert Taylor
		Lloyd Nolan
		Desi Arnaz
		Thomas Mitchell
		George Murphy
		Barry Nelson
		Lee Bowman
		Robert Walker
1943 THE CROSS OF LORRAINE	Direction (From the book *A Thousand Shall Fall*)	Gene Kelly
		Jean Pierre Aumont
		Hume Cronyn
		Sir Cedric Hardwicke
		Richard Whorf
		Peter Lorre
1944 MRS. PARKINGTON	Direction (From Louis Bromfield's novel)	Greer Garson
		Walter Pidgeon
		Cecil Kellaway
		Agnes Moorehead
		Edward Arnold
		Dan Duryea
		Peter Lawford
		Tom Drake
1945 VALLEY OF DECISION	Direction (From the book by Marcia Davenport)	Greer Garson
		Gregory Peck
		Lionel Barrymore
		Donald Crisp
		Gladys Cooper
		Jessica Tandy
		Dan Duryea
		Marshall Thompson
1946 THE POSTMAN ALWAYS RINGS TWICE	Direction (From the book by James M. Cain)	Lana Turner
		John Garfield
		Cecil Kellaway
		Leon Ames
		Hume Cronyn
1947 WILD HARVEST	Direction (From the original screenplay *The Big Haircut*)	Alan Ladd
		Dorothy Lamour
		Lloyd Nolan
		Robert Preston
		Richard Erdmann
		Allen Jenkins
1949 A CONNECTICUT YANKEE IN KING ARTHUR'S COURT	Direction (Thanks to Tennyson & Mark Twain)	Bing Crosby
		Rhonda Fleming
		William Bendix
		Sir Cedric Hardwicke

1950	FIREBALL	Direction (Original screenplay with Horace McCoy)	Mickey Rooney Pat O'Brien Milburn Stone Beverly Tyler
1951	CAUSE FOR ALARM	Direction	Loretta Young Barry Sullivan
1951	SOLDIERS THREE	Direction	Stewart Granger David Niven Walter Pidgeon Robert Newton Cyril Cusack Greta Gynt
1952	ONE MINUTE TO ZERO	Direction	Robert Mitchum Ann Blyth Richard Egan William Tallman Charles McGraw
1953	MAIN STREET TO BROADWAY	Direction	Ethel Barrymore Lionel Barrymore Mary Martin Rex Harrison Cornel Wilde Tallulah Bankhead Josh Logan Rodgers & Hammerstein Lilli Palmer Mary Murphy & T. Monaco
1954	THE BLACK KNIGHT	Direction	Alan Ladd Patricia Medina Peter Cushing
1956	CINERAMA DOCUMENTARY	Direction	A crazy Indian train
1960	THE NIGHTFIGHTERS	Direction (From the book *The Terrible Beauty*)	Robert Mitchum Richard Harris Cyril Cusack Anne Heywood Noel Purcell Niall McGinnis
1963	CATTLE KING	Direction	Robert Taylor Robert Loggia Joan Caulfield Robert Middleton William Windom

1970	THE DELTA FACTOR	Direction (Coscript & production)	Yvette Mimieux Christopher George Diane McBain
1972	THE MAD TRAPPER	Direction (Coscript with Chuck Keen)	Mike Mazurki Mari Aldon Fritz Ford
1972	84 CHARING CROSS ROAD (stage presentation)	Dramatization from Helen Hanff's Book Direction	Adrienne Moore Hedley Mattingley
1973	TIMBER TRAMP	Direction	Claude Aikin Tab Hunter Leon Ames Rosie Grier Bob Easton Stash Clemmens Cesar Romero Hal Baylor Eve Brent Shug Fisher Joseph Cotten Patricia Medina

Radio & Television Credits

Radio Series	Stars	Guests
Produced and directed twenty-six segments of *Three Sheets to the Wind*. Wrote or co-wrote 16 segments.	John Wayne Helga Moray	

Television

	Stars	Guests
Screen Directors' Guild Playhouse Wrote and directed original stories		Rory Calhoun Yvonne de Carlo Michael Wilding
4 Star Theatre Directed several segments with each star	Jack Lemmon Jane Powell	
The Loretta Young Show Directed many segments	Loretta Young	Eddie Albert Steve Cochran Ralph Meeker George Tobias
Wagon Train Directed several segments	Ward Bond Robert Horton Frank McGrath Terry Wilson Audrey Dalton Robert Loggia	Robert Fuller
The Deputy Directed several segments	Henry Fonda Alan Case	
The Tall Men Directed	Barry Sullivan Clu Gulager	
Riverboat Directed several	Darrin McGavin	
87th Precinct Directed a few	Various stars	

Laramie Directed several	John Smith Robert Fuller	
Overland Stage Directed a few	William Bendix Douglas McClure	Barbara Luna Robert Loggia Edgar Buchanan
The Untouchables Directed a few	Robert Stack Vincent Edwards	
Naked City Directed now & then	Paul Burke Horace McMahon	
Half a dozen Church Films for the Southern Baptist Church		
Rawhide Directed several	Eric Fleming Clint Eastwood Paul Brinegar	Barbara Stanwyck Maria Palmer
Gunsmoke Directed many	Jim Arness Dennis Weaver Ken Curtis Milburn Stone Amanda Blake	Lois Nettleton Barbara Luna
Beachcomber Directed several	Cameron Mitchell	Cesar Romero John Vivyan Ann Helm Glynis Johns
Death Valley Days Directed a scad		Ronald Reagan Keenan Wynn Joan Blondell Noah Beery, Jr. George Gobel Rory Calhoun Gilbert Roland Ken Curtis Denver Pyle Ken Murray
Bonanza Directed several	Lorne Green Dan Blocker Pernell Roberts Mike Landon	Patricia Blair Marlyn Mason Anjanette Comer Joan Blondell

Frontier Circus
Directed several

The Loner
Directed

The Legend of Jesse James
Directed

Please Don't Eat the Daisies
Directed

Richard Jaekel
John Derek
Chill Wills

Lloyd Bridges   Burgess Meredith

Alan Case
Christopher George

Pat Crowley